*Stokes Nature Guides*

by Donald Stokes

*A Guide to Nature in Winter*
*A Guide to Observing Insect Lives*
*A Guide to Bird Behavior, Volume I*

by Donald and Lillian Stokes

*A Guide to Bird Behavior, Volume II*
*A Guide to Bird Behavior, Volume III*
*A Guide to Enjoying Wildflowers*
*A Guide to Animal Tracking and Behavior*

by Thomas F. Tyning

*A Guide to Amphibians and Reptiles*

ALSO BY DONALD STOKES

*The Natural History of Wild Shrubs and Vines*

ALSO BY DONALD AND LILLIAN STOKES

*The Bird Feeder Book*
*The Hummingbird Book*
*The Complete Birdhouse Book*

*A Guide to
Amphibians and
Reptiles*

# A Guide to Amphibians and Reptiles

## Thomas F. Tyning

*Edited by Donald W. Stokes and
Lillian Q. Stokes*

Illustrations by Andrew Finch Magee
Range Maps by Thomas F. Tyning and
Timothy J. Flanagan

*Little, Brown and Company*
Boston   Toronto   London

FIRST EDITION

LIBRARY OF CONGRESS CATALOGING-IN-PUBLICATION DATA

Tyning, Thomas F.
    A guide to amphibians and reptiles/Thomas F. Tyning.
        p.   cm.
    Includes bibliographical references.
    ISBN 0-316-81719-8 (hc)
    ISBN 0-316-81713-9 (pbk)
    1. Amphibians. 2. Reptiles. I. Title.
QL641.T96   1990
597.6 — dc20                                    89-28444
                                                CIP

HC:        10  9  8  7  6  5  4  3  2
PB:        10  9  8  7  6  5  4  3  2

BP


Published simultaneously in Canada
by Little, Brown & Company (Canada) Limited

PRINTED IN THE UNITED STATES OF AMERICA

# Contents

# Part Two: The Reptiles

# A Note from the Stokeses

*A Guide to Nature in Winter,* the first Stokes Nature Guide, presented an unusual approach to enjoying nature. With traditional field guides you learn how to identify a plant or animal; with Stokes Nature Guides you learn all about its life history and behavior. For example, from a traditional field guide you can learn that a certain bird is called a red-winged blackbird, but with the Stokes Nature Guide on bird behavior you learn how it forms territories in spring, what its courtship methods are, when, how, and where it builds its nest and raises its young, and even the meaning of its calls.

We know from our own experience how exciting it is to learn about the lives of the plants and animals right around us. We find it adds immeasurably to the richness of our lives and makes nature a never-ending source of discovery and pleasure. Through Stokes Nature Guides we have tried to share our excitement about the natural world and our enjoyment of science's discoveries. Collectively, the eight books in the series form a useful reference to the lives and behavior of your favorite plants and animals.

Tom Tyning proposed to us that he write a Stokes Nature Guide on the behavior of amphibians and reptiles several years ago, and we were delighted. We knew that his expert knowledge of herpetology, his proven writing skills, and his extensive experience teaching the public made him perfect for the job. In addition, he shared with us a dedication to the Stokes Nature Guide approach, a belief in the importance of focusing on the life history and behavior of plants and animals. He had been using Stokes Nature Guides for years and had wished that there were one on amphibians and reptiles.

We worked with Tom on the format, design, and editing of this book, and he supplied the research, knowledge, and writing. We feel that the result is an informative and entertaining guide to all aspects of amphibians and reptiles. This book will help you find these fascinating animals, recognize them in all their life stages, and understand what they do throughout the year. In addition, it is a wonderful summary of all the most recent discoveries about these animals. It also contains some beautiful drawings of amphibians and reptiles. We hope you enjoy it as much as we do, and we want to thank Tom Tyning for creating a superb Stokes Nature Guide.

Yours in Nature,
*Don and Lillian Stokes*

# Acknowledgments

MANY PEOPLE gave valuable assistance to me throughout the production of this book. Without them, the task would have been much greater; their support was welcomed and wonderful. First and foremost, thanks are due to Don and Lillian Stokes not only for their help with organizing our thoughts on this book, but also for their advice and experience throughout its production. Somehow Donna Adams managed to survive the greater part of the year without any help around the farmhouse. She kept a good deal of sanity and humor floating around and that made a great difference. Andrew Magee's attention to detail and love for nature imparts a very special quality to his artwork. It has been a pleasure to have him as a friend and to work with him on this project.

Al Richmond, Scott Jackson, Terry Graham, Stephen Tilley, Kentwood Wells, and Diedra Cleary read parts of the manuscript and offered valuable thoughts and critical advice. Their suggestions and detailed remarks substantially improved early drafts. Tim Flanagan's assistance with range maps, general computer use, and field trips was above and beyond that of a friend. Other people who freely offered ideas, encouragement, and field trips include Dick Bartlett, Willie Bemis, Ann Flanagan, John Green, Kay Kudlinski, John Porter, Don Reid, John Goodrich, Keith Winston, Mary Rogers, and Dr. Ernest Williams.

I am grateful for the advice and support given by friends and current or former staff of the Massachusetts Audubon Society, including Martha Cohen, Marilyn Flor, James D. Lazell, Rene Laubach, James Baird, Chuck Roth, Tom Carrolan, John Mitchell, Chris Leahy, John Fitch, Larry Pottebaum, Doug Kimball, Mike Shannon, Cleti Cervoni, Widge Arms, Donna Munufo, Susan Rauchwerk, Helga Burre, Ray Ashton, Dick Walton, and Brian Cassie. The staff at several university libraries and museums were wonderful, especially Andrew Williams at Smith College, Doug Smith at the University of Massachusetts, and José Rosado at Harvard's Museum of Comparative Zoology. Debbie Roth, of Little, Brown and Company, and Larry Hamberlin were extremely helpful in editing drafts of the manuscript.

Part One

---

# THE AMPHIBIANS

# About Amphibians

Linnaeus, the great eighteenth-century biologist, had an apparent disgust for amphibians, summarized by his often repeated statement that they were "foul and loathsome creatures." Despite this, almost everyone who has spent any time with frogs or salamanders feels that, to the contrary, there is much to learn and enjoy by watching these animals.

Like reptiles, mammals, birds, and fish, amphibians are vertebrates. They are relatively easily distinguished from the other groups by their glandular skin and their lack of scales, hair, feathers, or claws.

The word *amphibian* has two separate meanings — one based on popular usage and one based more strictly on its etymological origin. While many people believe that it denotes an animal living both on land and in water, many amphibians in fact live in only one or the other.

A better definition of the word and of this group of animals is that amphibians have two lives (the literal meaning of the Greek *amphibios*) — a larval stage and an adult stage that are commonly very different from each other. Simply consider, for example, a tadpole and an adult frog. This definition has to be qualified a bit, because some amphibians retain many of their larval characters, such as external gills, all through their adult lives; still, most amphibians undergo a remarkable transformation as they pass from larval to adult stages.

There are three living groups of amphibians in the world. Frogs and salamanders are relatively well known, unlike the third group, the caecilians, which are legless, wormlike animals of the tropics.

### COMPLEX LIFE HISTORIES

While it is easy to assume that all amphibian larvae are doing their best to hurry up and become adults, more and more researchers are looking at the larval stage as an evolutionarily unique and significant life-history strategy. All of the factors that influence the lives of individuals and populations of adult animals also come into play at the larval stage. Field investigators are now looking at the role certain salamander larvae play as predators in temporary pond systems and at how the presence or absence of one species of tadpole affects the outcome of competition among several others in the same pond.

In a few species of salamanders, life as a larva is either so good, or life as an adult is so poor, that the larval stage is extended dramatically. Likewise it may well be true that a frog is simply a good way for tadpoles to get from one place to another.

### HOW THEY BREATHE

Most amphibians have a functional pair of lungs that work more or less the same as they do in any other vertebrate. There are many, however, including a widespread family of salamanders, that lack lungs completely.

All amphibians use their skin and the wet linings of their mouth and throat to take in oxygen and other gases. Some, of course, use gills as well. Often you will see the throats of frogs and salamanders rhythmically expanding and contracting; they are physically pushing air into and out of their bodies and exchanging oxygen and other gases at the same time.

## BODY TEMPERATURES

Overall, amphibians are relatively well adapted to cold, with wide tolerances for low temperatures. Several species range close to the Arctic Circle, and many southerly ones are active during the coolest parts of the year. Still, most species studied have preferred body temperature ranges and they must regulate body temperature accordingly, though they lack an internal heating mechanism like that of mammals and birds. Amphibians regulate their body temperature by choosing warm or cold places to rest.

Basking is a common method of raising the body temperature. However, moving under rocks or into leaves or other material may also raise their body temperatures without drying their skin as full sunlight might. Although some amphibians have even adapted to desert life, they are active only during the coolest times of the night or the wettest periods of the year. Most of the time they remain underground, insulated from the excessive heat and dryness.

## AMPHIBIAN REPRODUCTION

Each of the two North American groups of amphibians has its own method of reproduction. In most cases, frogs fertilize their eggs externally, the males simply releasing sperm in the water as the females release their eggs. This method is quite helpful to amphibian biologists who are interested in the social behavior of tadpoles and the breeding strategies of adults; one can be quite sure who the father is in any given breeding pair.

Salamanders, however, generally exhibit internal fertilization. Males do not have a sexual organ for this, but rather produce *spermatophores* that females are induced to pick up through the *cloaca* — the common opening for reproduction and eliminating wastes. Females in this case may pick up more than one spermatophore, confusing the paternity in any given clutch of eggs.

## MODERN VIEWS OF AMPHIBIANS

Rather than looking upon amphibians as an early, if not simple, step in the evolution of terrestrial vertebrates, modern field biologists are becoming more and more intrigued by the unique evolutionary methods amphibians use to cope with life. Just the dazzling variations in the ways frogs reproduce, for instance, are enough to contradict the idea that they are primitive animals. Present-day frogs and salamanders are not the ancestors to any other modern animals; they are not primitive life forms. Amphibians have evolved innovative behaviors and complex life-history patterns that are just beginning to be understood and appreciated.

## CONSERVATION OF AMPHIBIANS

Interest in the lives and welfare of living things other than mammals and birds has been spreading in many countries. For nearly twenty years Europeans have been installing tunnels beneath roads to help toads get to their breeding grounds safely. Recently, similar measures have been taken in North America for some salamanders.

You may be struck by the seasonal abundance of amphibians when, for example, frogs appear quite suddenly at nearby wetlands and begin to vocalize. Or, in the process of collecting firewood, moving rocks, or cleaning up debris, you may be surprised to learn how common and widespread some salamanders are.

Still, some species of frogs and salamanders are declining in parts of their range. Urbanization, overcollecting, soil and water pollution, some forestry practices, and other large- or small-scale projects are likely culprits. If you find your local frog pond paved under and destroyed or your salamander breeding pool "improved" by someone who deepens it and dumps in some goldfish, take action.

Conserving amphibians and the places they live requires also that more information about their biology be recorded, compiled, and analyzed. Direct field observation is an invaluable means of learning about these fascinating animals, and accurate records of sightings and behaviors can play an important role in the preservation of amphibians' habitats.

# Introducing Frogs

Early explorers traveling through the wilderness and modern condominum dwellers living near wetlands have at least one experience in common: it's impossible not to notice the myriad sounds of frogs during some parts of the year. Like the eighteenth-century naturalists who desired to know the wild inhabitants of the New World, many people today, with no less fervor, are drawn into the damp nights to try to glimpse the frogs that appear, almost magically, each year.

The invention of low-cost, portable tape recorders in the 1950s helped field biologists begin to understand the intricate behaviors and interactions that attend these vocalizations and the breeding strategies that come into play. The discovery of subtle variations in the ways adult frogs and their tadpoles balance numerous competing ecological and evolutionary forces has boosted interest in finding and watching the activities of frogs. As is typical with field biology, more questions continue to arise, promising that there will be rich discoveries to be made for many years to come.

Frogs are known scientifically as *anurans*—literally meaning "without tail"—in reference to the form of the adults. They evolved during the age of dinosaurs and have diversified into at least 3,500 species found throughout the world today, with more still being discovered every year.

There are nine families of frogs in North America, each with unique physical and behavioral adaptations that distinguish one from another. Four families include most of our species. The true toads (Bufonidae) include many of the brown, warty species we typically think of as toads. Some toads, however, are smooth skinned and brightly colored. All members of this family lack teeth and ribs, and have a thick skin and short hind legs. The spadefoot toads (Pelobatidae) are strange nocturnal creatures with vertical pupils, smooth skin, and teeth only on their upper jaws. The family name comes from growths on their hind feet that are used to dig into the earth.

Most members of the treefrog family (Hylidae) are aided in their arboreal haunts by rounded adhesive discs on their unwebbed toes. All have horizontal pupils, and most are relatively small animals. The true frogs (Ranidae) include many of the common "pond frogs" encountered by children and fishermen. Most have large, jumping hind legs and hind toes that are connected by extensive webbing. The vast majority live on the edges of ponds, lakes, and marshes.

No matter what their common or family names, all of them are anurans — frogs — in the largest sense of the term. That is to say, all toads, including spadefoot toads, are frogs.

## SEXUAL SELECTION AND MATE CHOICE

In some cases, a female frog may choose one particular male out of a pondful of frogs partly on the quality of his vocalizations. Or she may select a male on the basis of certain characteristics of his territory — water depth or temperature, type and amount of vegetation, or other factors yet to be discovered.

Males of some species must actively compete with each other for territories or directly for females. Aggressive encounters, including biting, pushing, and wrestling are very visible expressions of this competition. Age, size, and other qualities of individuals probably come into play in all these interactions.

## DIVERSITY IN BREEDING STRATEGIES

There are two basic reproductive strategies found in North American frogs. Some, such as wood frogs and spadefoot toads, are known as explosive breeders. All the sexually mature adults migrate to temporary ponds and large puddles within a few days, or even hours, of one another, go through a frenzied courtship, lay eggs, and then reverse their migration. Although the eggs and larvae of explosive breeders must deal with wide variations in water level and therefore temperature and oxygen supply, most species have compensated by evolving fast developmental rates to take advantage of the large amounts of food typically found in these communities.

Species such as bullfrogs and green frogs are called prolonged breeders because the males set up and sometimes defend territories in permanent bodies of water. They wait in these territories for females to move into the breeding grounds over a period of weeks throughout the spring or summer. The eggs and larvae that are left behind take longer to grow, leaving them more vulnerable to predators, but have the advantage over temporary-pond users of being able to metamorphose at larger sizes.

## HOW FROGS SURVIVE

All frogs have to deal with the basic necessities of life — finding food, avoiding predators, surviving bad periods of weather, and reproducing. How each species and family of frogs responds to these needs is the subject of numerous research projects.

It may seem at first glance that frogs — which lack claws, have only tiny teeth (if any), are unable to run away very quickly, and otherwise appear to be sitting ducks in the face of a barrage of marauding predators — must have a tough time surviving. All species have numerous predators at all stages of their lives, and individuals are continually eliminated.

But, in their favor, frogs have numerous methods for defense, ranging from camouflage to their enormous leaping ability, which allows them to catapult through the air where not a molecule of odor is left behind for a predator to follow, to their distasteful and even toxic skin secretions, which can immobilize or kill a predator. Perhaps even more important, frogs live relatively long lives and generally have large numbers of young each year, which almost guarantees that some will survive long enough to reproduce themselves.

It is difficult to misidentify a tadpole. Their heads and bodies are undifferentiated, combining in a round or oblong shape. Tadpoles also have a strong, muscular tail that efficiently propels them through their aquatic world. This unusual form has given rise to the two common names for larval frogs, both of which are derived from Middle English. The name *tadpole* means "toad's head," and the alternative name that most of us grew up with, *pollywog,* literally means "wiggling head."

When first hatched, tadpoles hang from their eggs or nearby vegetation by an adhesive disc appendage on their head. Within a few days, the gills are covered over and the head and body swell in size. The animal begins to use its tail to propel itself through the water, and it spends most of its active time feeding. Eventually, first the hind legs and then the front legs form and begin to grow. Numerous internal and external changes take place during the process of metamorphosis, and the tadpole is transformed into a frog.

## HOW TADPOLES SURVIVE

Far from being a short-lived, intermediate step between egg and adult, the tadpole is a unique form of vertebrate life that has evolved survival strategies very different from those of the adult it will become. The large diversity in the size and shape of tadpoles and in the length of time they exist is a response to adaptations for feeding, differences in the type of water they live in, and varied social behaviors.

By exploiting aquatic communities that are completely different from those of the adults (at least for most North American species), tadpoles have reduced the amount of competition from them. Most species of tadpoles in North America are classified as suspension feeders. In fact, they have been characterized as the largest freshwater swimmers that survive primarily by eating plankton. They filter minute algae (plants less than ten microns in diameter, called *ultraplankton*) and bacteria from the water as they swim or actively root around leaf litter and the surface of rocks to dislodge them. Most tadpoles have hardened, toothlike structures that help them loosen this plant material.

Like other animals, tadpoles are physically aware of their environment and when given choices prefer to live within certain narrow limits of temperature, water depth, current, acidity, and other conditions. As they get older, these preferences can change with changes in their own physiology. Tadpoles do not distribute themselves randomly, as you may observe.

Tadpole researchers have found that in some populations, a few tadpoles outgrow all the others, though the small ones will grow faster if moved to a new location. This led to the discovery of an algaelike organism that affects certain tadpoles by inhibiting their growth, allowing those unaffected to increase in size. In some species, a few tadpoles become carnivorous and even cannibalistic, developing huge jaws and teeth, while the others remain small in size and continue feeding on microscopic plants. As biologists continue to watch tadpoles much more will be learned about this life stage. Some already are finding that tadpole behavior is just as interesting to study as the behavior of adult frogs.

### SOME FROG TERMINOLOGY

Some behaviors or actions of frogs and some of the structures on their bodies that help in identification are referred to in special terms. A few frogs have two raised ridges of skin that run down the edges of their backs from the eyes to the tail, called the *dorsolateral ridges* or *folds.* The big lumps just behind the eyes of toads are the *parotoid glands,* containing a powerful toxin. The eardrum is covered by a circle of skin called the *tympanic membrane* or simply the *tympanum.*

When male frogs advertise at breeding locations they inflate their *vocal sac* with each call. Depending on the species, this can be a single, large structure beneath the chin or a pair of sacs that bulge out from each side of the head when inflated. The innermost toe on the front feet of frogs is usually referred to as a *thumb;* this can swell and develop growths on it to help males maintain their hold on females during the breeding season.

The typical mating posture in frogs, where a male is on the back of the female and holding on with his front legs, is called *amplexus*. The larvae of frogs are known as *tadpoles* (preferred term) or *pollywogs*. Soon after they metamorphose, young anurans can be referred to as *froglets* or *toadlets*.

In northern parts of North America frogs must cope with the prolonged cold and dryness of winter. Most become inactive and take refuge in ponds and lakes, dig into leaf litter, or enter underground tunnels on land. Biologists use the term *brumation* for the inactive periods of frogs and other ectotherms — animals that do not have the internal heating mechanisms that distinguish birds and mammals and allow them to stay active year-round.

### FROG VOCALIZATIONS

The courtship and mating behaviors of frogs are heralded by identifiable calls made by the adult males. Each species has at least one obvious call that can be learned relatively easily, and most make several others that can be heard by paying close attention to them. Standard terminology used to describe these vocalizations is becoming accepted, though various researchers continue to coin new terms. *Advertisement calls* are made by males during the breeding season to define their territories and serve as a signal to arriving females. *Aggressive calls* are usually made by males in the presence of other males who have entered or come close to the edge of an occupied territory. *Courtship calls* are given by males and some females shortly before amplexus takes place. When a male or nonreproductive female is clasped by another male, it may give a *release call*. The clasping male normally releases his grip in response. Finally, there are *defensive calls* that adults of both sexes and juveniles make when startled or attacked by a potential predator.

Vocalizations are important to frogs for many reasons, especially in helping individuals sort out which species, out of several in a pond at any one time, to mate with, defend a territory from, or ignore. Researchers test how effective these calls are by playing back tape recordings to territorial males or females to see what behaviors they exhibit in response. Advertisement calls clearly help frogs identify other members of their species; individual voices of frogs convey more intimate information to which other frogs may respond. Of course, frogs — especially females — are able to distinguish the calls made by others of the same and different species. Sound reception is complicated in frogs, but detailed studies have revealed that some species have remarkable abilities to discriminate between close frequencies.

The wonderful sounds frogs make are enhanced in males by the vocal sac. This loose pouch of skin inflates with air and acts as a resonating chamber that intensifies the sound made by the frog's larynx. By taking air into its lungs and closing off its nostrils, a frog can move a complex series of muscles and tendons that alternately inflate and deflate its vocal sac. Often, the sides of a frog's body expand and contract with each breath and call note.

Recently, some biologists have begun to focus on the energy costs that male frogs must pay for advertising their presence at breeding sites. Repeating a call hundreds or thousands of times in a night, and continuing this over a period of weeks, expends a great deal of energy. Constant calling from one place may also help predators locate the individual. Vocalizing is the most energy-expensive behavior a male frog engages in. It seems, however, that the reward of successful mating may be worth the effort.

*Adult American toad searching for food in a garden*

# AMERICAN TOAD / *Bufo americanus*

THROUGH AN OPEN WINDOW, the sweet sounds of American toads drifted in from the nearby pond. I put aside my papers and headed out into the warm, springtime afternoon. As I worked my way along the alders and willows of the shoreline, the toads nearest to me stopped calling. They didn't seem to be disturbed enough to leave, though, and I found a comfortable spot on the bank where I could sit, watch, and listen.

The male redwing blackbirds continued their territorial singing and displayed their brilliant shoulder patches by spreading their wings. The females hadn't arrived yet, but they were due any day. A nearby phoebe offered its vocalizations as well, and several species of bees were visiting some of the early flowers. Suddenly the vibrating trill of an American toad began, almost at my feet. There, just over the edge of the bank, a male was sitting, mostly out of water and facing the shoreline. Each time he called, his vocal sac swelled and became bigger than his own head. The song was a sweet, penetrating trill that lasted for nearly thirty-five seconds. His pouch deflated somewhat when he finished his call. He paused for half a minute and then began again. A few seconds into his next call, another male toad, about two feet further along the water's edge, started. Several more males joined the chorus, each

15

vocalizing from his own section of shoreline. I was thrilled to be able to distinguish the voice of each of the toads through differences in pitch and intensity.

## How to Recognize American Toads

### ADULTS

The sweet, trilling advertisement call of the American toad, ten to thirty or more seconds long, is easily distinguished from that of other frogs found within its range. These toads, moreover, are brown or reddish, and the number of warts within the dark blotches on their backs will generally distinguish them from other, similar-looking species.

American toads usually have only one or two warts in the black spots, while Fowler's toads (*Bufo woodhousei fowleri*) have up to six or seven. The separated ridges of skin on top of the head of the American toad will differentiate it from the western Dakota toad (*Bufo hemiophrys*), whose ridges join together between its eyes. The southern toad (*Bufo terrestris*) has very large knobs on its shoulder glands.

Not all toads are brown and warty, but many in North America are, including the American toad. The warts and large, oblong glands on the shoulders of toads secrete a thick, white toxin that can paralyze or even kill some predators.

American toads are in the true toad family, the Bufonidae, which includes more than 335 species throughout the world.

### DISTINGUISHING THE SEXES

Males are usually between two and three inches in length with a dark, almost black, throat. During the breeding season they have enlarged thumb pads and will chirp audibly if you pick them up.

Females are three to four inches in length; in the breeding season they often have a reddish hue. They have light-colored throats.

The small, dark-colored tadpoles often gather in large aggregations. Technical differences from closely related species are difficult to observe in the field.

### EGGS

Nearly all toad species deposit their eggs in long, double strings that may stretch for several feet in the shallow edges of ponds. This makes distinguishing the species of eggs difficult in the field.

## How to Find American Toads

**Habitat:** Suburban backyards, forests, meadows
**Months of Activity:** April to November

*Range of the American toad*

Outside the breeding season, it is easiest to locate American toads shortly after nightfall, when they are most active. Adults are particularly attracted to insects that in turn are attracted to porch and street lights left on after dark. Look for them at the base of a lamppost or the edge of a house during the warmer months of the year. During the day the toads take refuge from the drying heat of the sun. You can actively search for them by turning logs or boards or moving flat stones, and then carefully replacing them.

In the breeding season look for adult toads in ponds, lakes, marshes, and flooded meadows and along slow, meandering rivers. Search for them at the very edges of the water — they rarely venture far from shore. Though they are active mostly at night, American toads will be singing and courting throughout the warmer parts of the day during the height of their breeding period. This is the best time to watch them, and by using binoculars you can pick out many details of their behaviors.

## What You Can Observe

### SPRING EMERGENCE

In many parts of their range, American toads emerge from their land-based wintering sites and begin to move toward their breeding ponds in early April to May. This movement may take several days or even a couple of weeks to occur, though there is little evidence indicating how far toads migrate. Rainstorms, with their associated drop in barometric pressure, may be part of the natural trigger that signals the toads to move.

### TERRITORIAL BEHAVIOR AND VOCALIZATIONS

For most of the year individual American toads remain within a small home range. If you find a toad inside one of the small burrows that it digs with its hind feet and backs into before morning, expect to see it there regularly during the spring and summer.

American toads do not set up territories in their breeding ponds. Calling males tend to space themselves a yard or two apart, but this can be diminished as more males arrive. Males do not actively defend their calling site, though they investigate and attempt to clasp any toad moving near them.

American toads are known to make four vocalizations. The advertisement call is performed by the male only during the breeding season. This is a long, musical trill that can be easily imitated by whistling and humming a high note at the same time. A male sits upright in the water so that his vocal pouch, inflated to its fullest during this call, is above the surface.

The male chirp is a very short form of the advertisement call, lasting just a second or two. The vocal sac is slightly inflated during this call. It is given only rarely, by a male that is clasped by another male. It does not seem to be effective in causing the clasping male to release his grip.

The release call is also commonly given by a male when clasped by another male. This one- to five-second trill is usually accompanied by a strong vibrating movement of the toad's sides. There is some debate as to whether the call itself, the physical vibration, or a combination of the two causes the clasping male to release his grip.

A final, clicking vocalization has so far been recorded only in the laboratory. Known as an amplexus call, it is given by a male when clasping a female. It has been described as sounding like a regular series of drops of water hitting a puddle. The call can be short (eight repetitions) or long (ninety repetitions), with the rate averaging out to forty or fifty clicks per minute. It is extremely quiet and cannot be heard from more than a yard away. This call may not occur under natural conditions; patient field observers may confirm this.

### MATING

A chorus of male American toads is loud enough to attract females and other males from some distance away. American toads are explosive breeders; large numbers of individuals arrive at ponds within a very short time, and the entire breeding process is usually completed within two weeks. You may find singing males stationed near the edges of a pond, nonsinging males floating just offshore, females who enter the ponds and swim beneath the surface, male-and-female pairs clasped together, and a female with several males clinging to her. Calling and mating occur both day and night in most populations.

American toads exhibit an interesting variety of mating strategies in different parts of their range, at various population densities, and when given high or low male-to-female ratios. Size and age differences between males in a breeding pond and females' preference for particular males account for some of these variations.

Individual male American toads may remain stationary at the edge of a pond and continue to give the advertisement call. These males rely on their vocalizations to attract a female close enough for them to see and attempt to clasp.

Some noncalling males patrol the water by swimming about and remain silent. They investigate almost any moving object and attempt to clasp with females, other noncalling males, calling males, or pairs already clasping. In some populations these males are at least equally successful in securing mates as are calling males.

On some occasions you may actually see a female migrating toward the pond with a male already clasping her. In this case the male has intercepted the female on land and maintains his grip on her as they enter the water.

Some females have been observed to arrive at a breeding pond, swim underwater, and lift only their heads out from time to time. Field observations indicate that female American toads choose a particular mate by noting certain characteristics of his calls. Females tend to choose the largest males, and these generally have deeper voices. You too can clearly notice differences in individual male advertisement calls.

A female often initiates amplexus by surfacing near a male. Generally she will float or stand in shallow water with her head and back fully visible above the surface. She turns her back toward the male, and this causes him to approach and clasp her.

Male-and-female pairs are often approached by nonmated males who vigorously attempt to dislodge the male and clasp the female. Sometimes they are successful in gaining access to the female, but due to the strong grip of the first male this is not common.

A successful male holds onto the usually larger female by wrapping his front legs around her body just behind her front legs. In the breeding season males have swollen thumbs with a black growth of skin that allows them a strong grip on the females.

EGGS AND EGG-LAYING

When the female of a clasped pair is ready to deposit eggs, she swims to shallow water where there is abundant aquatic vegetation. She releases her eggs in groups at a time, and the male releases his sperm in response. Usually the female will slowly swim or crawl underwater throughout the egg-laying process; this forms two long strings of eggs, which emerge from her body and catch on the plant stems.

The double string deposited may be three or more feet in length and may contain several thousand eggs. When freshly laid, the eggs may be difficult to find because the outer jelly coating is so transparent. Over a few days, however, silt from the pond bottom and algae and other living things attach themselves to the strings of eggs, and they take on a conspicuous, cloudy appearance. Because of toxins, the eggs of closely related toads are known to be avoided by predators; this may be true for the eggs of American toads as well.

The eggs hatch within a week, or two at the most, as the jellylike coating of the strings begins to disintegrate. The egg strings last for a week or more after hatching, however. If you find them you know the toads have already bred.

## TADPOLES

Upon hatching, the tiny, dark tadpoles attach themselves to underwater vegetation or even their egg mass for a few days. They hang vertically, with their heads up. When disturbed, they may quickly dart away by vigorously wiggling their tails, but afterward they will return to a vertical position and remain still.

Within another week they will have grown and become conspicuous black tadpoles that forage in the shallow parts of the pond bottom. They swim by more or less constantly wiggling their tails, though they are not particularly fast swimmers. Tadpoles are known to be distasteful to many predators, but not to predaceous diving beetles.

It becomes obvious after a few observations that tadpoles tend to swim about in dense aggregations. Researchers have begun to investigate the possible functions of this behavior. These schools of tadpoles have been shown to be more efficient at filtering food, avoiding predators, and controlling their body temperature. At night, tadpole schools disperse, and individuals lie quietly on the bottom in deeper parts of their pond. When the sun rises, they move to the shallow edges of the pond; this seems to be how schools form each day.

The entire school of tadpoles may remain stationary, or the school may move about the edges of a pond. These differences can be easily seen. Stationary schools form when the tadpoles are feeding either on a dead animal (carrion) or material on the pond bottom. Moving schools can be composed of widely spaced tadpoles that swim relatively quickly from one place to another, or can be formed of tightly packed individuals that continuously feed while swimming forward.

One of the most remarkable aspects of these schools is the fact that related tadpoles (those hatched from the same egg mass) show a tendency to stay close to each other. Such aggregations are known as sibling schools.

Tadpoles begin to transform into toadlets about three weeks after hatching. These newly metamorphosed toads can be abundant in the vegetation around the pond or river in mid- to late summer. The toadlets may linger near their pond for days or weeks before moving away.

### OTHER FACTS ABOUT AMERICAN TOADS

When chased, American toads hop, often vigorously, to a safe hideaway; they also hop to close the distance between themselves and food (beetles, earthworms, or other small animals). Notice, however, that when they get within one or two feet of their prey, the toads walk, alternating feet on opposite sides of their body. The toad lifts its body off the ground and stalks its prey with considerable stealth and agility.

American toads have at least a couple of known defensive behaviors. Although the warts and the large glands on their shoulders contain toxic skin secretions, garter snakes, hognose snakes, some ducks, raccoons, and skunks are known to prey on American toads. When grabbed, the toads often inflate their bodies, making

*Adult American toad stalks an earthworm*

it difficult or impossible for some predators to eat them. Secondly, toads often hunch their bodies into a rounded form with their noses tucked under their bodies, almost touching the ground. This may make it difficult for a predator to grab the toad and also ensure that the first contact made is with the poison glands, which are now directed forward.

### OVERWINTERING

American toads are seen less often as autumn nights get chilly. Some researchers believe that the toads make a small but noticeable migration in the fall to reach a particular overwintering site. They seem to disappear completely by the first week in September (North) to the end of October (South) and remain in underground burrows until late March (South) to mid-May (North). American toads can either dig their own overwintering burrows or use existing mammal tunnels or natural crevices that are up to twelve inches below the surface. The toads apparently remain immobile during the cold weeks or months of winter, though they have rarely been studied at this time. At the end of winter, when the ground temperature rises well above freezing, the toads dig their way to the surface and begin to move toward breeding ponds. How they are able to navigate remains to be studied.

# Quick Reference Chart

*Life Cycle*

**Length of Breeding Season:** Late March (South) to mid-May (North)

**Breeding Habitat:** Usually temporary bodies of water

**Eggs Deposited:** 4,000 – 8,000 within a few days after reaching breeding ponds

**Eggs Hatch:** Normally within 1 week

**Length of Tadpole Stage:** 3 – 6 weeks

**Lifespan of Adults:** 5 – 10 years in natural situations; up to 35 years in captivity

*Vocalizations*

**Advertisement call:** A long (lasting up to 30 seconds), sweet trill by males in breeding season

**Male chirp:** A short (1 – 3 seconds) version of the advertisement call

**Release call:** Given by a male when clasped by another male; always associated with a strong vibration of the sides of the body

**Amplexus call:** Rarely heard and very quiet; sounds like regular drops in a puddle; given by male while clasped to a female

*Adult spadefoot toads in amplexus*

# EASTERN SPADEFOOT TOAD /
*Scaphiopus holbrooki*

The conditions were perfect. It was warm and raining hard. Lightning was flashing, and thunder crashed all around. Tonight we would look for spadefoot toads. A friend and I got into his car and headed out to an area that was reported to have had spadefoot toads ten years earlier. We were both anxious to see one but didn't hold out any real hope, since populations of these nocturnal amphibians can be relatively few and far between.

It was raining hard enough that water ran in sheets off the surface of the paved roads that wound through pastures and farmland. Incredible numbers of earthworms were on the roads, and we began to find spring peepers and American toads crossing as well. Each time a toadlike shape appeared in the headlight beams we stopped the car, ran out, and examined it. Finally, late in the evening one of the lumps at the edge of the road turned out to be an eastern spadefoot toad.

Small for a toad, it was also exceptionally smooth looking. The yellow lines on its back were especially brilliant. I picked the animal up to move it off the road and almost instantly felt the hard, crescent-shaped growths on its hind feet—the hallmark of the spadefoot toads—pressing into my hand. We continued searching but didn't find another spadefoot that night. In fact, it took two more years of nighttime searching during heavy downpours to locate the breeding pool of this particular population.

Spadefoot toads have gotten the reputation of being difficult to find because of their irregular appearances at breeding ponds, completely nocturnal habits, secretive, burrowing nature, and extremely fast developmental rates. Even as more field observers find and study them, spadefoot toads are not losing their aura of mystery. They continue to amaze everyone who has an opportunity to cross their path.

## How to Recognize Spadefoot Toads

### ADULTS

The weird, abrupt squawk of the male spadefoot toad is unmistakable. It has been compared to the sounds young crows make, the distant honking of geese, and the sound made by rubbing a balloon. Though obviously difficult to describe, it is unforgettable when heard. Spadefoot toads get their name from the dark growths on the inside part of their hind feet that allow them to dig so easily into the soil.

All spadefoot toads are squat, plump animals with relatively smooth skin and scattered, tiny warts on their bodies. In strong light, they have vertical pupils, while almost all other frogs in North America have round or horizontal pupils.

The eastern spadefoot is distinguished from others by the two wavy, yellow lines that run the length of its back. Also, unlike other species of spadefoot toads, its eardrums are obvious just behind and below its eyes. Eastern spadefoot toads grow to three and a half inches in length, slightly larger than other related species.

Eastern spadefoots are members of the spadefoot-toad family, the Pelobatidae. The eighty-three species in the family are distributed in North America, Europe, Asia, and North Africa.

### DISTINGUISHING THE SEXES

Male spadefoot toads have dark throats and during the breeding season develop dark growths on two or more of the toes of their front feet.

Females normally have light or white throats and in the breeding season are usually much fatter and larger than the males.

### TADPOLES

Spadefoot-toad tadpoles are dark brown on top with a gold iridescence that continues as a stripe onto the tail. Underneath, these tadpoles have more or less transparent skin throughout their larval life. They have relatively thin, short tails that are sprinkled with tiny spots.

### EGGS

Spadefoot eggs are deposited more or less in strings, though the strings are easily broken and rarely are as long as those of the American toad. Each egg is very small and dark; up to 2,500 eggs are deposited by each female.

## How to Find Spadefoot Toads

**Habitat:** Farmland, meadows, forests, dunes
**Months of Activity:** Year-round (South); April to October (North)

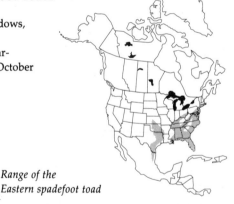

*Range of the Eastern spadefoot toad*

The burrowing and nocturnal habits of these animals make looking for them difficult and finding them a treasure. There are some conditions, however, that make the search a bit easier. During and after heavy rains, spadefoot toads make nighttime surface appearances to move about and perhaps feed. By searching on foot with a flashlight or by slowly driving along roads, you may spot one or more. They generally frequent fields and wooded areas that have very sandy soil, so here is where to begin.

Strong thunderstorms and heavy rains are the conditions that best encourage eastern spadefoot toads to emerge and search for breeding pools any time of the year. For only two or three nights following the storm you are likely to see and hear a fascinating concentration of these delightful animals. There is no annual, cyclic regularity to their migrations to and from breeding sites. Instead the event is usually triggered by a quick drop in barometric pressure, more than two inches of rainfall, and the cover of darkness. When a low-pressure front passes through your area and heavy rains swell rivers and flood low-lying fields, head out into the night and start hunting. Listen for their choruses or follow migrating individuals to their pools.

## What You Can Observe

### SPRING EMERGENCE

The precise time when spadefoot toads become active in the spring is difficult to ascertain since they are rarely observed. They may, in fact, be fully alert as spring approaches though they re-

*Spadefoot toad emerging from earth*

main concealed in underground burrows waiting for heavy rains and a drop in barometric pressure to draw them out.

Several observations of animals in February and March, at least in the South, indicate that they certainly can become active and function fully late in winter or very early in the spring.

### TERRITORIAL BEHAVIOR AND VOCALIZATIONS

Several different sounds have been heard coming from spade-foot toads. The only one you are likely to hear, however, is the male's advertisement call when he reaches a breeding pond. This is a loud, abrupt single note that is often repeated several times in succession. Both sexes also produce a release call that is accompanied by rapid vibrations of their sides.

There is no indication that male spadefoot toads set up and maintain territories during the brief breeding season. You are more likely to notice rather random movement by individuals that alternate calling with swimming and investigation of other frogs.

During the rest of the year, spadefoot toads are relatively sedentary animals, though they do move within a home range. This has been calculated to be about seventy square feet for eastern spade-foot toads in the southern United States. Individual animals can move much further than this, though most keep relatively near one or several burrows that they made and to which they often return. There does seem to be some spacing between individuals, as home ranges rarely overlap.

### MATING

The usually sudden and unexpected appearance of dozens or even hundreds of spadefoot toads on a single night is one of nature's most extraordinary phenomena. In the southern parts of their range, spadefoot toads have been known to breed every month of the year. Though there are reports of daytime activities, the strongest choruses and most breeding take place on warm, dark nights.

Males usually arrive at breeding pools before females and begin to give their advertisement calls. On at least a couple of occasions, males were found in burrows on the edges of ponds calling from underground as daylight was fading. Eventually they dug out and moved to the water. As night continues, more males and then the females arrive.

Though males may alternate vocalizing and swimming to new sites on the pond, they tend to remain relatively still when a female approaches and generally will not attempt to clasp her until she touches them. This is much different from the behavior of male wood frogs, which are also explosive breeders.

The male spadefoot toad clasps the female from the back but, unlike most other North American species, wraps his front legs around the female's waist, just in front of her hind legs. Biologists consider this a primitive amplexus posture in frogs. This position gives the male quite a bit of mobility; he can swim with the female underwater and use his legs to kick at other males attempting to clasp the pair.

### EGGS AND EGG-LAYING

Shortly after a pair gets into amplexus position, they dive underwater and the female searches for a place to begin laying eggs. Typically, this is a twig, grass blade, fern leaf, or other vegetation and is often near other spadefoot-toad eggs. She grasps the plant with her front legs and walks along the stem, occasionally pushing with her hind feet. The male fertilizes the eggs as the female ejects them in rapid spurts. The entire compliment of up to 2,500 sticky eggs may appear in less than a minute or two.

Females leave the breeding pool shortly after depositing their eggs, while males continue to call and search out new females. Rarely are any adults to be found, however, as dawn approaches. It is unclear whether they move back to their home ranges late in the night, or remain in burrows at the edge of the pool for some time. Generally, at least a few males will be found in the same pond on the second or third night, but unless there is another dramatic rainstorm the pond will be strangely silent, with hundreds of thousands of eggs left behind.

Spadefoot toads have evolved to live in desert and semiarid conditions. Even in more temperate parts of their range, spadefoot toads are normally found in the drier, sandiest areas. The rapid developmental rates of their eggs and tadpoles is one adaptation well suited to such water-poor environments. In most areas of their range, spadefoot eggs hatch in one to seven days, usually two to four, depending on water temperature. For the first few days after hatching, the tadpoles remain vertical, attaching themselves with a suckerlike appendage to the egg mass or vegetation. During the next three or four days, you may find most of the tadpoles dispersed around the pond swimming near the surface. At this stage, they are apparently feeding on plankton suspended in the water column.

In some ponds the number of spadefoot tadpoles can be astonishing. As early as a week after they hatch, but sometimes not until two weeks, spadefoot tadpoles form dense schools that can be several feet long and wide. At this stage, and for the rest of their tadpole life, they feed continuously, grazing on algae, dead animals, and suspended phytoplankton.

Three types of schools can be seen, though the differences in their functions are unclear. Large, oblong schools usually include animals moving forward at the bottom of the pond feeding together. Streaming schools are elongated in shape and tend to move along the shoreline. Circular schools maintain themselves as animals move in arcs around the outside and attempt to swim toward the center.

The temporary ponds that are often used by adults in laying eggs can dry quickly or even freeze, causing several events that are likely to affect the survival of the tadpoles. If the pond dries too rapidly, then all the tadpoles will die. Slowly drying ponds cause intense crowding of the tadpoles. They must consequently compete with each other and other animals in the ponds for scare resources.

Crowded spadefoot tadpoles tend to grow more slowly and

metamorphose at smaller sizes than those that have lots of room to roam. However, close examination of tadpole ponds indicates that there are many complex factors that may act to change the survival responses of the spadefoot toads. Cannibalism, reported in several populations of spadefoot-toad tadpoles, may be, in part, due to crowding.

In general, spadefoot tadpoles are fast growers and disperse from their ponds as soon as they metamorphose. Depending upon temperature and other factors, the larvae may transform from two weeks to two months after they hatch. Their tails are often not fully reabsorbed, though most of the toadlets already sport wavy yellow lines on their backs. Mass migrations during the day of young spadefoot toads have been reported.

## OTHER FACTS ABOUT EASTERN SPADEFOOT TOADS

Adult spadefoot toads characteristically burrow into the soil, where they may remain for days or even a week or two at a time. If you are lucky enough to find one on the surface, try to follow it and watch it. At some point, it will begin to shuffle its back feet, excavate a bit of earth, and turn its body to one side or the other. Once they get started, the toads take little time in completing the job by rapidly digging with their hind feet and turning the body first in one direction, then the next; they disappear, corkscrew fashion, in a matter of seconds.

During periods of extended drought, spadefoot toads excrete a fluid, curl into a tight ball, and lie dormant. The fluid hardens the earth around the toad and forms a compact chamber that will hold whatever moisture is there. When heavy rains soak deep into the ground, the toads uncurl and resume their normal activities.

## OVERWINTERING

In southern areas of their range, spadefoot toads may remain more or less active every month of the year, emerging during warm, wet nights to feed or perhaps breed. In northern and western parts of the range, spadefoot toads are rarely found between October and March. It appears they remain inactive when they are in their overwintering burrows, though ample evidence of this is lacking. Spring thaws and heavy rains may cause spadefoots to stir, but they rarely come to the surface before late April or May.

## Quick Reference Chart

*Life Cycle*

**Length of Breeding Season:** Spring to fall (North) or any month of the year (South)

**Breeding Habit:** Temporary bodies of water; flooded fields, woodland ponds, ditches, extensive puddles

**Eggs Deposited:** Up to 2,500 during 1 or 2 nights of breeding activity; a population may reappear to breed later in year

**Eggs Hatch:** 1–7 days

**Length of Tadpole Stage:** 2 weeks to 2 months

**Lifespan of Adults:** At least 5 years

*Vocalizations*

**Advertisement call:** A loud, abrupt wail, repeated several times in succession by the male during thunderstorm nights

**Release call:** Short, vibrating call notes like a soft trill; given by both sexes

*Singing male spring peeper*

# SPRING PEEPER / *Hyla crucifer*

O<small>NE WARM</small>, wet May night several friends and I drove out to a marsh that was cluttered with sedges, some cattails, and a few alder shrubs. Even before we stopped the car and turned off the engine we could hear the deafening chorus of male peepers. We put on our waders and slowly moved through the marsh looking for peepers and other species of amphibians who were also breeding. The males were intent on vocalizing and seemed to be fairly unconcerned with our presence or our flashlights; they continued singing as we watched. At one point I reached down and placed my hand beneath a male that was sitting on a small mat of dried sedge leaves. He climbed onto my hand and to my amazement continued singing, his throat pouch gleaming in the light as I lifted him up to show everyone.

For all their abundance and strong voices peepers are still, to many people, the unseen harbingers of spring. It's too bad really, because with just a little effort the tiny treefrogs can be found and observed in nearly every city and town throughout the animal's extensive range. With their breeding choruses, peepers give the impression of being incredibly abundant animals, their combined voices sounding like fields full of crickets. In contrast, at times of the year when the frogs are not calling in their wetlands, peepers are very difficult to find in any significant number. Concentrated searches by experienced field researchers are usually unsuccessful.

## How to Recognize Spring Peepers

ADULTS

The typical mating or advertisement call of the male peeper is distinctive throughout most of its range and is the source of the species' common name. This single, high-pitched whistling note is slurred upward at the end and is typically repeated about once a second, or even more frequently during high temperatures.

Though most peepers have an X-shaped dark mark on their back, this can be quite variable or even absent. Identify peepers by their voice and small size — the males are three-quarters of an inch and large females only an inch and a half from nose to tail. Peepers range from light tan to dark brown, and they can change their skin color within this range in as little as fifteen minutes. The only other small, brownish treefrogs found in some parts of the peeper's range (pine woods treefrog and squirrel treefrog) have hind feet that are webbed at least halfway to the tips of their toes, while peepers have almost no webbing in comparison.

The rounded disks on their toes will identify spring peepers as treefrogs in the family Hylidae, which includes about 14 species in the United States and Canada and a total of 630 species worldwide. The spring peeper is the most widespread treefrog in North America, ranging from the Great Plains eastward and from southeastern Canada to the Gulf Coast. Some recent evidence suggests that peepers are actually more closely related to chorus frogs (*Pseudacris*) than to other treefrogs. Future research will help decide this.

DISTINGUISHING THE SEXES

Males vocalize, are always under an inch in length, and have dark throats. Females are silent, grow up to an inch and a quarter in length, and have light throats.

These are tiny, dark tan on top, and metallic bronze beneath. They are often abundant in marshes and temporary pools.

EGGS

The eggs are attached singly or in small groups to underwater plants. Each is brown on top and light beneath. They are not easy to locate because of their size, but they are numerous.

## How to Find Spring Peepers

**Habitat:** Forested wetlands, meadows, floodplains
**Months of Activity:** Year-round (South); March to November (North)

*Range of the spring peeper*

It is best to locate these frogs by learning their single-note, high-pitched, slurred whistle call. Normally they call at night from the edges of marshes, swamps, and wet meadows during the breeding season. Isolated males also call from forested uplands during wet periods throughout the year. Peepers are generally nocturnal but will vocalize during the day at the height of the breeding season.

Trying to find an isolated male in a swamp where there are hundreds or thousands is not an easy task since a deafening chorus can be confusing and even disorienting. You can sit or stand quietly and wait for a frog to move into view. Some people use a simple method of triangulation to locate individuals at night, and this might help you too. Go peeper-finding with at least one other person, or preferably two others. Single out one peeper call, and, with the two or three of you standing about three feet apart, concentrate on where each one of you thinks the peeper is actually sitting. On the count of three simultaneously shine your flashlights toward where the peeper voice seems to be. Where two or more beams of light cross, begin your search. Sometimes it takes two or three attempts before you will actually locate a peeper, but your patience will be rewarded.

## What You Can Observe

### SPRING EMERGENCE

Adult frogs emerge very early in the spring and immediately migrate to temporary ponds, flooded meadows, or lake edges to begin their territorial and breeding activities. Peepers rely on stored fat reserves at this time since there is a scarcity of food for them. Often, individual males begin to vocalize even before they get to the breeding grounds. There are relatively few peeper predators this early in the season.

### TERRITORIAL BEHAVIOR AND VOCALIZATIONS

Male peepers defend small breeding territories — between four and sixteen inches in diameter depending on population density — from other males. An advertisement call is repeated by a male sitting on the ground or elevated on twigs or other vegetation. Watch as the large, single vocal pouch inflates with air when he calls. Occasionally you will hear one or more peepers begin to make a different call, their trilling, aggressive call. If you carefully search for the male who is doing this, you will probably find another singing male nearby, and you may be lucky enough to see more.

The advertisement call and the aggressive call are the two major types of vocalizations that male peepers make. You can detect and distinguish them quite easily in just a short time. The advertisement call is a single-note peep typically heard in a peeper marsh during the breeding season. The note is high in pitch and rises at the end as a clear, sweet whistle; it is repeated about once every second during evening choruses. Field researchers have calculated that a single male repeats his call about 4,500 times on any given night during the breeding season. Some males follow other males' peeps with their own and maintain duets or other combinations. Peepers are one of the few frogs in North America that will give this advertisement call during times other than the breeding season. Even in northern parts of their range peepers have been heard in every month of the year.

There is a slight variation of this call that you might hear when a female enters the calling male's territory. The male reduces the rate at which his peeps are produced but at the same time increases the length of each peep.

The aggressive call is a trill of variable duration given by a calling male when an intruding male enters his territory or when a neighbor vocalizes close to the boundary between them. Either or both may give the call, though the resident male, more than intruders, seems to be the one who initiates it. Individual males may lengthen their aggressive calls as intruders continue to approach. Early in the season, when nighttime temperatures are relatively cool and few peepers are singing, you can easily hear aggressive calls. During the height of breeding chorusing, aggressive calls may be more difficult to pick out from the background sounds. There is some evidence that as more and more males arrive at the breeding ponds, individual peepers become more tolerant of nearby males and the number of aggressive calls decreases.

### SATELLITE MALES

Some male peepers do not appear to defend territories and do not vocalize with other males, but may be successful in mating with females anyway. Called satellite males, they can be found close to calling males and are distinguished from females by their smaller size and dark throats. Satellite males maintain a low posture, holding their heads down close to their feet; this may serve to keep the resident male from giving his encounter call or attacking. In some populations, peeper satellites only rarely intercept females who are attracted to the nearby singing male. Instead they seem to wait for a singing male to amplex a female, and when they are off depositing eggs, the satellite will take over the territory and begin vocalizing. In other populations, however, satellites do intercept females and successfully resist attempts by the territorial male to dislodge them.

## MATING

Peepers have an extended breeding season that lasts for two months or more, depending on temperature and rainfall. A chorus of singing males is a clear signal to which males and females are attracted. A chorus of peepers is rarely continuous, but rather is characterized by fifteen-minute to half-hour periods of calling separated by five to ten minutes of silence during which few if any males call. There is variation in this, however. Some populations chorus continually for several hours. When calling, males tend to separate their individual advertisement notes from those of nearby males, thus reducing interference from them.

Field researchers have determined that females are able to distinguish individual males by unique characteristics of the call and may be choosing mates based on criteria unknown to us at this time. It has been suggested that larger males are older, and age, for a female, may be one measure of a fit and reproductively superior peeper. In support of this theory is the fact that older males tend to call at a much faster rate than smaller (and younger) males, and some researchers have found that females are attracted to faster-calling males.

The female chooses a male by moving into his territory, swimming nearby, and finally touching him. She will then allow the male to move behind and clasp her by putting his front legs around her body. Occasionally the male will clasp the female before she touches him.

## EGGS AND EGG-LAYING

At the height of the breeding season, many pairs in amplexus can be located, often beneath the surface of the water. This is where the female goes (she does all the swimming when the male is attached to her) to deposit up to eight hundred eggs, singly or in

*Adult peepers
in amplexus*

small groups, on plants. She deposits her eggs within the male's territory. A pair may remain in amplexus for up to four hours while the male fertilizes the eggs as they are extruded by the female.

After egg-laying, females leave the ponds and take up residence in moist woodlands. Males return to their calling perches and resume vocalizing.

### TADPOLES

Peeper tadpoles can be abundant, but their numbers are thinned by a myriad of predators, including insects, turtles, snakes, birds, mammals, and salamanders. It is not uncommon to see one struggling in the grip of a dragonfly larva or predaceous diving beetle. For the first two weeks after hatching, peeper tadpoles remain relatively quiet, living in the leaf litter at the bottom of the pond. Later they may be more easily found grazing on algae or other small plants in the shallow, open-water sections of the pond.

If you return to ponds near the end of the tadpoles' nearly two-month larval period, you may begin to notice tiny, hopping frogs on the edges. These are newly metamorphosed peeper froglets. Look closely and you will see that most of them still have their tails. Peepers leave their ponds at an earlier stage of development than most frogs, and they complete their metamorphosis on the ponds' damp edges. Young peepers appear to be active mostly at dawn and dusk and should be looked for in meadows near their breeding ponds on early mornings when dew covers the ground.

OTHER FACTS ABOUT SPRING PEEPERS

Few studies have investigated the feeding habits of spring peepers, but those that have indicate that peepers have a widely ranging diet that includes small invertebrates such as spiders, ants, and beetles.

Away from the breeding ponds and marshes, peepers are only occasionally discovered. Normally, this will be on damp, overcast days. When walking through wooded areas, be alert for the tiny frogs as they leap out of your path. Rarely will they be more than two or three feet off the ground in a small tree or shrub. Usually, they live on the forest floor in the leaf-litter area.

OVERWINTERING

Spring peepers spend the winter on the surface of the soil, covered by leaf litter, logs, tree roots, or other material. Air temperatures here can commonly get as low as 10° or 15° F, subjecting the peepers to freezing conditions several times during the season. Peepers' bodies actually freeze, with ice crystals forming inside of them. Recent research has shown that peepers use glucose as a sort of antifreeze that limits dehydration and protects their cells from damage.

---

## Quick Reference Chart

*Life Cycle*

**Length of Breeding Season:** November to March (South);
   March to June (North)
**Breeding Habitat:** Wet meadows, woodland ponds, lakes, bogs
**Eggs Deposited:** Up to 800, attached singly to underwater plant
   over a period of weeks throughout the breeding season
**Eggs Hatch:** Usually within a week
**Length of Tadpole Stage:** About 45–60 days
**Lifespan of Adults:** At least 3 years

*Vocalizations*

**Advertisement call:** A loud, whistling peep that slurs upward
   at the end, lasting just a fraction of a second
**Aggressive call:** An unmusical trill that also slurs upward
   toward the end, lasting a second or longer; given when 2
   calling males are within 4–5 inches of each other

---

*Two adult gray treefrogs and a sphinx moth*

# GRAY TREEFROG /
*Hyla versicolor, Hyla chrysocelis*

For several years I had an opportunity to work with students who were studying migratory fish in a major New England river. On the warm, humid nights of July some sections of the river resounded with the vigorous calling of male gray treefrogs. Their explosive trills rang from the treetops and backwater areas of the river and reverberated off the distant hillsides. Farther away great horned owls and occasionally barred owls hooted throughout the night. Bats flitted in the air, and the sparkles of lightning beetles dotted the shrubbery along the shoreline. All in all, it was a magical scene, dominated by the sounds of a well-camouflaged frog that few people ever see.

It was not too long afterward, however, that I was directed to a singing chorus of treefrogs that was not in the pristine setting where I was accustomed to hearing them. A friend called to explain that her family had been hearing strange calls in the backyard for several nights. They weren't sure what they were, but the calls were loud enough for me to recognize the distinctive trilling of the gray treefrogs through the phone lines.

I rushed over and walked into the backyard. I knew the frogs would be near water. The only source in sight was my friend's aboveground swimming pool, and it still had the cover on. Spring rains, however, had created numerous pockets of water on the crumpled surface of the plastic cover, and it was here that two dozen male treefrogs had set up their calling sites. They seemed oblivious to our presence, and we watched them for nearly an hour, their throat pouches ballooning with each vocalization.

Since then, I have come to expect these magnificent treefrogs to appear in a variety of locations. I never fail to be impressed by their size, color variations, and patterns. Each encounter with a gray treefrog outside of their breeding season is a matter of chance, at best, and is a treasured moment.

## How to Recognize Gray Treefrogs

### ADULTS

The large, rounded toe disks, which enable these frogs to climb, will distinguish this species as a treefrog. Adults are mostly gray on the back and legs and usually have a white spot or rectangle just below each eye. There is a brilliant, yellow-orange splash of color on the underside of their hind legs. They are large treefrogs, growing to almost two and a half inches in length, and are surprisingly dry and warty looking. Newly metamorphosed gray treefrogs are small, about an inch and a half in length, and are an unbelievably beautiful bright green in color.

There are two different species of gray treefrogs in North America that are identical in appearance. They are the greater gray (*Hyla versicolor*) and the lesser gray (*Hyla chrysocelis*). Both are found east of the Great Plains, though the greater gray is a northeastern species, while the lesser gray is south-central. Their calls, though distinguishable, are very similar. The species are differentiated by biologists, usually by looking at the frog's blood cells under a microscope or by using other laboratory techniques. Since their habits are also alike, the life-history details here can be used for either species.

Gray treefrogs are members of the treefrog family, the Hylidae, whose 630 or so species are found throughout much of the world.

Males can be identified by their gray or black throats, while the females have light or white throats. Only the males vocalize, and this behavior is limited mostly to the breeding season. Males also have larger eardrums than females.

### TADPOLES

Gray-treefrog tadpoles hatch at about a quarter of an inch in length and are light yellow in color. Their maximum size is two and a half inches, and the full-sized tadpoles have an olive green body with a brick red tail.

### EGGS

The eggs of gray treefrogs are light colored, gray above and white below, and are deposited in globular clusters, and sometimes singly, on underwater vegetation. They hatch in two to five days and are therefore hard to find.

## How to Find Gray Treefrogs

**Habitat:** Mixed forests; temporary wetlands
**Months of Activity:** Year-round (South); May to October (North)

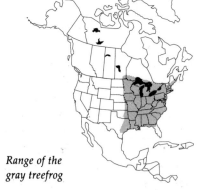

*Range of the gray treefrog*

The easiest way to find gray treefrogs is to follow their sounds as the adults migrate over a period of nights to their breeding ponds. They usually begin calling from upland woods a week or two before they actually start migrating. I have never been able to locate an isolated male that was calling from a mountainside in April or early May. For all I know they are hidden inside woodpecker holes or behind loose patches of bark when they vocalize. Only when you hear several or dozens of them calling from an isolated, usually temporary pond will you find the job of discovering adults easy.

These are late spring animals that do not call until nighttime temperatures reach 50° F or so. Although the males will sing in the daytime, especially during thunderstorms, they are usually well hidden. At night, however, they crawl onto fallen limbs, tree trunks, and branches and sing in full view. Use a flashlight to search likely calling sites. It is sometimes easier to do this than to try to isolate the sound of a single male. Gray-treefrog calls have a somewhat disorienting effect, making one think the sound is coming from a direction different from where the male actually is situated. Flashlights seem not to bother singing males at all.

Outside of the breeding season, there are numerous opportunities for a chance encounter with gray treefrogs. They are animals of deciduous or mixed deciduous and evergreen woodlands, and this is where they must be sought. They are quite often found around suburban and rural homes, so you should look for them along stone walls and wooden fences, under the eaves of houses and outbuildings, and around swimming pools and ponds. If you do find one, it is likely that you will see it several more times in or near the same spot; they remain in a home range.

## What You Can Observe

### SPRING EMERGENCE

Gray treefrogs emerge from terrestrial overwintering sites in April and move to unknown areas where they remain silent for several weeks. Then, the males begin to vocalize from wooded upland areas during warm days and just prior to thunderstorms. Not for another week or two will they begin to migrate to breeding ponds, though little else is known of their early spring behaviors.

### TERRITORIAL BEHAVIOR AND VOCALIZATIONS

Gray-treefrog males do not randomly situate themselves

around a breeding pond. Choosing a perch from which to call during the nights and on overcast days enhances a male's chance of successfully attracting a female, though after mating with one female, a male is not particularly likely to go back to the same perch. Characteristics of a good calling site have been analyzed by a few field researchers who have found that horizontal branches (arched over or fallen into the pond) with little or no leaves or adjacent vegetation correlated with the highest percentage of successful matings. If you find pairs together on a branch or other perch site early in the season it is likely that you will find others in the same place throughout the local population's several-week breeding period.

Males normally maintain a distance of at least thirty inches from each other during the breeding season. These territories are maintained by the use of aggressive calls and through physical interactions. Males have been observed in brief wrestling bouts.

Male gray treefrogs produce three different types of calls, though not all are easily distinguished in the field. They are the advertisement call, courtship call, and aggressive call. The easiest vocalization to hear during the breeding season is the loud, prolonged trill of their advertisement call. This has impressive carrying power. Researchers have found that the duration of an individual male's call varies with the distance of nearby males. The duration increases as other males come closer. The sound at a breeding pond filled with calling males is deafening. A second call, similar to the advertisement call but longer in duration, is the courtship call, given by a male who has been approached by a female and is about to clasp her. Finally, the aggressive call, a short, abrupt whoop repeated several times in succession, is given by a male when he detects another male calling or moving nearby.

MATING

When calling becomes more intense early in the breeding period, you can be sure that the females have just arrived. Females are attracted to singing males, and they will walk, not hop, toward them. Look for them near singing males; their white throats and movement toward the singing males will generally distinguish them from noncalling males. A gray-treefrog female chooses her mate by approaching a male and touching him with her nose or actually leaping upon him. The male usually responds instantly by moving behind the female and grasping her with his front legs.

The courtship and breeding season of gray treefrogs is prolonged, lasting for several weeks. While males will remain in and around the breeding pond for the entire period, individual females arrive, mate only once, and then leave within a night or two. Different females continue to arrive throughout the breeding season, however, so that there are always a few pairs of frogs interacting on any given night.

### SATELLITE MALES

Look carefully within a foot or two of the singing male and you may discover one or more satellite males sitting alertly but not

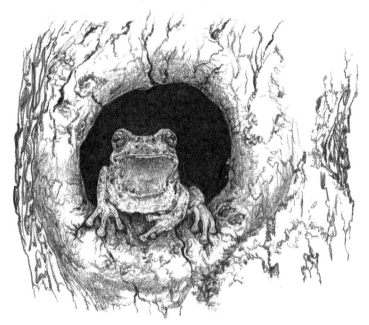

*Male gray treefrog peering out of tree cavity*

calling. Field observers of other species have found that occasionally satellite males have a fairly high percentage of success intercepting and mating with a female who is attracted to the singing male. In gray treefrogs, however, it is more likely that a satellite male will take over the singing perch of a resident male after he has successfully attracted a mate and they are off laying eggs.

## EGGS AND EGG-LAYING

Once a female has chosen a mate and the two are in amplexus, the pair will often stay on the calling perch for up to several hours. Eventually the female, with the male clasping her tightly, will crawl or hop down into the water and search for a place to deposit her eggs. The male maintains his grip and does not help in swimming.

Groups of ten to forty eggs are scattered on the surface of the pond, on and near emergent plants, until a total of nearly two thousand eggs is deposited.

## TADPOLES

The bright orange-red tail and green body of a gray-treefrog tadpole is a distinctive pattern among frogs. The colors may be disruptive — causing the outline of the tadpole to be broken — and therefore may make the animal less visible to predators. Gray-treefrog tadpoles also have some toxic skin secretions, and the red tail may be a warning signal to some predators. The tadpole stage lasts between one and two months.

## OTHER FACTS ABOUT TREEFROGS

One thing to notice is the hallmark of the treefrog family — the large, rounded pads at the ends of their toes. These disks are different sizes in different members of the family, but are particularly huge in the gray treefrog. The largest toes have pads about the same size as the frog's eardrum. The toepads allow the frog to cling to rough and smooth surfaces and actually to scale vertical barriers with little difficulty. Late in the summer, on humid nights, check your windows if your room lights are attracting insects.

Sooner or later, if they're in your area, you will see a big-eyed gray treefrog hanging on the glass.

After the toepads, note how rough the frog's skin is. It helps to dispel the myth that all frogs are smooth and all toads are warty.

If your gray treefrog is resting, you undoubtedly will see the standard posture for this behavior. The treefrog clenches its two front feet into fists and curls them beneath its chin. The whole body is in a compact mass and the edges of the skin are tightly pressed to where it contacts the frog's resting place. The belief is that in this posture the frog casts little or no shadow and its outline is completely obscured from foraging birds, snakes, or tree-climbing mammals.

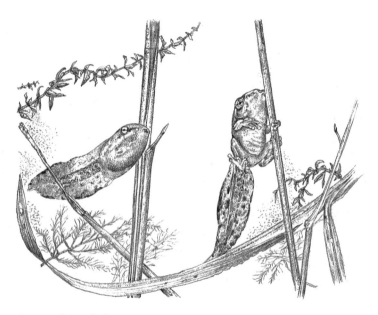

*Gray-treefrog tadpoles*

Gray treefrogs spend the winter beneath leaf litter, rocks, or perhaps inside mammal burrows or other undergound crevices. Laboratory researchers have found that this species has a remarkable ability to withstand freezing temperatures. Sexually mature gray treefrogs are able to survive for several days, partially frozen, at up to 20° below zero F by accumulating large amounts of glycerol in their blood. Juveniles also survived, but used both glycerol and glucose for antifreeze. In these experiments over 40 percent of the frog's total body water was frozen, and repeated bouts of thawing and refreezing seemed to have little effect.

---

## Quick Reference Chart

*Life Cycle*

**Length of Breeding Season:** Early May (South) to August (North)
**Breeding Habitat:** Temporary and permanent pools, ponds, oxbows, and floodwaters along rivers
**Eggs Deposited:** Up to 2,000 eggs per female, in masses of 10–40 eggs each
**Eggs Hatch:** 2–5 days
**Length of Tadpole Stage:** 30–60 days
**Lifespan of Adults:** Unknown, though sexual maturity is not reached for 2 years

*Vocalizations*

**Advertisement call:** A loud, explosive trill given throughout breeding season
**Courtship call:** A prolonged trill when a female approaches a calling male
**Aggressive call:** A short, abrupt whoop given by males within 30 inches of each other

---

*Female green frog emerging from pond*

# GREEN FROG / *Rana clamitans*

O<small>NE LATE</small> November day I was walking along a small, woodland brook searching for nothing in particular. There was very little water in the brook, and what was there was all but covered and clogged by the autumn leaves that had fallen not long before. Surprisingly few sounds came from the surrounding forest. Only a single chipmunk and a couple of chickadees made any vocalizations at all. The brook was seemingly lifeless, too, though small insects crawled along the bottom and an occasional fish darted through the shadows.

My feet crunched the leaves on the stream's bank, and simultaneously two things startled me. A loud, almost piercing yelp broke the silence, and a small form darted from under my feet and plopped into the water. I was lucky enough to be able to follow its swift motion under the surface, where it came to lie next to a small stone at the bottom of a pool. By carefully stepping on some large rocks I could lean over and see that it was a young green frog that had made the sound and abandoned its resting place when I approached too closely. Since the water was so clear, every detail of the frog was visible, including the clear membrane that covers frogs' eyes when they swim underwater.

After a few minutes, I continued on my way and, somewhat to my surprise, startled another green frog just a few steps further along the bank. For a few hundred yards more, another and another frog leapt to safety on my approach, and by the end of my stroll I had counted more than a dozen. All of these green frogs appeared to be young, much smaller than those that usually breed in the nearby pond. It occurred to me that there were no large green frogs to be found along the brook. I have looked for them without success on every late autumn trip that I've taken since.

## How to Recognize Green Frogs

### ADULTS

The voice of the male green frog has been aptly described as sounding like a plucked banjo string or tight rubber band. Individual notes are given at irregular intervals, and a small chorus of males sounds less coordinated than that of other species.

Green frogs are medium-sized frogs (about six inches long), with smooth skin and a single vocal sac. Two raised ridges of skin begin just above each ear and run on either side of the body most but not all of the way to the tail. Despite their name, green frogs may be brown or tan, as well as green. Individuals from southern populations have many spots on their backs, while northern ones are generally unspotted.

Other frogs that look like green frogs either lack the ridges on their sides (like bullfrogs), or have ridges that run all the way to their tails (leopard and wood frogs).

Green frogs are included in the family Ranidae, the true frogs.

### DISTINGUISHING THE SEXES

Males generally have eardrums larger than their eyes, and yellow throats. In the breeding season their thumbs enlarge and sometimes develop dark growths on them.

Female green frogs usually have white throats and eardrums the same size or smaller than their eyes.

TADPOLES

These can grow to be up to three and a half inches in total length. They are olive green above and have many small, blackish spots on them. Underneath they are cream colored with a coppery hue.

EGGS

The tiny, black eggs are imbedded in a filmy egg mass that, at least initially, floats on the surface of the water. The mass is about a foot in diameter and is usually found anchored by underwater plants in shallow water.

## How to Find Green Frogs

**Habitat:** Edges of ponds, streams, springs
**Months of Activity:** Year-round (South); March to November (North)

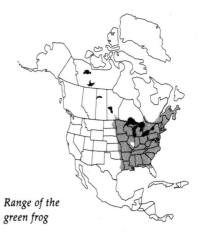

Range of the
green frog

These aquatic frogs are much more likely to be found in small brooks and streams than in the ponds or lakes that close relatives like bullfrogs prefer. Green frogs also frequent the margins of large lakes and reservoirs, the backwaters of larger rivers, and temporary woodland pools.

Though green frogs are active mostly at night, they can be found during daylight hours by carefully scanning the edges of the water, up onto the shore. Sometimes green frogs can be found moving through fields and woodland, especially during rainy weather, but again, they are usually close to ponds and streams.

# What You Can Observe

In southern parts of their range, green frogs usually begin to appear in late February or early March. In the far North, they may not become active until late April or May. Some observers have found that green frogs begin to breed shortly after they emerge, while others note a lag time of up to several weeks before they arrive at breeding sites in the backwaters of streams or adjacent marshes.

### TERRITORIAL BEHAVIOR AND VOCALIZATIONS

Like gray treefrogs, green frogs have a prolonged breeding season. Male green frogs set up and maintain territories all through the breeding season. Territories are set up in shallow water and may be from three to twenty feet in diameter. Within these areas, males generally have one or more favorite sites from which they vocalize. On occasion, males patrol the edges of their territory and change their vocalizations or behavior in response to other males. Resident males act differently depending on the population of the pond, weather, and probably other factors. Territorial males sit upright in the water with the head and back well out of the water.

Green frogs produce at least six vocalizations. The first four are associated with the breeding season and are given by males. The last two are given by both males and females.

The first is the common single-note advertisement call that sounds much like a plucked banjo string. Occasionally, males will give this single note two or three times in rapid succession, especially in a very active chorus. The second, known as a high-intensity advertisement call, consists of a further acceleration and number of single banjolike notes. Field observers have listened to males give this call when facing other males across a territory border, when another frog leaps through the territory of a resident male, or after having won a physical encounter with an intruding male.

When a resident male finds an intruder entering his territory, he may give an aggressive call. This is the same single-note advertisement call but is noticeably louder and more abrupt. This vocalization nearly always precedes some physical interaction between male frogs.

Male green frogs also give a soft, two- to five-second growl, though this may not be heard at a distance of more than ten feet or so. Researchers have heard this sound when males were actually wrestling or were about to. The function of the growl is not clear.

Both males and females give a long release call, consisting of a series of chirps. Females who have already deposited their eggs, others without eggs, and males who are losing wrestling matches give this call and are usually released by the male who is clasping them.

Finally, green frogs give a loud, sharp yelp when startled. This alert call is normally made as the frog leaps to the safety of water.

## SATELLITE MALES

Smaller males, unable to acquire and defend territories, are often found within the areas secured by larger, resident males. These satellite males remain low in the water, often with just their eyes and nose exposed above the surface. Resident males rarely bother the satellites, who often sit just inches away. The satellites have not been observed actively pursuing or otherwise intercepting females who enter a resident male's territory. Instead, they are much more likely to wait for the resident to attract a mate and move off to deposit eggs before taking over the territory and beginning to advertise.

## MATING

In green frogs, it is the female who chooses her mate. This decision seems to be based, in part, on how she perceives the quality of the male's territory. Females seem to prefer egg-laying sites that include a lot of underwater plants, such as *Elodea*; these plants make a mat upon which the film of eggs can rest.

Females enter the male's territories only when they are ready to deposit their eggs. During the day, they often remain in shallow water near shore, hunting, sunning, or resting. At night, they move in a very low posture through the territories of several males, apparently making some assessment of each one. When ready to choose a male, the female will surface just inches in front of him, turn away, and slowly back toward him. A male usually waits for the female actually to touch him before clasping her. This sometimes requires an hour or more of slow approaches by the female.

After egg-laying, females leave the breeding ponds and take up residence along the shore or in nearby streams and riverbanks. The males resume their territorial behavior and continue to vocalize. Females have been known to return to the breeding grounds within a few weeks, choose other males, and deposit second masses of eggs.

### EGGS AND EGG-LAYING

Once clasped, the female slowly moves around to find an appropriate egg-laying site. Often, the male will continue to give his

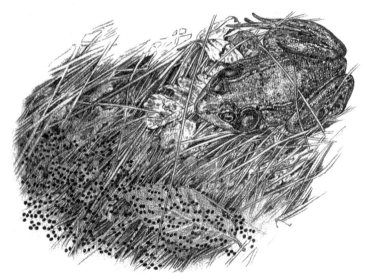

*Male green frog with eggs*

advertisement call, though it is usually muffled because his throat pouch cannot inflate very far as his chin is pressed on her head. The female usually deposits her eggs in the male's territory by arching her back upward toward the surface of the water. Up to thirty or forty eggs emerge at once, the male fertilizes them, and he seems to push them away from the female as more are extruded. Within ten minutes to half an hour, a large, flat mass of three to five thousand eggs floats on the water or is slightly draped on underwater plants.

## TADPOLES

Green-frog tadpoles show a fascinating variation in their adaptations to water levels and the prolonged breeding season of the adults. In most places, tadpoles that hatch early in the season will transform into frogs by mid- to late summer. Tadpoles that hatch late are likely to overwinter in their ponds (assuming the pond remains filled) and metamorphose late the following spring or early in the summer.

The numbers of green-frog tadpoles in a breeding pond can be very high. Field observers have estimated up to twenty-five thousand tadpoles to be active in a five-acre pond. Competition among individuals has recently been shown to be important to the survival of tadpoles. Also, not surprisingly, there are many tadpole predators you might easily observe. Chief among these are aquatic larvae of insects and wading birds.

## OTHER FACTS ABOUT GREEN FROGS

You might be able to watch green frogs stalk and catch their prey. Insects, spiders, snails, slugs, and aquatic crustaceans are known to be in their diet. While they feed mostly at night, patient observation of green frogs even in the daytime will eventually show you this behavior. Typically, green frogs sight moving prey from at least a foot or two away. A frog may walk slowly or take two or three short hops to close the distance before grasping the prey.

Over much of their range, green frogs overwinter at the bottom of ponds, lakes, rivers, and streams. Juveniles tend to remain active later in the season than adults, but most frogs of all ages disappear by late October. Green frogs have been found in water less than three feet deep, tucked into small crevices between rocks, fallen logs and branches, or other debris that accumulates underwater. No one has yet observed and reported any indication of a constructed overwintering form or other structure that the frogs might make and use.

Green frogs remain more or less inactive until the following March or April. In some overwintering locations, green frogs have been observed swimming and even feeding during midwinter warm spells. There is something special about seeing a frog swim beneath the surface of a cold, snow-circled spring on a sunny February afternoon.

# Quick Reference Chart

*Life Cycle*

**Length of Breeding Season:** 1–3 months

**Breeding Habitat:** Swamps, ponds, marshes, bogs, slow sections of rivers, oxbow lakes

**Eggs Deposited:** 3,000–5,000 eggs deposited in March and April (South); June to August (North); a second clutch is usually much smaller

**Eggs Hatch:** Usually within 3–7 days

**Length of Tadpole Stage:** 3–22 months

**Lifespan of Adults:** At least 5 years

*Vocalizations*

**Advertisement call:** Sounds like a plucked banjo string

**High-intensity advertisement call:** Faster repetition of advertisement call

**Aggressive call:** Very loud and abrupt advertisement call; usually precedes physical interaction between males

**Growl:** Faint call, lasting several seconds, given by wrestling males

**Release call:** A short series of chirps given by males and females; usually results in a male's releasing his grip on the calling frog

**Alert call:** A sharp yelp given by both sexes when startled; usually associated with an escape leap

*Adult female bullfrog*

# BULLFROG / *Rana catesbeiana*

I was on a June canoe trip down a slow, winding river. The voices of male bullfrogs bellowed from the shallow, plant-choked backwaters. In these old oxbow ponds, formed when meanders were left behind by the constantly shifting river, great mats of water milfoil, white water lily, and duckweed all but hid the dark water. We quietly slipped our canoes into the shallows and waited for the frogs to become accustomed to our presence.

In less than a minute they began again, the yellow throats of the males glistening in the sunlight and bulging out beneath their huge heads. It was clearly the height of the bullfrog territorial and mating season, and we were in for a fascinating day. There were more than a hundred different bullfrogs in the various areas we canoed into, and the largest males seemed most intent on proclaiming their territories. We saw numerous females as well, but they seemed to be on the banks in the main channel of the river, perhaps not ready to move into the breeding grounds.

At the last oxbow we checked, we finally got a spectacular look at a territorial skirmish between two huge males. They were only six inches apart when we first noticed them. Suddenly they lunged at each other; they hung on tightly with their front legs and feet. The water boiled with their activity as they wrestled for half a minute before breaking apart. In another minute they started again. We sat quietly and watched through our binoculars. Eventually one of the two frogs took several leaps away. The other followed closely on his heels. The territory dispute was over.

## How to Recognize Bullfrogs

### ADULTS

The easiest way to identify bullfrogs is by the male's familiar "jug-o-rum" call. Recognizing them by sight is not always easy. Bullfrogs are usually some shade of green, but brown, yellow, albino, and even blue individuals have been found. All bullfrogs have a ridge of skin that begins behind the eye, runs over the eardrum, and ends at the base of the front legs. Adult bullfrogs are large amphibians, often reaching seven inches in length from nose to tail.

Small bullfrogs look similar to several other semiaquatic species, especially pig and river frogs of the Southeast and the widespread green frogs. But bullfrogs have smooth skin (the river frog has rough) and webbing on the hind foot that doesn't reach the tips of the toes (the pig frog has webbing to the tips), and they lack a ridge of skin that runs along both sides of the back from eye to hind end (green frogs have this dorsolateral ridge).

Bullfrogs are members of the true frog family, the Ranidae. The bullfrog has been introduced into parts of this and other continents for food and for predator control. There is some speculation that introduced bullfrogs have displaced native species of frogs, though little evidence has been gathered to support this.

### DISTINGUISHING THE SEXES

Bullfrogs, like most amphibians, grow continually throughout their lives. The oldest and largest bullfrogs are almost invariably females, since males, because of their more active lifestyle, are exposed to predation much more than the adult females and don't live as long.

Male bullfrogs have yellow throats and eardrums much larger

than the diameter of the eyes. Females, by contrast, have white throats and eardrums that are about the same size, if not slightly smaller, than their eyes. Only males give vocalizations on the breeding grounds, though both sexes produce other calls.

### TADPOLES

The olive-colored tadpoles grow to five inches or more in total length, the largest of any in North America. Bullfrog tadpoles are white or cream colored underneath, which helps to distinguish them from other large species.

### EGGS

The eggs of bullfrogs are relatively easy to find and identify. They are deposited in huge, semifloating masses that look like mats of frothy, tiny bubbles. The whole mass may be two feet in diameter. Since the eggs hatch relatively quickly, the mass seems to disappear within a week.

## How to Find Bullfrogs

**Habitat:** Ponds, lakes, reservoirs
**Months of Activity:** Year-round (South); March to November (North)

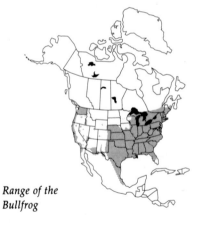

*Range of the Bullfrog*

If you want to find bullfrogs, visit a permanent body of water and, with a pair of binoculars, scan the edges. They might be sitting partially submerged or fully exposed on the bank. Sometimes the frogs are hidden beneath leaves and branches that arch over the edge; rarely will they be on top of floating logs. Along some streams with high banks I have found them on little ledges several feet above the level of the water. If you walk the edges, bullfrogs are usually very difficult to locate until they leap out from under your feet and take refuge in the soft mud beneath the water.

In general, most bullfrog behavior is best observed with the aid of a flashlight at night. During the height of the breeding season and the heat of summer temperatures, however, bullfrogs are actively finding food, avoiding predators, and otherwise attending to their needs all day long. The largest populations exist where both underwater plants and those growing near the margins of the water are particularly lush.

## What You Can Observe

### SPRING EMERGENCE

The youngest bullfrogs usually appear first in the spring in any given population, sometimes weeks before the largest adults emerge. Increasing air and water temperatures are probably responsible for bullfrogs' becoming active each year, and those in the South are typically active long before individuals in northern and upper-elevation areas. Gulf Coast bullfrogs, for example, may appear in January, while Canadian populations are not expected until April or May. When pond-bottom temperatures of 55° – 60° F are recorded, bullfrogs become active.

### TERRITORIAL BEHAVIOR AND VOCALIZATIONS

When the males begin singing, get a pair of binoculars and some method of surviving mosquitoes and go down to their pond. Try to spend a little time every few days or nights over a period of a month or so in order to see most of the behaviors and activities that can occur. Males will call during the day, though not as vigorously as they will at night. They move offshore to their territories, situated near an abundance of underwater plants.

When the first males begin singing in the season, the females are still on the edges of the ponds and marshes. They don't move out to where the male territories are for a week or more after the males commence their choruses. Only a few females at a time enter the choruses to breed.

A male bullfrog's territory is a roughly circular area that may be anywhere from six to twenty feet in diameter. Males who are singing have established territories and tend to be the largest and oldest individuals. They usually sit high in the water, with their head, throat, and back fully exposed and in clear view.

Sometimes another large male will challenge a resident male for his territory. The resident will give another vocalization sounding like a loud "hick." The challenger may return this call and then be vigorously attacked by the resident. The two may actually lock themselves in a wrestling hold and try to gouge each other with their thumbs. The victor might hold the loser underwater for minutes at a time, but will eventually let him up and then chase him to the edge of the territory.

### SATELLITE MALES

Occasionally smaller males will enter the territories of larger, singing males but will not be attacked. These males, usually young, take on a much different posture than the residents, maintaining a low profile on the surface, most often with just the top of the head out of the water. Their low swimming posture is very similar to that of approaching females, and there is some belief that this mimicry causes the territorial male's passive behavior.

Because of their small size, these satellite males are unable to compete successfully for territories. However, satellites have been observed to intercept females who are approaching a larger male. Occasionally, the smaller male is successful in his attempts to mate, though most are dislodged by the larger male. Satellite males have also been observed taking over the territory of a larger male who has successfully attracted a female and is engaged in fertilizing her eggs. Since the satellite males spend very little energy defending a territory or even in vocalizing, their mating strategy may give them at least a modicum of success in leaving behind some offspring. Estimates of the number of satellite males in a breeding chorus indicate that they may make up anywhere from 14 to 43 percent of the total breeding population.

OPPORTUNISTIC MALES

At least in a few populations, observers have found that some singing male bullfrogs do not maintain a territory but will nonetheless attempt to attract a female. These individuals, called opportunistic males, are generally larger (and therefore older) than satellite males, but smaller than territorial males. Opportunistic males retreat from advances by any large male who is defending his territory.

The displaced opportunistic male will begin singing from a new location and will change his position in the pond each time he is threatened. There is some speculation that this may in fact be an intermediate behavioral stage between the satellite- and territorial-male mating strategies.

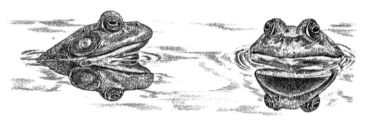

*Female bullfrog (right) approaching male*

MATING

When a female is ready to deposit her eggs, you may be able to observe her choosing her mate. Her choice is based primarily on the quality of the male's territory. She surveys potential mates by maintaining a low swimming posture and moving slowly through the chorus of males. Calling males allow her to approach very closely but do not clasp her until she actually touches one with her leg or nose.

Then the male swims behind her and wraps his front legs around her upper body near her front legs. She swims a short distance and begins to look for a place to deposit her eggs. Usually, the pair remains clasped to each other for a half hour or less, but they can remain together for several hours as she releases her enormous number of eggs and he fertilizes them.

EGGS AND EGG-LAYING

When ready to extrude and fertilize the eggs, a pair of bullfrogs dives just beneath the surface of the water. The female slightly arches her back to bring the end of her body close to the surface. The male stretches out his hind legs and, as she extrudes fifty or sixty eggs at a time, he fertilizes them. An average of six or seven thousand eggs are eventually deposited in a thin sheet on the water's surface, though the largest females may lay nearly twenty thousand eggs. When the entire complement of eggs is deposited, the female will leave the breeding ground to take up a summer residence along the shoreline. The male will return to his territory in the hope of attracting more females. Only recently has it been discovered that some female bullfrogs can deposit a second clutch of eggs within a couple of weeks. The number of eggs extruded in the second mating is relatively small, perhaps two thousand.

Predation upon the eggs, especially by leeches, takes a large toll. Eggs whose temperatures increase above 82° F develop abnormally, and most such embryos die. It is curious to think that a frog chooses the warmest months of the year to lay eggs, but has to find the coolest areas of the pond to keep its eggs from dying.

In normal situations at least some of the eggs in the clutch survive and hatch within two weeks. The newborn tadpoles initially remain near the plants where the egg mass was deposited.

TADPOLES

Bullfrog tadpoles can be found anytime of the year in most areas. Their large size (they can grow to five or more inches) makes them conspicuous members of pond-bottom communities. During the heat of the summer many lounge in the warm, shallow edges of their ponds. If you carefully walk to the edge of a pond you may see them before they spot you and scurry away to deeper water. You must look carefully because the tadpoles are a muddy green color, matching the plant and silt bottom of their aquatic communities.

When not resting, bullfrog tadpoles spend much of their time feeding, which they do, like most tadpoles, by vigorously swimming forward with their head and mouth in the substratum or along a plant stem. Bullfrog tadpoles graze on small food particles and detritus and apparently get much food value from bacteria and other microorganisms that they ingest. It has been demonstrated that bullfrog tadpoles have a fairly inefficient digestive system, so that only a small part of the food they take in is actually utilized. The tadpoles are known to ingest their own feces, perhaps incidentally, but this may contribute to their growth. Larger and older tadpoles are able to outcompete smaller ones for all types of food, including feces, and this puts the larger ones at a distinct advantage. Larger tadpoles also have fewer predators.

In most parts of their range, the tadpoles will metamorphose into juveniles during the summer following their hatching. Some, especially northern, populations, will spend a second winter as tadpoles before sprouting legs, lungs, and a host of other adaptations for juvenile and adult life. Tadpoles appear to be inactive during the winter when ice covers their ponds.

### OTHER FACTS ABOUT BULLFROGS

There are three additional bullfrog behaviors that you can observe. The first of these is the bullfrog's regulation of its body temperature. You may see bullfrogs sitting in full sunlight make small but important adjustments in the angle of their body to receive more or less radiation. Following this, they may cool off by diving into the water or moving to a shady location. Field researchers have found that bullfrogs prefer to remain between 78° and 92° F.

You may also watch bullfrogs feeding. They usually wait for prey to move before lunging or leaping forward, mouth agape, to

*Adult male bullfrog*

snare their meal. Don't be shocked if you see a bullfrog going after "unfroglike" meals. They are known to eat mice, small turtles, fish, snakes (including rattlesnakes), birds, and other frogs, including bullfrogs. However, the bulk of their diet is insects, spiders, crayfish, and other invertebrates, and many of these are active on warm days when bullfrogs sit on the shoreline.

Because they usually see you long before you see them, you can sometimes watch bullfrogs escaping. As they leap off the shore they often give what can be described as an alert call. This is a short note that some researchers have suggested may warn nearby frogs of a potential predator, implying some sort of altruism. It is equally possible that the alert call may simply function to startle a potential predator, who might hesitate just long enough for the frog to make good its escape.

With one or two immensely powerful kicks of its hind legs, an escaping bullfrog glides to the pond bottom where it remains motionless. You must be very patient if you are to outwait an underwater bullfrog. They can stay there for dozens of minutes. Bullfrogs have a large number of predators against which this escape behavior may be helpful. Known predators are snakes, herons, alligators, raccoons, snapping turtles, otters, mink, large- and smallmouth bass, pickerel, pike, and others. When caught by a predator, bullfrogs can emit an incredibly loud distress call that may last up to five seconds or more. When doing this vocalization, the frog's mouth is wide open.

OVERWINTERING

Juvenile and adult bullfrogs seem conspicuously absent from their ponds as the air temperature drops toward 40° F. Adults retreat to the mud and leaf litter of the lake bottom days or even weeks before the juveniles. Occasional reports of winter kills of this species thus usually include a high percentage of young frogs.

Before disappearing underwater for the winter, bullfrogs spend progressively less time on riverbanks and pond margins and more time floating on the surface. In the North, bullfrogs burrow completely beneath leaf litter or into the mud at a pond bottom in mid-October, while in the South they remain active year-round except during cold spells.

# Quick Reference Chart

*Life Cycle*

**Length of Breeding Season:** February to October (South); May
   to July (North); March to July (West)
**Breeding Habitat:** Permanent bodies of water—lakes,
   reservoirs, ponds, and marshes
**Eggs Deposited:** Up to 80,000 eggs in a floating mass per
   coupling, throughout the breeding season
**Eggs Hatch:** Within 14 days
**Length of Tadpole Stage:** 4 months to 2 years
**Lifespan of Adults:** Minimum 5 or 6 years

*Vocalizations*

**Male advertisement call:** The familiar deep bass "jug-o-rum"
**Male challenge call:** A loud "hick" or "hic-cup" call
**Alert call:** A short "miaow" note made when leaping to safety
**Distress call:** A very loud and long (up to five seconds in
   duration) wailing cry

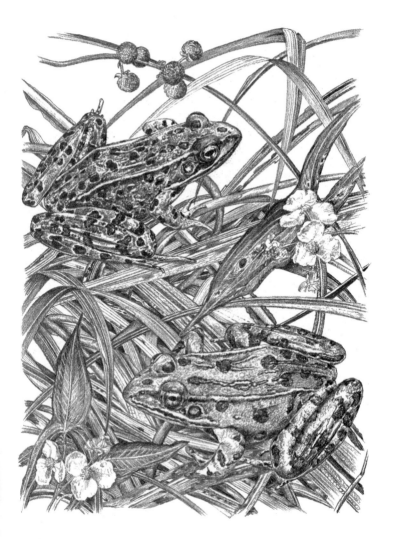

*Variations in northern leopard-frog spot pattern*

# NORTHERN LEOPARD FROG / *Rana pipiens*

W<small>HILE SOME</small> friends and I were camping in a state park some years ago, the sounds of calling leopard frogs reached us from a nearby lake. We got up and went to look for them, but for a long while our searches were unsuccessful. No amount of stealth or careful scrutiny of the shoreline would reveal the presence of the males, who continued to call all around us. Frustrated, we returned to the campsite to discuss the situation over supper.

About an hour later, with the frogs still calling, we returned to the water's edge to try again. This time we were successful, but only because someone accidentally dropped a flashlight into the lake. The light illuminated a pair of leopard frogs, already in amplexus, and the male was still singing — underwater. His two vocal sacs, located on both sides of the body near the armpits, swelled each time he called. This was the first time any of us had seen frogs vocalizing beneath the surface; we found two or three others that night doing the same thing.

Leopard frogs are familiar to most high-school and college students in North America since they have been commonly used for dissection in biology classes for many years. While many students find the experience less than delightful, researchers have gleaned enormous amounts of information from laboratory studies of leopard frogs.

Five different species of leopard frog are now recognized in North America. Their identity and relationships with each other are not adequately understood, and the release of captive pets and laboratory animals outside their original ranges has only added to the confusion. It is easy to find leopard frogs with the characteristics of any given population anywhere in the country.

## How to Recognize Northern Leopard Frogs

### ADULTS

The vocalizations of this frog are not as easily distinguished from those of other species because their advertisement call has quite a bit of variation. It includes a series of clucking notes, often following a two- or three-second snoring sound. It is something like the sound produced by rubbing your hands irregularly over an inflated balloon.

As their name suggests, leopard frogs are marked on the back, sides, and legs with numerous dark, roundish spots that usually have light borders around them. The spot pattern and color are quite variable and may be used to identify individual leopard frogs. The base color is usually brown or green but can also be yellow or even blue.

These are typically slender, long-legged frogs with two dorsolateral ridges. Leopard frogs grow to about five inches in length. Other leopard frogs may be distinguished from the northern in that they have smaller or fewer spots or incomplete ridges along their sides.

Northern leopard frogs are in the true frog family, the Ranidae.

### DISTINGUISHING THE SEXES

Both sexes look quite similar, though males are generally smaller than females, reaching only three and a quarter inches. Males have two vocal sacs that swell out from their armpits when the frogs are calling. In the breeding season, the thumbs on the males' front feet swell in size. Females usually grow to three and a half inches or more in length. During the breeding season they are much fatter than males.

### TADPOLES

Leopard-frog tadpoles are not easily distinguished in the field from those of other species of true frogs. They are olive or tan on top and creamy white below. They grow to a maximum size of three inches.

### EGGS

Up to five or six thousand tiny, black eggs are deposited in oblong egg masses about six inches long and two inches wide. They are loosely attached to twigs and other material underwater.

## How to Find Leopard Frogs

**Habitat:** Fields and meadows, from coasts to mountains
**Months of Activity:** February to November

*Range of the northern leopard frog*

For most of the warmer parts of the year, you should seek out leopard frogs in meadows and grasslands, especially those near streams, rivers, and ponds. Cultivated hay fields or meadows inhabited by grazing cows or horses are likely locales. Here leopard frogs are active mostly at night, but on any afternoon stroll through the area you will see numerous leopard frogs as they dart off in all directions. During the spring, search the banks of slow-moving rivers for basking leopard frogs. A canoe is an especially good way to approach the frogs slowly; they often allow an observer to get within inches.

During the breeding season adult leopard frogs are found in water on the edges of shallow ponds, lakes, rivers, and streams. During hot and sunny periods, leopard frogs may construct small burrows on muddy banks; they back into these burrows and sit facing outwards.

In early summer, young leopard frogs can be incredibly abundant in those areas that still have populations. They rarely get far from where they hatched. You should search for them on the pond margins where there is a thick growth of plants. Most likely, many of the young frogs will leap frantically out of the way and into the water before you see them. They are especially hard to locate underwater, so concentrate on finding them before they leap.

## What You Can Observe

### SPRING EMERGENCE

Leopard frogs emerge from their underwater winter retreats in the early spring. This is often in February in southern parts of the range but not usually until late April in the North. Adults may move into a terrestrial home range for a week or more, but soon after they become active they migrate to breeding ponds and begin their courtship activity.

### TERRITORIAL BEHAVIOR AND VOCALIZATIONS

There is not much evidence of leopard frogs' maintaining territories either during the breeding season or during the summer. Individuals do live in a home range that includes several small burrows that they use repeatedly. On rainy nights the frogs may move some distance away to other meadows, but often return to their home area within a few days. The significance of these movements is unclear.

Both male and female leopard frogs make sounds. The male advertisement call is a hoarse croaking followed by two or more clucks. This is given during the breeding season on land or in water.

Males also produce a short, chuckling aggressive call when they are clasped by another male or held by a human observer. This sound can be heard throughout the year, even from overwintering frogs who have been lifted out of water. Females that have finished egg-laying also give an aggressive call when they are clasped by males as they are leaving the ponds.

## MATING

Little is known of the breeding strategies employed by male and female leopard frogs. Males generally arrive first at breeding ponds and begin to give their advertisement call. Females appear to approach males and may or may not touch them before the male moves behind and attempts to clasp her with his front legs.

In some populations leopard frogs have a second breeding period in September or October.

## EGGS AND EGG-LAYING

Once a pair is joined, the female will swim to egg-laying sites that are often adjacent to other egg masses. Females have been observed in a characteristic posture where they turn their hind legs inward and stretch their thighs.

While the female extrudes the eggs, the male fertilizes them; this activity is accompanied by a series of slight adjustments in both of their postures. The whole process may take only five minutes or so. Once finished, the female arches her back in an apparent attempt to signal the male to release his grip. Once he does, she leaves the water. He may start his advertisement call again. It is not known how successful male leopard frogs are in mating with additional females.

The eggs of leopard frogs are deposited in elongated masses that may be up to six inches long and two or three inches wide. From four to six thousand eggs are deposited in a single mass or occasionally in several masses. Females tend to deposit their eggs in communal nesting sites. The eggs hatch within two to three weeks.

Leopard-frog tadpoles are known to congregate in shallow water, but the significance of this behavior remains unstudied in this species. They transform into small frogs two to three months later, usually in August. Some tadpoles in northern parts of the range are known to overwinter in ponds.

## OTHER FACTS ABOUT NORTHERN LEOPARD FROGS

The main food eaten by leopard frogs is apparently the large insects, worms, and spiders commonly found in meadows and fields. These include grasshoppers, crickets, and beetles, though their diet changes as populations of prey change. If you sit and watch a leopard frog for a while, you may see it hunt and feed.

The motion of a crawling insect or worm attracts the frog's attention (although recent research has shown that leopard frogs are also able to find food by smell). If the movement of an insect is within a few inches, the frog simply leans forward and with an incredibly rapid movement snaps it up with its tongue. Move-

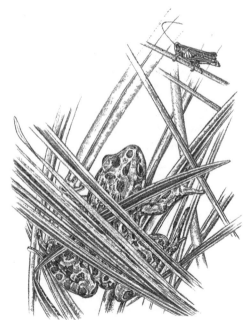

*Northern leopard frog stalking prey*

ments made by large beetles or worms that are further away from the frog may cause it to step forward within grasping reach.

OVERWINTERING

Leopard frogs have been found to overwinter in the mud at the bottoms of lakes, ponds, streams, and marshes and in some situations inside terrestrial caves. Close observations of overwintering leopard frogs indicate that they are usually found near underwater trees or rocks. They may construct oval-shaped underwater pits within which they stay for the winter.

Even at winter water temperatures not far above freezing, adult leopard frogs can move at least a bit. There is no indication that they are feeding, but it is believed that they may adjust their positions from time to time. Laboratory studies indicate that leopard frogs are not able to withstand freezing as are wood frogs or spring peepers.

---

## Quick Reference Chart

*Life Cycle*

**Length of Breeding Season:** March (in South) to June through October (in North and West)

**Breeding Habitat:** Temporary and permanent ponds, marshes, lakes, streams

**Eggs Deposited:** Up to 6,000 deposited in oblong masses in March (South) to early June (North), occasionally in September (West)

**Eggs Hatch:** In 13–20 days

**Length of Tadpole Stage:** Usually 9–12 weeks, but tadpoles may overwinter in some locations

**Lifespan of Adults:** At least 3 years

*Vocalizations*

**Advertisement call:** A series of snoring croaks 1–3 seconds in duration, given by the male during breeding season

**Aggressive call:** A short chuckle, given by both male and female above or below the water

*Well-camouflaged adult wood frogs on forest floor*

# WOOD FROG / *Rana sylvatica*

On a sunny and warm March afternoon a friend and I took a walk along an old trail that winds through a forested hillside that was once a farm. Now the forest has grown back, stone walls are wrapped in poison ivy and grapevines, and only a stone porch foundation exists where a large house once stood. Even before we got to the home site we could hear the sounds of male wood frogs coming from the small abandoned stone quarry nearby.

The quarry is small, only about fifty feet long, thirty feet wide, and five feet deep, but it is ample enough for the several amphibian species that use the flooded basin for an early-spring breeding site. The hole fills with melting snow and spring rains, and wood frogs, peepers, and spotted and Jefferson's salamanders from the adjacent woodland migrate here by the hundreds each year. On this particular visit ice still adhered to one edge of the pond. The wood-frog activity seemed like a final call for the end of winter.

To many people the calls of wood frogs in the spring sound so much like quacking ducks that they are slow to believe that amphibians actually make these sounds. Often when a nearby pond is investigated all of the animals stop vocalizing and dive to the bottom of the pond as the observers approach, making any attempt to find out just what is making the sounds especially frustrating. For the rest of the year, wood frogs are found away from water and can be seen on forested hillsides.

## How to Recognize Wood Frogs

### ADULTS

The ducklike quacking of the males is distinctive during the short and early breeding season. Wood frogs have a dark, raccoonlike mask and no spots or other markings on their back except for a small percentage that may have a light stripe down the middle. The two- or three-inch adults are some shade of brown, from very dark to a reddish hue, and have two distinct dorsolateral folds. Underneath, they are unmarked and white or cream colored.

Wood frogs are members of the true frog family, the Ranidae, all of whose members are smooth skinned and have thin waists and long hind legs. Wood frogs are found within the Arctic Circle and therefore have the northernmost distribution of any member of the family. The wood frog's range encompasses over ten thousand square kilometers.

### DISTINGUISHING THE SEXES

Males are usually darker, almost black in color, especially in the breeding season. During the breeding season, males develop a pad on their thumbs to help maintain a grip on the female. The edge of the webbing between the male's hind toes is convex.

In some populations, females are larger than males and redder in color. In breeding ponds females are much fatter than males due to their eggs. The webbing edge between their hind toes is concave.

### TADPOLES

Wood-frog tadpoles are olive or brown on their body and tail, often with a greenish tint. They have few markings on their belly, which has a pinkish iridescence. Maximum size is up to two inches.

Up to a thousand or more eggs are tightly packed in rounded masses about the size of a tennis ball. When fresh the outer jelly covering is transparent, but within a couple of weeks it becomes imbedded with a green alga, which obscures the eggs and developing embryos.

## How to Find Wood Frogs

**Habitat:** Wet, mixed woodlands, tundra, grasslands
**Months of Activity:** February to October

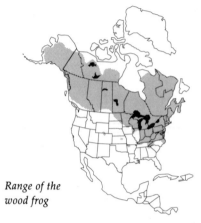

*Range of the wood frog*

Though they have a short breeding season, this is the best time to find wood frogs. Follow the sounds of their calls to temporary woodland ponds, bogs, or open meadow pools. If they become quiet, sit still and scan the surface of the water for their heads as they begin to move again. At the height of the breeding season they can be found both day and night.

Away from the breeding ponds, wood frogs are most often discovered early in the morning or just after soaking rains along the forest floor. Their habitat consists almost exclusively of woodlands, and this is where you should begin your searches.

## What You Can Observe

### SPRING EMERGENCE

Wood frogs emerge from their overwintering sites and immediately migrate to breeding ponds. These migrations appear to be synchronized, with most of the adult population arriving within a few days of one other. Heavy rains and a strong thaw brought on by unseasonably warm temperatures, from January in the South to May in the North, are associated with the emergence and breeding migration of wood frogs.

## TERRITORIAL BEHAVIOR AND VOCALIZATIONS

Male wood frogs do not defend territories. They simply float on the surface of the water, calling intermittently. A few observers have reported that a slight spacing (about a foot or two) between males is maintained, but this may not be true for all populations. Males approach and attempt to clasp almost any object that moves or floats nearby, including other males, inanimate debris, and even other species of frogs.

Wood frogs have two vocal pouches near their front legs, and these gleam bright white when inflated. There is some belief that these flashes of white are visual signals to other males, incoming females, or both.

There are two typical sounds made by male wood frogs: the advertisement call and the release call. Males give their ducklike quacking advertisement call only in water, repeating the call several times. Males do not seem to synchronize their calls, so that from a short distance a pond appears to have a continuous chatter. A disturbance, such as the careless approach of a human observer or a predator, may silence the whole pond, at least for a short period.

The release call is a quiet but audible chirp given by a male that is clasped by another male. This happens frequently in breeding ponds, and you should hear this call easily. The call almost always results in the clasping male's releasing his grip on the one who gave the release call.

Females not ready to mate have been reported to make a call when approached by males that seemed to repel the advances of these males. Little is known about this vocalization, however, and it has not been well described.

When a female enters a breeding pond, her swimming actions usually attract at least one nearby male, unless she immediately dives beneath the surface and rests on the bottom. When she is ready to mate she will allow the male to swim up and clasp her from behind, with his front legs held tightly beneath her front legs. There has been little investigation of female wood frogs' role in choosing mates, though they can be seen to avoid certain males by easily outswimming them. Some females also have been observed trying to dislodge males that have clasped them.

Pairs will stay clasped together for varying lengths of time, from an hour or two to three or more days, until the female deposits all her eggs. Often other males are attracted by the swimming movements of a pair and will attempt to dislodge the male. For short periods of time an aggregation of five or ten males can be seen clasping a single female. Field biologists have occasionally found females killed by this activity.

Males who have already mated attempt to clasp other females, but due to the very short breeding season they are not likely to be successful. After laying their eggs, female wood frogs immediately leave the ponds. Within two weeks all the males will leave as well.

### EGGS AND EGG-LAYING

Find a clasped pair of frogs and try to follow their movements in the pond. Notice that it is generally the female that propels the pair as she searches the pond for an egg-laying site. She usually finds a small twig or branch just under the surface of the water and grabs hold of it with her front feet. As she releases her several hundred to a thousand eggs, the male fertilizes them. They adhere to the twig and initially look like a black mass about the size of a quarter.

Female wood frogs prefer to deposit eggs in a communal nesting location. After the frogs have left the pond, dozens or even hundreds of egg masses can be found within just a few yards of each other while other likely-looking sites in the pond are devoid of eggs. Theories explaining communal nesting sites have been suggested by several researchers. One idea is that egg masses at the center of the nesting area have higher temperatures, due to the insulation effects of surrounding masses, and therefore faster developmental rates. This allows the eggs to hatch more quickly, an advantage in latitudes where refreezing might occur after the eggs are laid.

Another advantage may be that the chance of predation on any individual egg or embryo is reduced when there are many more targets around for prey species. Having many thousands of other eggs nearby reduces any one's chances of actually being eaten. Additionally, some researchers have found that in ponds that begin to dry after the breeding activity, the eggs in the center of communal nesting sites may retain moisture longer, allowing them to hatch and escape to the deepest part of the pond, where they might survive until future rainstorms refill the basin.

After a week or two you will notice that each egg mass begins to turn green. This is due to a symbiotic alga that infuses the outer

*Adult wood frog. Note dark mask*

jelly coating of the egg. Even though it is widespread in many populations, the effects of the alga on the developing embryos have not been investigated to any great extent.

During the three weeks that wood-frog eggs take to hatch, you have an opportunity to observe the many predators that eat the developing eggs and embryos. Foremost among these are several species of caddisflies, whose aquatic larvae are sometimes able to burrow through the outer jelly coating. In some areas adult red-spotted newts take a heavy toll on the eggs as well as on recently hatched tadpoles. Leeches, snapping turtles, and spotted turtles are also known to feed on the eggs of wood frogs.

Because they breed in ponds that fill with spring rain and snow-melt, wood-frog eggs are exposed to a wide variety of acidic conditions throughout their range. A few researchers have noted that increased acidity causes some eggs to die and larvae to deform. Populations probably have varying tolerances to acidity overall, but each one is likely to have a threshold level above which reproduction is severely affected.

TADPOLES

Newly hatched tadpoles hang motionless alongside the rapidly deteriorating egg mass. This is accomplished with a suckerlike mouth that will soon begin scraping bacteria, algae, and tiny animals from the surface of underwater plants and rocks. Within a few days, wood-frog tadpoles are capable of rapid escape movements. They will disappear into the leaf litter or stands of underwater plants when disturbed.

As they grow, wood-frog tadpoles are known to become distasteful to some aquatic predators such as diving-beetle larvae. Toxins in their skin seem to develop early, and this makes them unpalatable.

Typically, wood-frog tadpoles are in a race against time. They have to find food, grow, avoid predators, and begin to develop into frogs before their temporary ponds dry. In some drought years none of the tadpoles survive; mortality is 100 percent. To overcome this, wood frogs have evolved an early breeding season, a prolonged embryonic development, and a rapid tadpole growth period.

OVERWINTERING

As fall approaches, few adult or juvenile wood frogs are encountered during woodland outings. When cold weather begins, they take refuge beneath leaf litter, crawl under rocks or logs, or enter small burrows beneath the soil. It is believed that they do not go very far underground and are, in fact, subjected to freezing temperatures, especially in years when there is little snow cover. Wood frogs are known to have antifreeze compounds in their bodies that allow them to survive periods of freezing and thawing throughout the winter and early spring.

# Quick Reference Chart

## Life Cycle

**Length of Breeding Season:** January to March (South); March to May (North); May through July (far North)

**Breeding Habitat:** Temporary ponds, beaver swamps, streams

**Eggs Deposited:** Up to 2,000 eggs in at least 1 globular mass, deposited within 2 or 3 days of female's entering pond

**Eggs Hatch:** Usually within 3 weeks, depending on water temperature

**Length of Tadpole Stage:** 60–70 days

**Lifespan of Adults:** At least 3 years

## Vocalizations

**Advertisement call:** A ducklike quacking of males during the breeding season

**Release call:** A short chirp, given by a male when grasped by another male

# Introducing Salamanders

## ABOUT SALAMANDERS

Salamanders are relatively easy to identify by their smooth skin, long tail, and four legs, though there are several exceptions to this simple description. Unlike frogs, the other major group of amphibians, all salamanders possess tails. Superficially, salamanders resemble lizards, but the latter are easily distinguished by their dry, scaly skin, ear openings, and clawed toes. Except for a few sounds made by some species, salamanders are entirely silent. Different families of salamanders have remarkable and unique life histories and methods of survival.

## WHERE SALAMANDERS ARE FOUND

Some adult salamanders are fully aquatic, while others are decidedly terrestrial. In fact, though they are usually small and remain hidden from casual view, some species of salamander may be the most abundant terrestrial vertebrates in much of North America. Salamanders are found throughout the world, except for Antarctica and the far North, and are especially common in the northern hemisphere.

## COMMON FAMILIES OF SALAMANDERS

Throughout the world, there are nine recognized families of salamanders divided into about 350 different species. Of the eight families found in North America, four comprise the vast majority of species in our region, and each of these families has unique characteristics.

The family Necturidae, the mudpuppies and waterdogs, includes large, fully aquatic animals, usually over a foot in length. They have an unusually high number of chromosomes (thirty-eight) and retain many of their larval characteristics, including external bushy gills, throughout adulthood.

Another group of salamanders, the newts, make up the family Salamandridae. All fifty or so members of the family have toxic skin secretions, often coupled with brightly colored markings that signal potential predators. Some can deflate their bodies, allowing their sharp, pointed ribs to emerge from their sides as an additional deterrent to predators. Adults may be found on land or in water. The family is found mainly in Europe and Asia, with only two genera in North America.

The mole salamanders make up the family Ambystomatidae. These are thick-bodied animals that live most of their lives underground. A few of the thirty species in this family retain their gills and aquatic life as adults, and the majority breed in ponds or temporary pools.

The woodland or lungless salamanders, in the family Plethodontidae, include well over half of all the species of salamanders in the world. Almost all of the 220 species in the family are found in North and South America. All lack lungs and breathe by taking in oxygen through their skin or the membranes inside their mouths. The family exhibits many and varied survival strategies. Some have webbed feet, others grasping tails. Some grow to only an inch or so in length; others reach nearly ten inches. Some are entirely aquatic, while others spend their entire lives on land.

SALAMANDER LIFE HISTORIES

As you might guess from the number of species, many different evolutionary paths have been taken by salamanders. Information on most species is incomplete; some salamanders, especially in the American tropics, remain unknown. Even with the great many details that are known about our common species of salamanders, there is much to learn, and many people, from casual observers to ardent researchers, are finding ample areas for study.

Reproduction in most families is internal. Males deposit small packets of sperm atop a jellylike base called a spermatophore. At the height of courtship, the female picks up the spermatophore with her cloaca, the common opening for reproduction and eliminating wastes. The eggs are thus fertilized inside her body.

Most female salamanders lay their eggs in water, but numerous species deposit their eggs on land instead. Some terrestrial eggs hatch directly into juveniles; others hatch into aquatic larvae when the nesting site is flooded by rains. Shortly after hatching, aquatic larvae have teeth, swimming fins, and small legs.

Typically, salamanders go through egg, larval, juvenile, and adult stages. Most North American salamanders have aquatic eggs and larvae, while the juvenile and adult stages are terrestrial. In some, the larval stage is passed mostly in the egg, and the young hatch into juveniles similar to, though smaller than, the adults. In others, the juveniles are quite distinct from the adults in their shape, their color, or the places they live.

Some salamanders are paedomorphic (sometimes called neotenic). That is, they remain in a relatively larval state physically — with external gills, no eyelids, long tail fins, and other larval characteristics — even though they become sexually mature. Some populations within the same species exhibit very different life histories.

All feeding stages of salamanders are carnivorous; the size of the prey is determined by the size of the salamander. Aquatic adults and larvae stalk underwater insects and other invertebrates. Terrestrial salamanders hunt prey underground, in the leaf litter, on the surface, or even in shrubs and trees.

## CONSERVATION OF SALAMANDERS

There has been a growing interest in the common, small animals that, like salamanders, have been able to survive from prehistoric times to the present. Some salamander species have drawn attention when, during concentrated breeding migrations, they have been compelled to cross roads. Concern for maintaining salamander populations, in the wake of increasing development and highway mortality, has spawned ingenious measures by conservationists.

While some people attempt to help the migrating animals cross the roads, lifting them one by one, others have been able to convince their town officials to close certain roads during the few nights of movement. Recent international interest in installing tunnels to allow large numbers of animals to cross safely without impeding highway traffic is very encouraging.

Still, the biggest threat to many populations of salamanders is the loss of habitat. This is unfortunate because, with relatively little care, patches of upland forest and small, temporary ponds can be saved, thus providing required winter, summer, and breeding sites for many salamanders. Indiscriminate draining and filling of wetlands, in general, has been a major reason for the decline of aquatic and semiaquatic species. Pesticides, herbicides, lawn-care and orchard products, and other toxic wastes also continue to take their toll.

Only if people show concern for the diversity and health of their local communities will we be able to keep salamanders and other small animals around for the foreseeable future. Find out what your nearest museum, nature center, or area conservation organization is doing and support them with your money, time, or ideas. Salamanders' genetic diversity makes even the most local, isolated populations worth every effort in their behalf.

### SOME SALAMANDER TERMINOLOGY

Throughout the species accounts that follow, you will encounter a few words that have special meaning for this group of animals. Becoming familiar with them will help you to better understand their interesting lives.

An adult salamander is composed of a head, body, and tail. In aquatic adults, there may be a swimming fin on the tail, called the *caudal fin*. Most salamander adults have four toes on the front feet and five on the hind feet. In some salamanders there are a number of wrinkles or folds along the sides of the body, between the front and hind limbs. The actual indentations are called *costal grooves,* while the bulges in between are the *costal folds.* The number of grooves or folds is generally unique among species and can help to identify some salamanders.

All salamanders have a vent or *cloaca,* the opening for reproduction and eliminating wastes. Males generally have glands on the sides of their cloacas that produce *spermatophores*—small structures with a packet of sperm on top that the females pick up in their cloacae to breed.

Newly hatched salamanders are simply called *larvae,* having no alternative name (though some researchers do refer to them as tadpoles). They have bushy *external gills,* a caudal fin that continues onto their back as a *dorsal fin,* and tiny legs.

*Adult mudpuppy encountering common prey*

# MUDPUPPY / *Necturus maculosus*

On a beautiful summer night, several of us slipped our canoes into a small, hilltop lake. The air was warm, the winds were calm, and we slowly paddled just offshore. We were looking for nothing in particular, but had brought lights to see into the lake. The clarity of the water allowed us to see the bottom and anything that might be walking there, especially near the shoreline.

Among other things, we watched large crayfish investigating some debris, numerous water beetles, an occasional leech, huge snails, and several different types of fish in various states of activity. When the first mudpuppy came into view we were not particularly prepared for the encounter.

We could see it, large and white, without the flashlights. All the mudpuppies I had seen before were somber brown in color and seemed particularly well camouflaged among the gravel and leaf litter of their pond or river bottoms. But this ghostly mudpuppy, like another we found that night, was particularly obvious as it patrolled the lake bottom. Though many aquatic salamanders, like some fish, undergo a dramatic color change at night, becoming quite light, this was the first time any of us had seen a mudpuppy in that state.

Like most people who encounter mudpuppies, we were impressed by its size. Adults can grow to be about twenty inches in length, though most commonly they are about a foot long. The large, maroon-colored, bushy gills that sprout from each side of their heads and slowly wave seem out of place on a salamander of this size. In fact, the mudpuppy is one of several salamanders in North America that retain most of their larval characteristics (such as gills, a swimming tail fin, and an absence of eyelids) throughout their adult lives.

## How to Recognize Mudpuppies

### ADULTS

Their large size, obvious external gills, and fully aquatic nature are good clues for identifying this species. Adult mudpuppies are brown to gray-brown with numerous dark spots along their backs and sides.

Some populations of tiger salamander (*Ambystoma tigrinum*), who also retain their gills as adults, may be nearly as large, but usually they are light in color and have a golden stripe along their sides. Also, mudpuppies have only four toes on their hind feet, while tiger salamanders have five.

Mudpuppies are members of the mudpuppy and waterdog family, the Necturidae, though some authorities use the name Proteidae for this family.

### DISTINGUISHING THE SEXES

Males are generally the same size as females and can be identified best by looking at their vents. In the male, the vent is long, wrinkled along the edges, and has an arch-shaped groove crossing near the posterior end.

Females' vents are shorter, have smooth edges, and lack the obvious groove at the far end. Otherwise, their overall body dimensions, coloration, and length of tail are about the same as the males'.

Newly hatched mudpuppies are almost an inch long. Though their front legs and toes are discernible, their hind legs are small and toes undistinguished. Young mudpuppies are striking in color pattern, having a dark brown top surface with light, yellowish stripes along the sides.

EGGS

Mudpuppy eggs are oblong in shape, normally cream colored or yellowish, and deposited singly. They are found on the underside of submerged logs, flat stones, or other debris in quiet sections of rivers or lakes.

## How to Find Mudpuppies

**Habitat:** Aquatic; lakes, ponds, rivers, and streams
**Months of Activity:** Year-round

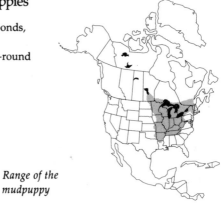

*Range of the mudpuppy*

Since they are predominantly nocturnal, the best time to search for mudpuppies is after sunset, when they come into shallow water and forage on the sand and leaf-litter bottoms of streams and ponds. Use a flashlight or lantern to illuminate areas near rocks, underwater logs, or other debris.

During the daytime adults and young may be found by wading into shallow water and turning over logs, boards, and rocks. In the spring, females with eggs and newly hatched young are relatively easily found this way.

# What You Can Observe

Even in northern parts of their range, mudpuppies remain active throughout the winter and do not appear to speed up or change much of their behavior from winter into spring. Some researchers have noted at least small autumn migrations from the interior of a lake to incoming rivers and streams where adults collect for breeding.

### COURTSHIP AND MATING

It is unlikely that you will actually observe any of these behaviors in mudpuppies since they usually occur in deep water and at night. Unlike many other salamanders, mudpuppies breed during the autumn, from September to November.

A male courts a female by continually walking around, beneath, and over her body. Females may remain relatively passive and stand on the bottom with rigid legs. Males deposit large, clear spermatophores on the substrate, and the females pick them up through their cloaca. The spermatophores are just under an inch in length and ought to be easy to find. There have been relatively few observations of mudpuppy courtship under natural conditions, however, and much still needs to be learned.

### EGGS AND EGG-LAYING

While adults court in the fall, females do not deposit their eggs until the following spring, normally in April, May, or June. In preparation for egg-laying, females construct a nest of sorts. It normally consists of little more than a hollowed-out depression beneath a large, flat object — a board, log, or rock — lying in relatively shallow water (two to five feet deep). From thirty to almost two hundred eggs are attached individually to the underside of this flat object in a stream, river, or lake. The female must somehow invert her body to press the eggs onto the underside of the rock or log. Actual observation of this has been reported only with captive females, who remained upside down for several hours while depositing eggs. It would be fascinating to see this in wild animals. The eggs take up an area of six to twelve inches in diameter. The female remains with them throughout the incubation period of five weeks to two months.

On at least a couple of occasions, females have been found close to (within a foot or two) other females with eggs, even under the same boards or logs. This communal nesting may be in response to a lack of other nesting sites.

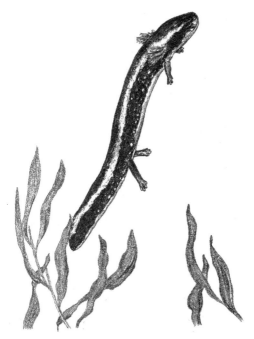

*Immature mudpuppy*

## LARVAE AND METAMORPHOSIS

Newly hatched mudpuppies remain relatively near each other and the female, though the duration of this behavior is not known. In natural situations larval mudpuppies grow about an inch and a half a year. They lose their stripes after the second year, indicating metamorphosis into a juvenile. Mudpuppies become sexually mature at five years of age, when they are about eight inches long.

The attainment of sexual maturity in mudpuppies is manifested by few outward signs, since the salamanders retain most of their larval characteristics. As noted, unlike most other salamanders, mudpuppies never develop eyelids or molt their skin, and they keep the fin on their tail and the large, bushy gills.

FEEDING

Throughout their lives mudpuppies, like all other salamanders, are carnivorous. Generally, their prey — aquatic insects, snails, fish, frogs, other salamanders, eggs of fish and amphibians, worms, leeches, and crayfish — changes as they get older (and therefore larger). Among adults, crayfish are the major food item, at least in some locations. Mudpuppies also take in a large amount of plant material, though it is unclear how much nutrition is gained from it. Plants may simply be eaten incidentally as the salamanders grab their prey.

OTHER FACTS ABOUT MUDPUPPIES

Mudpuppies in the Mississippi and Ohio River drainages are the only known hosts for a freshwater mussel whose larvae attach themselves to mudpuppy gills. The immature clams drop off the salamander eventually and in this manner are able to colonize new areas of the watershed.

Even with their large, bushy gills, mudpuppies do possess functional, though simple, lungs. Though they may be useful in extracting oxygen from the air, the lungs' main function is to help the animal control its position in water by inflating and deflating like a fish's swim bladder. The large tail fin may also help extract oxygen from the water by having numerous blood vessels close to the surface where oxygen can diffuse.

Suspected predators of adult mudpuppies include large fish such as bass, pike, and pickerel; some mammals; and large turtles. A large number of species, including insects, fish, other salamanders, other mudpuppies, and leeches, feed on the eggs and young.

By most observations, it appears that mudpuppies do not undergo any reduction in activity during the winter. Though some of the first researchers of this species indicated that mudpuppies became lethargic and even buried into the mud during winter periods, this has not been substantiated.

People who ice fish are likely to encounter mudpuppies since the salamanders readily feed on worms and small fish used as bait, even in the winter. Often, when mudpuppies are caught through the ice, the incident is reported in local newspapers, where they are often identified as lizards, or animals "new" to science.

## Quick Reference Chart

**Length of Breeding Season:** Autumn: September to November
**Breeding Habitat:** Shallow, slow-moving water in tributaries-of larger rivers and lakes
**Eggs Retained by Female:** 7–10 months
**Eggs Deposited:** Up to 190 cream-colored eggs deposited singly on the underside of a rock, log, or board
**Eggs Hatch:** 5 weeks to 2 months
**Length of Larval Stage:** About 5 years
**Lifespan of Adults:** Unknown; at least 6 years

*Red efts (above) and adult eastern red-spotted newts*

# EASTERN OR RED-SPOTTED NEWT /
*Notophthalmus viridescens*

Not too long ago, a friend and I decided to walk along an abandoned road that led through a mixed forest of sugar maples, cherries, and small patches of hemlocks. It was late in the summer, the day was rainy but warm, and the woodland smelled rich with decaying humus. We began to notice juvenile red-spotted newts, called red efts, crossing our path and saw others in the woods. We decided to make a count of those on the road; in the distance of a mile we recorded 523 individuals. I have since come to anticipate encountering the red efts during damp weather, and my spirits never fail to be lifted when I see one.

I also enjoy looking for adult newts late in winter, when the edges of beaver ponds and lakes begin to thaw. In January or February I find adult newts walking over the submerged leaf litter, amid a rich, living world that includes aquatic beetles, caddisflies, snails, and many other invertebrates. The newts are massive compared to these other inhabitants of the shallow zones of the pond. At this time of year, no matter how long I watch, the salamanders rarely, if ever, come to the surface to gulp air into their lungs. The cold water must be highly oxygenated, diffusing oxygen directly into their bodies through their skin.

There are many different species of newts in the world. Their unusual behaviors often cause people to think that they are not salamanders. But when one examines the life histories of all the various families of salamanders in the world, one realizes that the newt's life cycle, though unique, is no more unusual than that of many others. It's just that most other families of salamanders remain hidden from our view.

Newts are mostly diurnal and the efts especially are easily seen walking on the surface of leaves, or on roads, driveways, and in backyards. For these reasons they are very familiar throughout their wide range in the eastern half of the United States and Canada.

## How to Recognize Red-Spotted Newts

### ADULTS AND JUVENILES

Adult red-spotted newts are olive to dark green above and yellowish below, and are about four inches in length from nose to tail tip. Close inspection reveals small, red dots encircled in black sprinkled on the sides, back, tail, and legs. Adults are mostly aquatic, though some can be found under logs adjacent to ponds, lakes, and streams.

In dramatic contrast, the brilliant, orange-colored red eft, which lives on land, looks nothing like the adult newt into which it will mature. These juveniles can range from just over an inch to four inches in total length. Efts also are speckled with a variable number of small, deep red spots each surrounded by a black circle, though some individuals and populations of adults and juveniles lack the spots.

There are six members of the newt family, the Salamandridae, in North America. The red-spotted newt has a wide range throughout the eastern half of North America, while the other five species are restricted to small areas on the Gulf and California coasts.

For most of the year, male newts show the majority of the sexual characteristics important during courtship and breeding. These include a very wide fin on the top and bottom edges of their tail, enlarged glands around their cloaca, and dark growths on the inside of their hind legs and toes. Males also tend to be dark in color. Females have only slight swellings near their cloaca and a very small development of a tail fin, and in the breeding season are very plump due to the presence of developing eggs. Females tend to be lighter in color than males, often appearing tan.

### LARVAE

At hatching, red-spotted-newt larvae are just under half an inch in length and yellowish green in color. There is a grayish stripe on each side of the body that runs from the head onto the tail. At full size newt larvae grow to be about an inch and a half in total length. They have branched, soft, external gills.

### EGGS

Each egg, deposited singly and attached to underwater vegetation, is somewhat elliptical in shape. The fertilized egg itself is brown on top and yellowish underneath. Newt eggs are very small and difficult to find.

## How to Find Red-Spotted Newts

**Habitat:** Adults are aquatic in ponds, lakes, slow rivers; efts are terrestrial in moist forests
**Months of Activity:** Year-round (South); January to November (North)

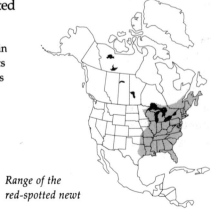

*Range of the red-spotted newt*

Throughout their range, red-spotted newts are active during the warmer parts of the year. Even in northern states and Canada, however, adult newts are often active during winter in open water and beneath the ice. Look for adult newts in permanent bodies of water where they are active both day and night and can be seen along the shoreline hunting for food or looking for mates. In small ponds they are easily seen if you wade in just a few feet from shore.

Efts are easily seen when they are walking on the surface of wet woodlands during the daytime whenever temperatures are above freezing and there is no snow on the ground. They seem to be entirely absent from grasslands and other open areas and prefer second- and old-growth forests with deciduous trees, evergreens, or both. Walk casually along trails and stream edges when looking for them. During dry periods, roll logs, boards, or rocks and sift through leaf litter on the forest floor. Often the efts, and some-times adults, take refuge in these places.

## What You Can Observe

### EMERGENCE AND MIGRATION

From mid-March to early April adult newts can be found emerging, sometimes in large numbers, from their overwintering sites on land. They immediately begin to migrate back to the same breeding ponds they inhabited the previous autumn.

After the larval newts begin to metamorphose into efts late in summer, a distinct migration out of and away from the pond takes place. Some populations, due to the various ages and migratory patterns of the adults, will exhibit two or more waves of migrating, transformed larvae. Throughout the range of the species, these larvae can be looked for from July through November. These young efts tend to leave the ponds and move at night, especially following a rainy afternoon.

Among some populations of red-spotted newts there is also a marked autumn migration of red efts who are transforming into adults. These young adults go to ponds or lakes; they will either leave them again to overwinter on land, or remain in the pond permanently.

COURTSHIP AND MATING

The breeding activities of both sexes of newts are easily observed from the shoreline from spring to late summer, and in some ponds courtship activity renews again in the autumn. The black growths on the feet and hind legs of male newts develop during the breeding season and function, apparently, to give the male a better grip on the female during their courtship. Often you will find pairs of newts in a courtship embrace. This can take several forms, though the male is always above the female and grasps her with his hind legs. In the most typical posture, he will be clasping her just in front of her front legs. Less often he will grasp her around her body near the hind legs. Follow a pair and you may see the female slowly crawling about the pond bottom, seemingly unconcerned with the attached male.

Repeatedly, the male will arch his body and rub his chin on the top and side of the female's head. When doing this, he is rubbing onto her the secretions of a gland found on his cheeks that proba-

*Two female red-spotted newts and a male (far right)*

bly act as a stimulant for the female. At some point, the male will slowly begin to wave the tip of his tail. Watch to see if he releases his grip. If so, he may next walk ahead of the female, continuing the tail wag, and then stop suddenly.

If the female remains attentive, he may deposit a spermatophore on the pond bottom. If she is ready, the female will walk forward, behind the male, and pick up the spermatophore with her cloaca (vent). After this, females generally discontinue any courtship activities, though the male may remain attentive.

### EGGS AND EGG-LAYING

After picking up a spermatophore, females normally swim or walk to heavily vegetated sections of their pond. Here, they begin to climb underwater plants and, while grasping the stem with their hind feet, press their body close and extrude a single egg. The outer egg capsule adheres to the stem, and the female walks further up the plant, or moves to another, and continues depositing more eggs. She will lay eggs over a period of a week or more, until all three or four hundred of them are deposited.

The eggs are subjected to many hazards. These include predation by insects and leeches, accidental damage caused by large animals walking in the shallows, bacterial and fungal attacks, and incidental ingestion by aquatic herbivores.

### LARVAE AND METAMORPHOSIS

The tiny eggs hatch in three to five weeks, depending on the water temperature. Newborn newt larvae sink to the bottom and remain relatively inactive for several days. At this stage they are susceptible to insect predators such as diving beetles and dragonfly larvae. Within a week of hatching they become active and feed on the abundant bloom of life in a summer pond.

Newts remain as larvae for about three months. By late summer and early autumn they begin to reabsorb their gills and caudal fin. They develop lungs and a rough-textured skin. Red efts then begin to emerge from the ponds to take up life on the land.

Red efts are always exciting to find. If you keep track of your observations you will note that they are almost always discovered during or after rains and during daylight hours. Apparently they prefer both high humidity and daylight for most of their terrestrial life.

Sit nearby and watch a red eft move. They seem to take deliberate steps but do not appear to have any particular destination in mind. Watch how they negotiate around rocks, logs, and stream gullies.

An interesting aspect of watching newts is the behavior of other wildlife toward them. Field biologists have surmised that the eft's bright color advertises its toxic skin secretions to potential predators such as birds. In fact, experiments have shown that some birds quickly learn to avoid eating the red efts after they taste one. Efts are more toxic than adults. The larvae are also distasteful, though several species of fish, insects, and even adult newts are known to eat them. Of course, the toxic properties of newts come into play only when they are attacked by predators and their skin is bruised. Gentle handling produces no ill effects at all.

## FEEDING AND PREDATORS

Adult newts eat a variety of aquatic animals and occasionally terrestrial animals that enter the water. Insects, water fleas, and other invertebrates make up the bulk of their diet, but many other small animals, including larval newts, are potential food sources. Larval newts feed on similar, though smaller, items among the thick, underwater forests of submerged vegetation.

The toxic skin secretions of newts repel most, but not all, predators. Populations of newts are kept in check by a number of factors, and predation by the amphibian blood leech (*Batrachobdella picta*) seems to be a major one. This may be especially significant in the spring, when large numbers of newts are entering ponds and the leeches are abundant. In addition to feeding on the tissues of adults, the leeches kill and eat larval newts and are known to transmit a parasite into the newts' blood that eventually weakens and kills them. Because newt toxins are concentrated only in their skin, animals that can penetrate into the body cavity, such as leeches, are able to feed on newts without ill effects.

## OTHER FACTS ABOUT NEWTS

It has been suggested that the newts' distinctive life history has evolved in response to and association with temporary, ever-changing, and ever-moving ecological communities. The coupling of the distinctive land-dwelling eft with the aquatic, long-lived adult seems to fit very well with the activities and behaviors of North American beavers. The red eft is viewed as a wandering stage able to find and colonize new ponds, which are constantly created by beavers or the meanderings of streams and rivers. Adult newts show strong tendencies to remain in one pond, even if they leave seasonally to overwinter on land. When beavers abandon a pond the adults presumably do not migrate, but live out the rest of their lives along the stream edge and reproduce little or even never again.

## OVERWINTERING

While some permanent bodies of water have newts in them year-round, many, if not all, of the individuals in some populations leave the water in August or September to overwinter on land. In ponds that are dry in the winter, all the adults must leave to take up a terrestrial existence, though some take refuge beneath leaf litter, logs, and bark in the pond basin. On land, adults overwinter beneath logs, rocks, or leaf litter. Some may enter mammal burrows or follow natural crevices below ground.

## Quick Reference Chart

**Length of Breeding Season:** Spring and summer, March–August, sometimes beginning again late in autumn or early winter

**Breeding Habitat:** Permanent or temporary bodies of water

**Eggs Retained by Female:** 1 or 2 hours to a few days

**Eggs Deposited:** Up to 375 eggs deposited singly on underwater plant stems and leaves

**Eggs Hatch:** 3–5 weeks

**Length of Larval Stage:** 2–3 months

**Length of Juvenile Stage:** 2–5 years

**Lifespan of Adults:** 5–15 years

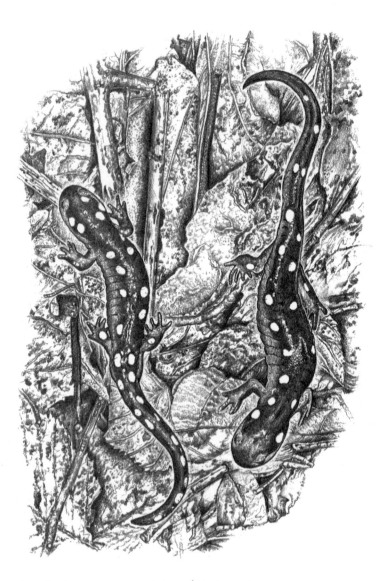

*Individual spot patterns on adult spotted salamanders*

# SPOTTED SALAMANDER /

*Ambystoma maculatum*

L IKE MANY PEOPLE'S, my first view of a spotted salamander was in school, when my fifth-grade science teacher walked up and down the aisles with one in a terrarium. It was spectacular, but the view hardly prepared me for my first encounter with one in the field. I happened to look beneath a flat piece of bark, and there was a tiny spotted salamander, barely three inches long. Its sleek, polished black body, punctuated by a dozen or more brilliant yellow polka dots, looked more like an enameled sculpture than a living animal. The next spring I was ready to try to find an adult during the breeding season. When I discovered them I was again not really prepared for what I saw.

The first striking thing about spotted salamanders is their size: adults grow up to eight or nine inches in length. The bright yellow polka-dot pattern is variable and has been used to identify individual animals in local populations. I was also impressed by the number of adults migrating downhill through an oak and hickory forest to reach a small pond where they bred. After a single circuit of the pond, I had recorded over five hundred adults, and more were still arriving. Several remained in the pond over the next few days, but the large concentration of them on the first night is part of their very short courtship and breeding season. My luck in seeing them at their breeding pond this first time fueled my fascination with these animals. Since then I've enjoyed many wet, spring evenings with friends, watching the salamanders and recording bits and pieces about their life histories.

## How to Recognize Spotted Salamanders

### ADULTS

The large, yellow spots scattered on the glossy black head, body, legs, and tail make this an easy species to identify. In some, especially southern, populations, the spots on the head and neck are orange in color. Occasionally some are found that lack spots at all, and albinos have been reported as well.

In some areas the much thinner slimy salamander (*Plethodon glutinosis*) may look similar. Spotted salamanders are stout and their spots are large, round, and bright yellow. Some tiger salamander (*Ambystoma tigrinum*) individuals are spotted, but their olive or brown background color helps distinguish the two species.

Spotted salamanders are members of the mole-salamander family, the Ambystomatidae.

### DISTINGUISHING THE SEXES

From February through April, females are filled with eggs, giving them a fatter, more plump appearance. Males have glands next to their vents (cloacae) that are especially swollen during the same season. Even from above, the swollen vents of the males are obvious, while the vents of the females are not.

### LARVAE

These larvae are dark on top and whitish below. At full size they are less than two inches in length. Typically they have large, feathery gills that sweep up and back from the base of their head. It is not easy to distinguish them in the field from closely related species, however.

Eggs are deposited in a single oval mass about the size of a tennis ball. Each black egg is imbedded in a jellylike matrix that holds them all together. In some populations the jelly coating around the eggs is milky white, making the entire mass highly visible and easy to find. More typically it is clear, or somewhat translucent, and is usually attached to underwater twigs, fern leaves, or grass blades.

## How to Find Spotted Salamanders

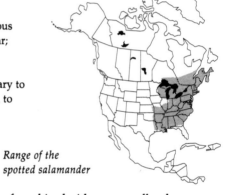

**Habitat:** Mixed or deciduous forests throughout the year; temporary ponds during breeding season
**Months of Activity:** January to November (South); March to October (North)

*Range of the spotted salamander*

Spotted salamanders are found in deciduous woodlands or areas of mixed hardwoods and evergreens. Like most members of their family, spotted salamanders spend most of their time in the leaf litter or in burrows beneath the surface of the ground. They are not commonly encountered outside of the breeding season, though they can be looked for beneath logs, boards, and flat rocks. They often get trapped in window wells, swimming pools, and even in smooth-sided pet dishes.

You should search for this species during its spring migration, associated with the first warm, rainy night of late winter or early spring, though several other factors may actually initiate it. When the air temperature first rises above 40° F and an extended rain begins in the afternoon and continues into the evening, get your raincoat, flashlight, and boots. The adults are less disturbed by light if a red filter of some type is used.

Dozens, hundreds, and, in some places, thousands of adult spotted salamanders congregate at night to breed in small, temporary, woodland ponds. They can be found crossing roads, walking down wooded hillsides, and swimming in the ponds. They can be perhaps most easily observed crossing roads in many rural and some suburban locations. If you drive slowly, you will spot them in ample time. This is an effective method for locating these (and other) salamanders if you are not sure where a breeding pond is located.

At a pond, carefully walk along the edge at night with a flashlight, searching the shallow areas for the obvious pattern of yellow spots. While the majority of the adult breeding population of any given year is concentrated in the pond for just a day or two, many individuals remain in there for varying lengths of time up to several weeks, giving you ample time to search during the season.

If you are unable to get out at night there are things to look for in the daytime. Normally, adults remain hidden beneath vegetation at the pond bottom, although some do move about, and females might lay their eggs in daylight. More likely, however, you will see clusters of spermatophores in various shallow areas of the ponds. If you find these, you know that there has been some recent activity in the pond, and you might still see some.

## What You Can Observe

### EMERGENCE AND MIGRATION

The appearance and migration of spotted salamanders is one of the more predictable events in nature. Adult spotted salamanders generally use the same breeding ponds yearly, and these are likely to be the same ones where they were born.

In response to rain (or very high humidity) and warming temperatures, adults make their way to the surface of the ground on wooded hillsides and at night head downslope to reach their breeding ponds. The migration is often very abrupt, with hundreds or even thousands of spotted salamanders migrating through the woods in the course of a single rainy evening.

In the North the migration usually occurs in late March or April, while in southern portions of the range it might be as early as January. In many cases, again, there may be one major night of movement, but some individuals will get to the ponds days or even weeks later. It is unknown if these late animals are coming from farther away or if they are returning for a second or third time.

Often, when the rain stops, individual animals will take cover beneath the leaves before continuing. Notice that the males precede the females, often by several hours, and, if the conditions are unfavorable (such as if it stops raining after a couple of hours), females may be delayed by several nights.

### COURTSHIP AND MATING

The terrestrial adults show no hesitation when they reach the pond; they simply walk in and swim for a few feet before settling down on the sunken leaves. Males usually arrive before the females and eventually gather into groups, called congresses. In ponds with large breeding populations, there may be several groups scattered about. While a congress may consist of four or five males, some include a hundred or more. Try to watch a single individual in a congress and notice that every few minutes it will swim to the surface, undulating its body and pressing its limbs against its trunk, take a gulp of air, then slowly drift back down to the bottom.

When females arrive at the pond, they too head underwater. Once one approaches a group of males, you will notice much more movement by both sexes. As of yet, no one is able to explain just how females locate a congress of males, though pheromones are suspected. In some cases, the courtship of the female and a male is difficult to observe with all the commotion of the congress. Try to locate a female away from the group; she will usually have a male or two nearby who are trying to get her attention.

The courtship dance of the spotted salamander consists of a single male and female circling each other on the pond bottom. Occasionally one or the other will swim up for a gulp of air, but then will slowly drift back down and resume activity. Males and females nudge each other and try to push their heads beneath the other's body, especially near the tail. Males attempt repeatedly to rub their chins along the back of the female.

At some point the male will walk away and slowly wiggle the tip of his tail. The female may follow and, if so, he will deposit one or more spermatophores onto a leaf or twig. If fully stimulated, the female will walk forward and cover one with her cloaca and, in so doing, transfer the sperm to her oviducts. Generally, the female will then show little or no interest in this or other males and head out to deeper parts of the pond. The male may return to a nearby congress and search out another female in the pond.

### EGGS AND EGG-LAYING

It is not difficult to find females depositing eggs if you look carefully and often. Normally, they don't lay their eggs for at least a day or two after they court. Go back to the ponds on succeeding nights and, with a flashlight, slowly search the twigs and branches of fallen tree limbs that are underwater. These are the main egg-laying sites. One corner of the pond may be more attractive to females than others. Often, several females will deposit eggs on the same or adjacent branches so that in the daytime huge clusters of eggs are visible.

As she prepares to deposit her eggs, a female will slowly crawl along a small twig (usually less than a quarter inch in diameter). Somewhere near the surface of the water, she will stop and grasp onto the twig tightly with her hind feet. Watch as she touches the branch with the lower part of her body; the black eggs will be extruded, several at a time, in a gelatinous mass. She may deposit up to two hundred eggs in a single mass, in a process that takes about half an hour. Many young females, however, lay only a few dozen eggs at a time and then move up the stem, or perhaps to a different branch, to lay the rest of their eggs.

Notice how tiny the newly deposited cluster of eggs appears. In a few hours, however, the mass will swell from its original size, two inches or so in diameter, to enormous proportions, with all the black eggs embedded in a mass of jellylike material the size of a tennis ball. Female spotted salamanders may produce a jelly coating for eggs that is completely transparent, allowing a clear view of all the individual eggs, or one that is opaque, giving a milky white appearance that obscures all but the most surface-dwelling eggs.

### EMBRYO-WATCHING

Once the eggs are deposited you can watch the developing embryos and the changes that occur in the egg mass itself. Since each mass is firmly attached to an underwater twig or plant stem, it is easy to keep track of one and watch its progress.

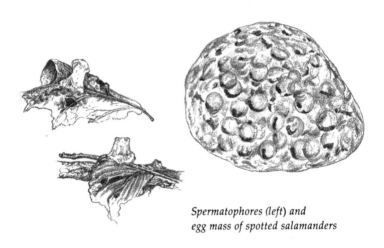

*Spermatophores (left) and egg mass of spotted salamanders*

If you keep brief notes on the size and appearance of the developing embryos it will become apparent that not all survive to hatching. There are many predators on the eggs and embryos that you will see. In the course of a few weeks look for adult red-spotted newts crawling over the masses and snapping at the embryos. Caddisfly larvae — the insects who build impressive houses around themselves — also feed on the eggs and embryos. Watch how they cling to the surface of the mass and try to break through the outer jelly layer to reach the eggs.

One field observer watched spotted turtles feeding on the eggs in a clear mass, but apparently ignoring those in an adjacent opaque one. Patient observations in your own pond could shed light on this and other aspects of the breeding biology of spotted salamanders. Leeches and fly larvae are also known to feed on spotted salamander eggs. Pond chemistry, especially its acidity, may also affect the embryos, as can temperature and water-level fluctuations.

After a week or two you may notice that some of the egg masses in the pond tend to take on a greenish hue. This is caused by algae (*Oophilia amblystomatis*) that grow particularly on salamander and frog eggs. This growth may be just a fortuitous event, but there is speculation and some evidence that a symbiotic relationship exists between the plant and embryos. The simplest explanation is that the developing salamanders give off carbon dioxide, nitrogen, and other nutrients that the algae make use of. In return the algae produce excess oxygen that the embryos, crowded in the mass as they are, need.

### LARVAE AND METAMORPHOSIS

Upon hatching, larval spotted salamanders race against the summer sun that evaporates their pond. In some dry years, the larvae are unable to grow fast enough to metamorphose before their world evaporates. In other years, there is ample water, but cool temperatures slow their development, and the larvae will remain in the ponds throughout the winter and emerge the following spring.

Larval spotted salamanders become major predators in their temporary ponds. They hunt small animals living on the surface of the leaf litter at the pond basin and drifting prey in the water column, such as mosquito larvae and fairy shrimp. At the same time, they are fed upon by a variety of predators, from diving beetle larvae to herons.

### JUVENILES

Newly transformed juvenile spotted salamanders are about an inch and a half to two inches in length. They are now ready for life on land. For a week or more, they linger along the nearly dried pond's basin edge, taking refuge under logs, fallen bark, or stones. Eventually, they move on to find underground retreats, where they remain for a year or two before becoming sexually mature.

Interactions between adult and juvenile spotted salamanders have been observed in laboratory situations and the field. Apparently, juveniles are excluded from adult territories or they avoid them. It appears that the adults mark their territories, or at least parts of them, with chemical scent markers.

### OTHER FACTS ABOUT SPOTTED SALAMANDERS

Spotted salamanders have long been recognized as important research animals in the fields of genetics and embryology. Twenty years ago researchers discovered their sensitivity to pond acidity, and this opened up investigations of the problems associated with acid rain pollution. (It now appears that in some isolated locations, populations of spotted salamanders are somewhat more tolerant to pond acidification.)

Increasing suburbanization is making it difficult for some populations of this species to survive. Many adults are killed when highways bisect their wintering sites and breeding ponds. It is easy to spot the animals as they move across roads, and in fact many people stake out exact distances on the roadside and keep track of the local population by making annual counts. Some enterprising salamander conservationists have convinced town officials to close certain roads on the nights the animals are crossing.

### OVERWINTERING

Spotted salamanders remain in underground retreats during the coldest parts of the year throughout their range. It is still unknown how deep individuals go or what conditions they prefer, but it is likely that they either make use of burrows and tunnels excavated by mammals or enter natural crevices. It is not known whether individuals move around during the winter or if they remain completely inactive, though spotted salamanders are able to move even when temperatures are close to freezing.

In one or two field studies, researchers have found that spotted-salamander larvae can overwinter in some ponds and metamorphose the following spring. This is apparently not a widespread phenomenon, however.

# Quick Reference Chart

*Life Cycle*

**Length of Breeding Season:** January to March (South); February to April (North)

**Breeding Habitat:** Temporary woodland ponds, primarily; also shallow coves of lakes and reservoirs and roadside ditches

**Eggs Retained by Female:** 2–7 days

**Eggs Deposited:** Up to 250 in at least 1 oval mass

**Eggs Hatch:** 1–2 months

**Length of Larval Stage:** Normally 1–4 months, but some larvae can overwinter and metamorphose 13 months after hatching

**Length of Juvenile Stage:** 1–3 years

**Lifespan of Adults:** At least 10 years

*Adult tiger salamander in burrow*

# TIGER SALAMANDER / *Ambystoma tigrinum*

I<small>T'S HARD</small> not to be impressed with tiger salamanders. As the larg-est land-dwelling salamander in the world, these huge animals normally evoke a strong response in people. Often, people first encounter a captive animal in an exhibit. It was some time before I actually did see a free-ranging tiger salamander. When I did, it was nothing like I had imagined. In a cool, shallow pool near the en-trance of a cave, a hefty-looking animal with huge gills swam past my view. It was a very light-colored larval tiger salamander, al-most half a foot in length.

The larvae of tiger salamanders (sometimes erroneously called "waterdogs" or "axolotls") are collected in some areas and sold as live fishing bait. They are thus transplanted into many areas out-side their natural range or mixed with unique tiger-salamander populations. Some states restrict or regulate the sale and importa-tion of tiger salamanders due to the potential disruption of local, native salamander populations. In addition, researchers are warn-ing of the potential confusion of data through the use of laboratory animals from unknown locations.

Tiger salamanders may be quite common in some areas, and their larvae can be especially abundant in small pools, brooks, or streams.

# How to Recognize Tiger Salamanders

An extremely variable species throughout its extensive range, tiger salamanders are best identified by their large size (up to thirteen inches). Most individuals have some sort of bold markings, often yellow or tan on an olive, black, or brown body. Some populations are lightly sprinkled with spots, others with tigerlike stripes, and some with a complex netlike pattern.

Unlike most other salamanders, maturing tiger salamanders may retain their external gills, remain aquatic, and become sexually mature. In some populations these adults, which can grow to be nine inches long, are quite common.

In contrast, spotted salamanders are black with yellow polka dots. Ringed salamanders (*Ambystoma annulatum*) are dark with a few yellow rings meeting the gray color that reaches up from the underside.

## DISTINGUISHING THE SEXES

During the breeding season, males have swellings around the base of their cloacae while females do not. Males are generally longer than females and have longer tails and hind legs. Females, when breeding, are especially plump and filled with eggs.

## LARVAE

Even in areas where they do eventually transform, tiger-salamander larvae grow to be quite large — up to five inches long. They are yellowish green in color with a wide, golden stripe running the length of their body. Their large size and light side stripe should distinguish them from most other salamander larvae in ponds.

## EGGS

Females in some tiger-salamander populations deposit their eggs in globular masses, somewhat similar to those of spotted salamanders, while others attach them individually along an underwater leaf, twig, or grass blade. In other locations, tiger-

*Tiger Salamander*

salamander eggs are deposited in groups of three to ten, all within a common jellylike matrix. Tiger-salamander egg masses are not firm and easily handled like those of spotted salamanders; the eggs and parts of the mass tend to fall apart when lifted out of the water.

## How to Find Tiger Salamanders

**Habitat:** Forests, meadows, deserts, canyons throughout the year; temporary ponds and streams during breeding season
**Months of Activity:** Year-round (South); April to September (North)

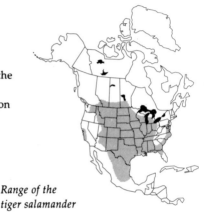

*Range of the tiger salamander*

Despite their widespread range and large populations, tiger salamanders are rarely encountered because they spend most of their time hidden and usually emerge only at night.

They can be found throughout the year by turning over logs, bark, rocks, or other material in wooded areas and grasslands, or on the edges of ponds and streams. Adults are most common near their breeding ponds, where they typically use the dens of medium-sized mammals for shelter. Often individuals are accidentally captured in window wells, sunken water tanks, and swimming pools. This occurs most frequently during their spring migrations to and from breeding ponds.

## What You Can Observe

### EMERGENCE AND MIGRATION

Except in the South, where they are active all year, tiger salamanders become active during the latter part of winter, as rains and warming temperatures stimulate them to come to the surface and migrate to breeding ponds. Tiger salamanders migrate primarily at night, probably to avoid being seen by potential predators such as birds, snakes, and some mammals. They do not display the concentrated migration and large congresses of spotted salamanders; rather, several dozen or more individuals will congregate at first while others may arrive over the next few weeks.

Though their congresses are smaller, the actual courtship between male and female tiger salamanders is somewhat similar to that of spotted salamanders.

A pair of adults will circle and nudge each other on the pond bottom. The male rubs his head and chin on the head, neck, and back of the female. She may or may not respond immediately, but eventually will follow him as he walks forward. Some males strongly push the female through the water, leading some researchers to wonder if this might be a method by which males ensure their access to females at the expense of other competing males.

The male will stop and deposit a spermatophore, which in this species is large — up to half an inch tall. Sometimes he will slowly undulate the tip of his tail afterward. The female will walk forward as the male moves ahead and stop to pick up at least the packet of sperm on top, if not the entire spermatophore. Generally, she will show no more interest in the male and move off into deeper water.

EGGS AND EGG-LAYING

Typically, a female begins to deposit her eggs within two or three days of courting with a male and picking up a spermatophore. A wide variation in methods and forms of egg-laying exists among populations of tiger salamanders. Females in the eastern half of the continent normally deposit up to 125 eggs in globular clusters somewhat resembling those of spotted salamanders but smaller (only about two inches by four inches at most). South-central females normally attach their eggs one at a time or in small grapelike clusters to the tops of underwater vegetation. In other regions, females may deposit several clusters of eggs over a period of days spent in the pond.

A large female may deposit a maximum of nearly five thousand eggs in a season, while smaller females deposit several hundred. The maximum number represents the largest number of eggs known for any salamander in the world.

After depositing all her eggs, a female pays them no more attention and leaves the pond. Depending upon water temperature, the eggs may begin to hatch in three to five weeks.

### LARVAE AND METAMORPHOSIS

The hallmark of this species is its extremes in life-history strategies; these have evolved in response to the many different ecological requirements of regions throughout North America. In many, if not most, populations, tiger-salamander larvae feed and grow during spring and early summer. They metamorphose in midsummer, two to five months after hatching. Frequently, however, those in mountain regions of the American West will remain as larvae for ten months or longer. They will overwinter in their ponds and metamorphose the following spring.

Some populations also exhibit a number of unique larvae who develop differently and feed almost exclusively on other tiger-salamander larvae. These cannibals have longer heads, much larger mouths, and longer teeth. They appear in areas with extremely high populations of larvae, so this variation may take advantage of the unique food resource or be a response to the difficulty of competing for food with close relatives.

In some populations of tiger salamanders, larvae never fully metamorphose, yet they become sexually mature. They retain many of their larval characteristics: external gills, wide tail fin, underwater habits, and general body shape. This process of becoming fully mature while retaining a larval form is called *neoteny* and is found in a surprisingly large number of salamanders. Individuals, populations, and species that develop this way are called *paedomorphic* (or sometimes *neotenic*). Of course, neoteny is found only in salamanders whose larvae exist in permanent bodies of water. In tiger salamanders, neotenic populations exist in fishless ponds, while nearby populations in ponds with fish metamorphose normally.

The existence of neoteny seems to be an adaptation for dealing with adverse conditions on land, such as extreme temperature fluctuations, arid conditions, or relatively poor food or plant cover for adults.

*Pattern variation in tiger salamanders*

### OTHER FACTS ABOUT TIGER SALAMANDERS

Tiger salamander adults and larvae are predators of a wide variety of smaller organisms. When aquatic (including breeding adults who may remain in the pond to feed), tiger salamanders feed mostly on aquatic invertebrates such as insects, crustaceans, worms, and snails. Their varied diet also includes fish, tadpoles, and other salamander larvae. At least some larvae have long, coiled intestines, indicative of a vegetarian diet, though this does not appear widespread.

In turn, tiger salamanders are hunted by numerous other predators at all stages of their lives. Aquatic larvae and neotenic adults are susceptible to snakes, otters, diving beetles, turtles, herons, alligators, and fish. At least in one location, a large concentration of tiger-salamander larvae helps sustain a nesting population of white pelicans who migrate to the freshwater ponds to feed. Tiger-salamander eggs are fed upon by caddisfly larvae and other aquatic invertebrates.

Predation is not the only factor, of course, that keeps tiger salamander populations in check. Diseases, lack of food, sudden freezes, or extended droughts may also take their toll. In some years, none of the larvae survive, while in other years many hundreds transform and become adults.

OVERWINTERING

Tiger salamanders in northern parts of their range and in high mountains may overwinter as terrestrial adults, normal larvae, recently transformed juveniles, or neotenic adults in water. Only the terrestrial adults spend the winter in underground burrows (usually made by other animals) or natural crevices, remaining relatively inactive during the coldest months. All the other forms overwinter in permanent ponds that normally lack fish. In most locations these aquatic forms remain active and feed during the winter months.

---

## Quick Reference Chart

**Length of Breeding Season:** November to February (South and Southwest); April to June (North and higher elevations)

**Breeding Habitat:** Normally in temporary ponds in fields and meadows adjacent to forests; also in overflow areas of streams and pools in small, slow-moving brooks; occasionally in permanent ponds without fish

**Eggs Retained by Female:** 2–5 days

**Eggs Deposited:** Often, 10–100 eggs in flimsy clusters, underwater; also deposited singly, often near each other, on underwater stems, twigs, leaves; up to 5,000 eggs total

**Eggs Hatch:** About 3 weeks after being deposited

**Length of Larval Stage:** From 3 months to a year and a half

**Lifespan of Adults:** Up to 25 years

*Two banding patterns of marbled salamanders.*
*Female on top, male below*

# MARBLED SALAMANDER /

*Ambystoma opacum*

As a habitual roller of fallen tree trunks and lifter of rocks, I'm always excited about what may be hidden underneath. Of course, there are many times when I find nothing. Sometimes just the tunnels of a shrew or channels made by earthworms are visible. Other times ground beetles, centipedes, or cave crickets will scurry out of the way. But on occasion a log will reveal a striking scene, herpetologically speaking. So it was when, in the oak and hickory forest that I travel, I turned a weathered, old log and saw there, adjacent to a young spotted salamander and two redbacks, the first adult marbled salamander I had ever found. Its striking black and white bands were a brilliant spectacle, and I simply stared at it for several minutes. While all of the close relatives of the species are stocky animals, this marbled salamander impressed me as being even more so. It was just three inches long but looked massive next to the sleek redback salamanders.

This was not the first of the species I had ever found, just the first adult. For several years at a nearby temporary pond I had watched the larvae of marbled salamanders swimming and resting in the leaf litter. When I go to watch the courtship of spotted salamanders late in the winter each year at several ponds, the tiny larvae of marbled salamanders are already active in the shallows.

These small larvae are easy to find and observe.

Marbled salamanders are unusual members of their family (Ambystomatidae) because the females deposit their eggs on land. Because their courtship and egg-laying take place in the late summer or early autumn, they also represent one of the few species of amphibians in this country that dramatically abandon the typical spring breeding season stereotype.

## How to Recognize Marbled Salamanders

### ADULTS AND JUVENILES

There really are few other animals that sport this dramatic black-and-white pattern of crossbands from the neck to the tip of the tail. Marbled salamanders grow only to about four inches in total length, so they appear very stocky. The top of the head is varyingly patterned with black and white; these differences can help to identify individual animals in a local population. Newly transformed young are dark brown with varying amounts of light-colored flecking that develops into the adult pattern within a few weeks. Little or no research has been done to determine if the banding changes substantially over the years on individuals.

Some populations of tiger salamanders may appear to have crossbands on their bodies, but tigers are usually much larger and the bands are yellow. The same is true for the ringed salamander (*Ambystoma annulatum*) of the Ozarks and eastern Oklahoma: its few bands are thin and yellow.

### DISTINGUISHING THE SEXES

While both sexes have the same pattern, the white bands of the males are exceptionally brilliant and glossy. The white areas on the females tend to be much grayer and duller.

### LARVAE

These are dark-colored animals that grow to an inch and a half in length. Their fully expanded gills look like feathered fringes at the base of their heads. The best way to identify the larvae of this species is to note the time of year they are found. Throughout the range of the marbled salamander, very few other species deposit their eggs in late summer or early autumn and have active larvae throughout the winter.

The eggs are not connected to each other by a common, jellylike matrix like the eggs of most other members of this family. Instead they are separate and tiny (less than three millimeters wide). Each egg is transparent when first deposited but soon becomes covered with soil or bits of leaves. Then they are difficult to see.

## How to Find Marbled Salamanders

**Habitat:** Deciduous woodlands and temporary pond edges
**Months of Activity:** Year-round in South; April to October in North

*Range of the marbled salamander*

Look for marbled salamanders on land, especially in deciduous woodlands near temporary pond basins. In coastal areas, they inhabit woodlands with sandy soils. They are rarely found walking on the surface of the ground, so you must turn logs, rocks, and other debris on the ground to find them.

During their late summer and early autumn courtship and breeding season, adults can be discovered if you carefully lift matted leaf litter or live vegetation in the shallow sections of damp, partially evaporated temporary ponds.

### FINDING NESTS AND EGGS

To find nests and eggs, carefully lift fallen tree limbs that lie in damp basins of temporary ponds or intermittent streams. Search along the edges of the channels left by the trees for females who might be with the eggs or just the cluster of eggs left unattended. The nest cavity is generally oval shaped, about three inches long, two inches wide, and an inch deep. This small size makes them somewhat difficult to see, so search carefully.

### FINDING MARBLED-SALAMANDER LARVAE

Larvae are relatively easy to find compared to the adults. From late autumn to early spring, before most other amphibians have deposited their eggs in temporary ponds, you can sit quietly on the edge of such ponds and look in the water for the dark-colored larvae resting on the leaf litter in the shallows. They are tiny— only about an inch in length. Often they are the only amphibian larvae in the ponds at that time of year. To increase your chances of seeing them, use a small branch to move leaves at the pond bottom.

## What You Can Observe

### EMERGENCE AND MIGRATION

We know little about adult marbled salamanders' emergence in the spring after overwintering beneath the leaf litter, in natural crevices, or in mammal burrows. In fact, they are rarely reported in the spring, though they begin feeding and moving about not long after the ground thaws.

The breeding-season migration of adult marbled salamanders from their underground, woodland retreats to the relatively dry basins of temporary ponds can be anticipated each year. Appearance of the adults in and near their breeding sites usually occurs just after heavy rainfall, so keep a check on the local weather and the condition of small, woodland basins that fill up each year when autumn storms occur.

### COURTSHIP AND MATING

Marbled-salamander courtship occurs on land and has been

rarely observed in the field. Sometime between their first appearance near the pond basin and when rainfall begins to fill it, adult males and females go through a courtship that includes much nudging, circling, and body posturing. This may occur either in the daytime or at night and usually is accomplished beneath a protective covering of leaf litter.

Fertilization of eggs is accomplished by a spermatophore that the male deposits, at the height of courtship, on a twig, grass blade, or leaf stalk. If sufficiently excited, the female will walk over the spermatophore and straddle it so that her cloaca engulfs all or just the top part of it. It is believed that once the female picks up the sperm packet on top of the spermatophore, she shuns advances from the same or additional males and walks away. The male may look for other females to court.

EGGS AND EGG-LAYING

Often the female will find a natural depression, or perhaps scour out her own, in which to deposit from sixty to two hundred eggs. The most fascinating aspect of this species' behavior is that the female usually stays with the eggs, curling her body about them. The function of the female's attentiveness has been discussed by several researchers. In controlled experiments female marbled salamanders vigorously attack small mammmals, such as shrews, and large insects, such as beetles, who are potential predators on the eggs. Another function of her remaining with the eggs may be that the female helps keep them from drying out by moistening her clutch with her body fluids and insulating them from surface heat.

The bond between the female and eggs is not particularly strong, however. If you find a female with eggs one day, she may just as likely not be there a few days later. Just how long a female will remain with the eggs has never been determined, but it is clear that she leaves by the time autumn rainfall begins to refill the pond and her egg chamber.

The eggs always hatch within a few days of being inundated. If autumn rains are insufficient to fill the pond, the female will leave

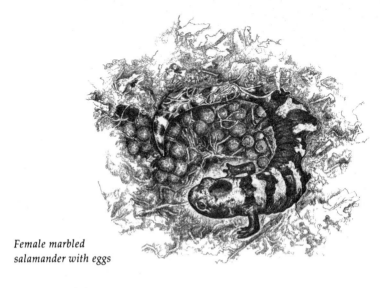

*Female marbled
salamander with eggs*

anyway and the eggs will be covered by leaves or snow. They will hatch the following spring when snowmelt and rains refill the pond.

### LARVAE AND METAMORPHOSIS

In the daytime, most marbled-salamander larvae rest on the pond bottom, although some feed in the leaf litter. At night you can use a flashlight to watch them swimming or drifting in all levels of the water. When newly hatched the larvae are actually attracted to light, but within a few weeks are generally disturbed by it. Placing a red filter over the flashlight will help reduce their aversion, and they may be watched at some length.

Some populations of marbled salamanders respond strongly to intensities of light and dark. On dark nights following bright, sunny days, field observers have found marbled-salamander larvae commonly swimming in the open water of their ponds. But on nights following cloudy days or on clear nights with a bright moon, fewer larvae strayed into the open water.

Marbled-salamander larvae hunt both large and small prey, from tiny daphnias to earthworms. Follow a single larva and perhaps you will see it lunge suddenly forward and then float back down to the leaf litter. This lunge-and-gulp movement is a common method of feeding whether they are stalking along the pond bottom or drifting in the water column. After feeding, their tiny bellies are bulging, so much so in some instances that their feet are unable to reach the ground.

These same feeding movements may make them more visible or bring them into proximity with any number of aquatic predators. Dragonfly larvae are particularly common predators, but many others exist. These include adult red-spotted newts, snapping and spotted turtles, damselfly and water-beetle larvae, and more. Many of the larvae that hatch in the autumn will not survive, but enough generally do to keep the local population viable.

Typically, the larvae begin to metamorphose late in the spring. By May or June most of the juveniles have left the ponds to take up a terrestrial existence. Juveniles are very small and little is known of their lives.

OVERWINTERING

It is unclear just how far away from their breeding ponds individual marbled salamanders go. Since the adults breed from late summer into the autumn, they must head for underground retreats shortly afterwards. The assumption is that they remain relatively inactive during this period.

---

## Quick Reference Chart

**Length of Breeding Season:** September and October (North); October to December (South)

**Breeding Habitat:** Temporary ponds in deciduous woodlands

**Eggs Retained by Female:** Several days to 3 weeks

**Eggs Deposited:** Up to 200 eggs, deposited singly in a small depression; eggs only slightly adherent to each other

**Eggs Hatch:** Within a few days after being covered by water; may overwinter as eggs and hatch the following spring

**Length of Larval Stage:** 4–6 months; usually transform in May and June

**Lifespan of Adults:** At least 4 years

---

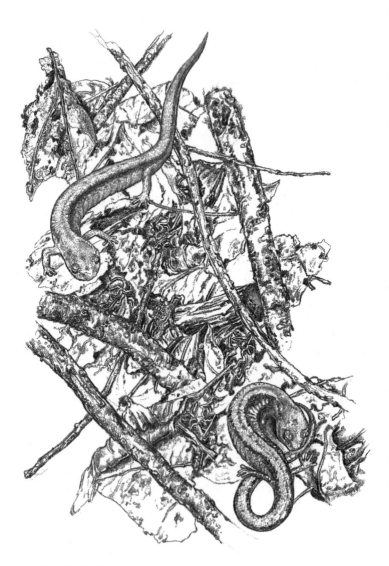

*Adult redback salamanders*

# REDBACK SALAMANDER / *Plethodon cinereus*

Over the years I have led or been part of many natural-history walks where a group of us would wander with no apparent focus, enjoying the variety of plants and animals that happened to be around at the time. Invariably, questions about certain animals come up. Most of these concern the large, impressive species like deer, bear, eagles, or owls. People are immediately fascinated with large wildlife, especially mammals and birds; an appreciation of smaller life forms generally comes later. It delights me to see people turn their attention to the small creatures around them.

Rarely am I disappointed in a quick search for a small, woodland salamander under fallen limbs and tree trunks. In many areas of the eastern part of the continent, the most common salamander is the redback, a slim, quick-moving animal that can help turn a person's view of amphibians completely around. These animals do several things that most people think salamanders shouldn't do.

I remember one particular walk that I was leading. It was a night hike, and we were listening for sounds of the forest and searching for nocturnal species of wildlife. Our flashlights illuminated beautiful spiders, courting daddy longlegs, many beetles, and a redback salamander that had climbed a three-foot-tall blueberry shrub. Although I knew they were supposed to hunt during humid evenings for small prey and that they often foraged in small shrubs, I had never seen one there. It amazed everyone that such a spindly legged and long-tailed salamander was able to negotiate the delicate and numerous branches of blueberry. But here it was, somewhat startled by our attention. The experience has often since lured me outdoors at night to watch them.


## How to Recognize Redback Salamanders

### ADULTS

These are small and slender animals, rarely growing more than four inches in length. Redbacks resemble many other small, woodland salamanders, and it may take close inspection to identify them at first. They lack any markings on the sides of the head and there is no pinched-in appearance where the tail connects to the body.

The species is interesting because individuals can come in one of several distinct colors. An individual salamander does not change its colors, but starts life either entirely gray (called the lead-back or unstriped phase), gray on the sides with a brick-red stripe down the back (called the redback or striped phase), or, in a few locations, may be bright orange-red overall, with a mottled-tipped tail (called the red or erythristic phase).

The predominant color in a local population of redbacks is often related to elevation. Those with the stripe down the back are usually found at upper elevations, while the gray redbacks are usually found in the lowlands.

Redbacks are members of the large family of woodland or lungless salamanders, the Plethodontidae. Over 220 species are known, all but two of which are found in the New World. The lungless salamanders are especially diverse in both eastern North America and Central America.

### DISTINGUISHING THE SEXES

Male redbacks are generally smaller than females, rarely exceeding three inches in length. The head shape is a bit different, with the males' snouts appearing more rounded. Males also are light-colored around their cloacae.

Females can grow longer than three and a half inches and in the breeding season usually are quite plump with eggs. They tend to have dark pigment around their cloacae.

### LARVAE

The larval stage of redback salamanders is spent within the egg capsule, and therefore even at hatching most redbacks show only the smallest hint of external gills. The remnants are absorbed within a few days. The juveniles then take up residence in the leaf litter on the forest floor, often seeking refuge under, or even inside, rotting logs. They become sexually mature in one to two years.

### EGGS

Up to fifteen cream-white eggs are deposited in an adhesive cluster inside rotting logs, beneath boards, or in leaf litter. They hang like tiny bunches of grapes from a stalk at the top of the cluster.

## How to Find Redback Salamanders

**Habitat:** Forested areas away from floodplains
**Months of Activity:** Late April or early May to October (North); year-round (South)

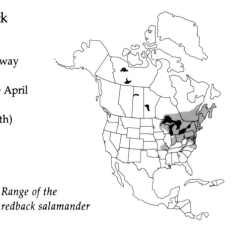

*Range of the redback salamander*

This is a forest animal that is equally widespread in deciduous woodlands, evergreen forests, and mixed wooded areas with both conifers and hardwoods. The redbacks' world is a magical and generally unfamiliar one to most of us. They hunt in the thickness of the leaf litter and come to the surface when there is ample humidity and moderate temperatures. During the driest weather they take refuge in damp spots—up to a foot below the surface, within the leaf litter, or beneath logs and rocks. It is here that you should seek them out.

You must look carefully since redbacks can be difficult to see at first. Their color may match the earth, leaves, or other debris, and they are so slender that they may look like plant roots or underground stems.

During the day you can casually sift through the leaves of the forest floor. This is exactly what some birds and small mammals do in their search for redbacks and other animals to eat. On damp nights, take a flashlight and carefully search the tops of the leaves and small shrubs. Redbacks often hunt for their food in these places and can climb at least the lower portions of tree trunks.

## What You Can Observe

### EMERGENCE AND MIGRATION

Since redback salamanders spend the majority of their life under cover, few observations have been made of their early spring appearance. Certainly, in most areas, redbacks become active near the surface again when the ground temperature and humidity increase.

The discovery of large numbers of redbacks that overwinter together indicates that some sort of migration must occur to get them all to the same point. There is no evidence indicating if this is widespread or not.

### COURTSHIP AND MATING

Several investigators have found that redbacks court and mate both in the fall and spring, and perhaps throughout the winter in southern parts of their range. The courtship behaviors of males and females are still poorly known, but a general pattern of activity has been observed.

Both sexes are able to detect and probably use odors to find and identify each other. A tail-straddling walk, typical of many members of the lungless-salamander family, is known to occur between redbacks. The female places her chin on the base of the male's tail with her front legs straddling his tail. As he walks forward, she maintains her position. The male may rub his chin and head on the female's body and slowly wave his tail shortly before he deposits a spermatophore on the ground. A few observers have seen male redbacks press their chins onto the back of a female and then snap their bodies back and away. Since male redbacks and other close relatives have a gland beneath their chin that produces a substance only during the breeding season, chin rubbing must have something to do with stimulating the female.

Eventually, the female picks up the top of the spermatophore in her cloaca and may move away from the male. In some cases, females deposit their eggs in a few days. In others, they retain the sperm in special structures within their reproductive tract. The sperm is then used to fertilize the eggs the following spring. In this way, sperm from redback salamanders is known to survive for several weeks or months within the female's body.

EGGS AND EGG-LAYING

A female invariably chooses an enclosed place to deposit her eggs. The most typical sites are spaces and crevices inside a well-rotted log, though eggs have been found beneath rocks, logs, leaves, boards, and other materials on the surface of the ground. There is a pronounced preference for nesting inside conifer logs. Females make their way through tunnels that have already been excavated by ants or other insects. Once inside, they find openings that are just a little larger than their own bodies and deposit from three to fifteen eggs, connected in a grapelike cluster.

The eggs are fairly large for such a small, slender salamander and are cream-white or yellowish in color. All are deposited within a day of each other, usually within a few hours. They hang by a common stalk from whatever material is above them, indicating that the female must somehow turn upside down to deposit each egg. Females remain with their eggs during the entire period of their development, which averages about two months. After hatching, young redbacks tend to linger with their mother, even climbing on her back and head.

Females are known to defend their eggs aggressively from other redbacks (who may eat the eggs) or other potential predators, including snakes. Lunging, biting, and grappling may occur when intruders get too close to a female redback defending her eggs and nest.

### LARVAE AND METAMORPHOSIS

The two-month incubation period allows the larval stage to be spent entirely within the egg capsule. This developmental trait has undoubtedly coevolved with the terrestrial eggs and eliminates the need for this species to find standing water for successful completion of one of its life stages. Metamorphosis is nearly completed within the egg capsule, as well. Final development is finished within a few days following the emergence of a three-quarter-inch juvenile redback.

### PREDATION AND DEFENSE

Redbacks are preyed upon by many other animals, including shrews, snakes, screech owls, and songbirds, particularly thrushes. For their part, redbacks have at least a few behaviors that enhance their chances of survival.

When you uncover a redback you will often find it in one of three different positions. Their typical resting posture is one in which they are relatively stretched out, perhaps with the head and tail bent at some small angle. Second, a redback may bend its body to be in a partial coil when it is uncovered. Third, you may find one coiled with its head and tail touching, or nearly so. If you reach out to it and come close, it may quickly snap its head to the side or straight up into the air, sometimes doing this several times in succession. This is probably some sort of defensive behavior.

The redback is also able to detach most of its tail, which continues to move and wiggle on its own. This is an effective means of distracting a predator while the salamander moves away. In addition, numerous glands in the skin of the tail may be distasteful to the predator and possibly function to prevent further attacks, at least by that particular animal. A redback that has lost part or all of its tail will regenerate a nearly complete one at some time in the future.

The all-red color phase of the redback salamander is widely distributed, being known from Ohio and southern Ontario to New England and Nova Scotia. In a few areas, the local population of the all-red color phase approaches 25 percent of all the redbacks in an area, a high percentage indeed. Field biologists have surmised that this color phase is especially common where large populations of red-spotted newts exist and where the red eft stage is prevalent. The belief is that the all-red redback is a mimic of the toxic red eft. Laboratory and field experiments indicate that birds learn to avoid the edible redbacks if they've had an unpleasant experience tasting a red eft.

FEEDING

If you travel to a redback habitat on a damp night, be prepared to see redbacks searching for food in deliberate and sometimes energetic ways on the surface of the ground. Sometimes you will see them with their noses touching the leaf litter, while at other times they will have their heads lifted high off the ground.

Most impressively, you may find them a foot or more off the forest floor on branches of small shrubs or on the trunks of trees. It is thought that redbacks are thus able to take advantage of the large number of small insects and other invertebrates that abound in these places on damp nights. In fact, the salamanders may be more or less fasting during the nights that are too dry for them to forage at the surface.

*Gray form of redback salamander*

### OTHER FACTS ABOUT REDBACK SALAMANDERS

Within most of their range, redbacks are very common. A New England study showed several years ago that redbacks were actually far more abundant than all the bird species added together and equaled the live weight of the entire population of small mammals in the study site. It seems clear that redbacks are important members of forest communities and play a role in nutrient recycling, predator-prey relationships, and energy flow.

Although salamanders are likely to be the most abundant terrestrial vertebrates in many forest communities, little research has been conducted with them in mind. Forest-cutting practices, woodlot management, application of herbicides or pesticides, and habitat manipulation all affect populations of redbacks and other salamanders in poorly understood ways.

#### OVERWINTERING

During the winter, redback salamanders take refuge as far as three and a half feet below the surface of the ground in subterranean crevices, tunnels, mammal burrows, and ant mounds. Often the salamanders congregate in large numbers, leading to a belief that they must perform some migration to reach a particular site.

Several observations indicate a surprising amount of activity for redbacks during the winter, even among some females that have recently mated. Many other redbacks seem actively to feed during the winter.

---

## Quick Reference Chart

**Length of Breeding Season:** Fall and spring, perhaps continuing through the winter

**Breeding Habitat:** In small nesting cavities inside rotting logs (evergreens especially) and under rocks, boards, and leaves

**Eggs Retained by Female:** Several days to 4 months

**Egg Number and Form:** Up to 15 cream-colored eggs adhering to each other and hanging by a common stalk from the top of the nest chamber

**Eggs Hatch:** About 2 months

**Larval Stage:** Spent entirely within the egg capsule; young hatch with only tiny remnants of gills

**Lifespan of Adults:** At least 3 years

---

Part Two

---

# THE REPTILES

# About Reptiles

Reptiles are vertebrates, like birds, mammals, amphibians, bony fish, and cartilaginous fish. Their unborn young develop in a special chamber (the *amnion*) that is, in essence, an aquatic environment. Around this are other specialized layers, all enclosed in a tough, shelled layer giving the outer form to their leathery eggs. All reptiles have scales, hardened growths attached to the outer layer of skin. They also have at least one functional lung, requiring them to be air-breathing no matter where they live, and a three-chambered heart (though the crocodilian's heart has four chambers).

## MAINTAINING BODY TEMPERATURE

For the most part, reptiles are *ectothermic* animals; that is, they maintain their body temperatures (sometimes at surprisingly even levels) by relying on external sources of heat. Many reptiles bask on conspicuous perches to accomplish this. This is often thought of as a handicap to reptiles, as compared to the self-reliance allowed by the internal heating mechanism of mammals and birds. Because they don't have to keep an internal heating mechanism going all the time, however, reptiles can be more efficient eating irregularly and are able to go for long periods without eating at all.

In mountain regions and northern latitudes, reptiles become dormant for a few days to several months at a time during cold periods. For the most part, reptiles simply slow down their body processes and become inactive until temperatures increase again. It is unclear just how reptiles, tucked safely some distance below the surface of the ground, sense these increased temperatures.

All reptiles reproduce by internal fertilization. Male snakes and lizards have a sex organ called the *hemipenes*, which is actually composed of two separate and functional organs. They use only one at a time when copulating. Turtles and crocodiles have a single copulatory organ.

Female reptiles show a wide array of reproductive methods. Some lay eggs; many retain the eggs inside their bodies until they hatch, and the live young then emerge. Others give birth to live young directly. All young reptiles are independent at birth — they don't require any assistance from, or generally ever see, their mother. There are a few exceptions to this, such as the care given to their young by female alligators, and the recently discovered scent trails laid down by some female snakes, which may help guide their newborn young to wintering sites.

## MODERN VIEWS OF ANCIENT REPTILES

Modern reptiles have long been thought of as mere holdovers from the great age of dinosaurs, sort of the last gasp of those giants in a world dominated by "higher" vertebrates. In fact, many reptiles today exhibit recent evolutionary adaptations and complex behaviors that should help us rethink this myth.

In addition, there is nothing implicitly wrong with having a long lineage. Turtles, for example, are superb examples of survival through the ages. Few other vertebrates on earth have come close to achieving the longevity this group has had, and despite the current dire condition of many species brought on by human-caused pressures, turtles might very well continue to exist on the planet long after we and other sophisticated species disappear.

Paleontologists continually debate the long history of the group, investigate the possible warm-bloodedness of dinosaurs, and question what caused the extinction of the large reptiles while all the others survived and continued to evolve. Some wonder whether dinosaurs are extinct at all, or have merely grown feathers and taken a new name—birds.

Biologists interested in living reptiles are finding among them complex social behaviors long thought to be the sole domain of birds and mammals. New species are being discovered and relationships between groups constantly rearranged. There is no shortage of material to study.

Reptiles are a diverse and varied order of vertebrates that rarely evoke neutral responses in anybody. Of course, these responses are not evenly distributed; snakes are still feared and killed by so many people that sociologists wonder if there really isn't some innate human aversion to them that goes back to the time when humans were just beginning to make tools and communicate with each other.

The crocodilians, including the American alligator, are potential predators of humans, like many other large species of animals. Yet unlike lions and some other large predators treated with respect, alligators and crocodiles are commonly loathed and have been exterminated over much of their former range.

On the other hand, turtles are almost universally accepted, if not for their intrinsic worth, then at least as a food source. Lizards too are tolerated, since they are usually small and dart out of the way quickly. They are rarely paid any attention—until they show up inside the house.

To those of us who have shed the burden of superstition or unwarranted fears, reptiles offer an almost unbeatable combination of features as animals to watch. Many are easy to find and observe, they allow relatively close approach, and their colors, shapes, and daily activities invite attention. So much is unknown about the lives of even common species that there is a superb opportunity for anyone to add to the growing body of knowledge about them.

# Introducing Turtles

Nothing else living on earth today is like a turtle. Certainly, there are plenty of animals with shells, but they either have fewer than four feet (clams and snails) or more than four (lobsters and crayfish). Turtles' unique design — their ribs fused to their shell and their leg bones tucked inside their body cavity — has been a hallmark of the group since they evolved about 250 million years ago. Turtles were around before the dinosaurs, and they watched them emerge, prosper, and disappear altogether. Without changing their body plan at all, turtles further observed the rise of birds and mammals. They are still here today, waiting to see what happens to all of us.

## TURTLE LONGEVITY

Besides having a long and distinguished evolutionary lineage, turtles are believed to attain greater individual ages than any other existent vertebrates on earth. In some groups, notably the sea turtles and huge land tortoises, ages over one hundred years may be common. Even small species tend to live twenty to fifty years or more, much longer than most amphibians, fish, birds, and mammals.

## COMMON FAMILIES OF TURTLES

Today, there are twelve different families of turtles in the world, totaling about 250 species. In the United States, seven families are represented, with about forty-eight species known. Three of these families include the vast majority of species in our area. All of these are relatively easy to find, watch, and identify.

The snapping-turtle family (Chelydridae) includes only two species. They both grow to large sizes, have reduced bottom shells, live in semiaquatic conditions, and eat both plants and animals. The common snapping turtle is well known because of its large size, relative abundance in suburban and urban areas, and the facts and fables about its life.

A similar-looking but unrelated family is that of the musk and mud turtles (Kinosternidae). Found only in the New World, the twenty-two total species include nine that are found north of Mexico. All have scent glands opening near where their top and bottom shells meet, a small, rounded top shell, and at least one hinge on the lower shell.

The largest family of turtles in the world is the Emydidae, known as the pond, marsh, or semiaquatic, turtles. Found throughout the world, there are thirty-four different genera and up to ninety-one species currently known. Many of these turtles are found in the United States, where seven different genera and twenty-six species are known. This large family includes such diverse animals as the box turtle, painted turtle, and pond slider.

CONSERVATION OF TURTLES

Many people, including biologists, are very concerned with the rapid rate at which many turtle populations are disappearing. The commercial collecting of their eggs by people, drowning in shrimp nets, and ingesting ocean trash are problems for the magnificent sea turtles. Box turtles and sliders are collected in great numbers for the pet trade. The great construction boom in the southeast and southwest is putting pressure on the few surviving land and desert tortoises. Even once-common species are disappearing because of wetland drainage and other habitat alterations or because of deaths suffered as they cross the numerous highways that bisect their home ranges.

*Hearing*

The ears of a turtle are not generally visible, though some species do have visible a large, circular area on both sides of the head behind the eyes. These are the *tympanic membranes* that cover the middle and inner ears.

Most if not all turtles hear to varying degrees. You may have tried walking along the bank of a pond or stepping through a woodland to peer at painted turtles, only to find ripples on the surface where they plunged into the water upon sensing your approach.

*Smell*

Turtles seem to have at least an adequate sense of smell. Many field observers report females nosing the ground near nest sights. Snapping turtles and other underwater scavengers are able to locate food at night by odors. Terrestrial species can distinguish various odors as well.

*Sight*

Obviously, all turtles can see, though their spatial perception varies greatly. Early experimenters noted that box turtles hesitate when they come to an edge of a precipice (like a table) but painted turtles hurl themselves off with wild abandon. These differences, of course, have to do with the two species' varying evolutionary strategies, which have resulted in contrasting life-styles and habitat preferences. When danger threatens painted turtles, all they normally need to do is launch themselves off their basking perch into water. Box turtles, which are terrestrial, usually have to negotiate uneven terrain where hills and valleys may abound.

Most turtles are probably able to distinguish colors, and there is some belief that this discrimination helps with many social interactions between individual turtles, helps them locate food items, and perhaps also serves other functions.

## Sound Production

Some turtles can and do make sounds, though all lack vocal chords. Most commonly heard by people are various hisses that occur when a turtle quickly withdraws its limbs inside its shell and expels air from its lungs. Little is known about the value to turtles of these and other vocalizations, such as whistles and grunts, which have been reported.

### BASKING

Most biologists believe that basking is important to turtles because they are thus able to increase their body temperatures to a range where they are most efficiently able to move, digest food, escape predators, and perform other activities. Often this optimal temperature is substantially higher than that of their surroundings. It is clear that few, if any, semiaquatic turtles bask when the air temperature is colder than the water temperature or during cold rainy periods; this takes into account the chilling effects of the wind. Turtles can be seen basking, however, on warm but overcast days and on days when a warm rain is pouring down. In some situations, semiaquatic turtles have been observed basking by floating on the surface of the water, resting on the top of another, larger turtle that was floating on the surface, or simply sitting motionless in very shallow, sunlit water. These actions may cause small but important changes in the body temperature of the turtle.

There are other benefits of basking besides regulating body temperature. During long periods of basking, and in some cases immediately after an individual turtle emerges, it can be seen to stretch out its head, legs, feet, toes, and tail for many minutes at a time. One explanation for this is that any parasites such as leeches, which commonly attach themselves to turtles, might be encouraged to drop off in the heat of the sun and dryness of the air. Exposing their shells to the air can reduce the growth of algae, a potentially harmful problem for some turtles.

In addition, observations of captive semiaquatic turtles indicate that diseases of their shells occur much more frequently in individuals that are unable to bask than in those allowed to. Finally, there has been much interest in the role that ultraviolet radiation from the sun has upon the ability of a turtle's body to assimilate vitamins. There is mounting evidence that exposure to UV light is required for many semiaquatic turtle species to synthesize vitamin D, which, among other benefits, promotes strong, healthy shell growth.

TURTLE TERMINOLOGY

Because of their unique design and structure, turtles seem to have acquired a particularly large number of terms specifying minute parts of their bodies. The following are some of the most useful in field observations of turtles.

The shell of a turtle is divided into halves, an upper section called the *carapace* and a lower section called the *plastron*. Turtles cannot, except in cartoons, leave their shell, both halves of which are solidly fused in an area on each side of the body called a *bridge*. Both the carapace and plastron are made up of a number of bones, and these are covered with *plates* or *scutes* (sometimes called *laminae*) that give the turtle its color and design. These scutes are shed periodically as the shell grows. They meet in regular and distinguishable ways; the joint or space between them is called a *seam*.

The head of a turtle is covered with numerous small and large scales. There is no indication of an ear opening at all, though it appears that most turtle species can hear very well. Turtles do not have teeth, but the strong, sharp edges of their upper and lower *jaws* form a *beak*.

## Turtle, Tortoise, and Terrapin

These terms are used with varying frequencies and with different meanings by many people. All reptiles with shells are turtles. Tortoises are turtles that have developed specialized features for living on land, such as thick, elephantlike legs and no webbing between their toes. Small species of turtles that have been collected commercially for food are often called terrapins. Terrapin soup in many parts of the country is actually made from snapping turtles.

*Basking male painted turtle*

# PAINTED TURTLE / *Chrysemys picta*

On a sunny but chilly early spring day, some friends and I took a long walk near a reservoir surrounded by woodlands. Most of the ice was gone from the water, but patches of it still hung on in the quieter and shadier coves. A brisk wind coming off the water sent us inland where the trail wound up and down small hills. Between two hills was an isolated pond, perhaps half an acre in size. The north-facing side was still covered with ice, but the southern half was open and the sun was shining down on it. From the top of the hill we almost didn't notice that on some of the sedge hummocks that emerged from the water were several dark shapes. We looked closely with our binoculars and discovered fifteen painted turtles basking in the afternoon warmth. Their appearance on such a cold day was a bit surprising.

I was reminded of an earlier experience. During one winter trip to the local ice-skating pond situated in a nearby woodland, I was entranced by the view of underwater plants, snails, and insects afforded by the clear ice. I wasn't quite prepared then when an adult painted turtle swam leisurely by. Although I have not seen this since, other people have reported similar experiences.

Throughout most of their wide range from coast to coast, this is the small turtle commonly seen basking on logs and soft vegetation in ponds, marshes, rivers, and reservoirs.

# How to Recognize Painted Turtles

ADULTS

True to their common name, these turtles often have a beautiful top shell with bright red and orange markings along the margin. The individual plates on the top shell are black edged with yellow. The turtles also have yellow and red stripes on their legs, neck, face, and head, and a pair of bright yellow spots just behind each eye. They have a distinctly flattened carapace that can grow to a total length of ten inches.

The closely related slider, cooter, and red-bellied turtles are usually much larger as adults and lack the often bright lines that run between the plates on the carapace.

Painted turtles are members of the Emydidae, the pond- and marsh-turtle family. The painted has the widest range of any species of turtle in North America.

DISTINGUISHING THE SEXES

Males have very long front claws and long, thick tails. Their cloacae are relatively close to the tip of the tail. Female painted turtles have short front claws and their cloacae are closer to the base of the short tail. Females grow to much larger shell dimensions than males.

EGGS AND NESTS

Throughout their range, painted turtle females lay from two to twenty eggs, the largest number being associated with populations in the Northwest. Typically a nest will contain about half a dozen eggs.

Normal eggs are white or have a slight yellow tint. The surface is somewhat granular, not glossy smooth. Eggs are about an inch and a half long and three-quarters of an inch wide.

Nests are often found in sandy soils, lawns, mowed fields, gravel pits, roadsides, or railroad beds. Each cavity is about four inches deep and an inch and a half or two inches wide. After laying the eggs, females cover the nest so well with soil that there is usually little or no visible sign of its presence.

## How to Find Painted Turtles

**Habitat:** Aquatic; usually permanent bodies of water
**Months of Activity:** In most of range, year-round; in the North, March to November

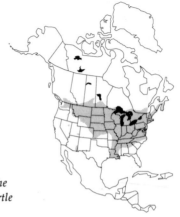

*Range of the painted turtle*

The best place to start when looking for this species is in a lake, river, pond, or reservoir. Occasionally they are found in temporary ponds, but their preferred locations are permanent bodies of water. Painted turtles rarely leave their ponds or rivers, so throughout the year they can be expected to be found there. The wetland that they survive in does not have to be any particular size or shape, but some locations seem to support larger numbers of turtles. One of the factors that may come into play here is the abundance and location of basking sites. It is on these logs, branches, tree trunks, rocks, or floating debris that you are most likely to see your first painted turtles. Ponds with few of these may be avoided by the turtles, and if there, they may be more difficult to find, basking in hidden areas on the bank.

Early spring and mornings are the best times to look for painted turtles, since they bask more then. They are very attentive, however, and in remote areas will slide off their perches long before you can approach. If this happens, sit still for a few minutes and one or more turtles will probably reemerge. Use binoculars to get a good look from a distance first.

# What You Can Observe

Painted turtles can be found moving beneath the ice in northern parts of their range during late winter and early spring. On some particularly sunny days, individuals are induced to haul out onto the melting edge of the ice and bask. For adults, this period of time between their first becoming active and the complete thawing of the pond's surface is especially dangerous; higher mortality of adults is recorded during March and April than at any other period, and is usually attributed to a small food supply. In some populations, males may become active earlier than females, though not all field researchers have found this to be true.

Once they do become active under the ice in March, painted turtles may respond to periodic cold spells by burrowing into the mud at the bottom of the pond. When temperatures again warm they resume their activities. In at least one field study, painted turtles did not begin feeding until May, after air and water temperatures increased substantially, even though the turtles initially became active as early as March.

## TERRITORIAL BEHAVIOR

Interactions between two or more basking painted turtles can range widely; they may totally ignore one another, or they may engage in aggressive visual displays and physical encounters. A common display between two turtles inhabiting the same basking site is an "open-mouth" gesture in which one animal simply opens its mouth and directs it at another turtle. The second turtle may respond by turning away from the first turtle, moving its position on the basking site, or even returning the same behavior. Biting another turtle's shell or limbs has also been recorded in some well-studied populations, though this is not believed to be particularly common.

In some cases where basking sites are at a premium or the population of turtles is especially high, an interesting behavior can be seen among turtles that are stacked on top of one another. The turtle at the bottom pushes with its hind legs to elevate the rear part of its shell and then either rocks side to side or up and down. This is especially noticeable when large turtles are on top of smaller turtles, and it seems to be a clear attempt by the lower animal to dislodge the one on top.

COURTSHIP AND MATING

The activities of adult painted turtles are easy to observe during the breeding season, which extends from March into late summer, with peak periods of courtship and mating from late April to mid-June. If you station yourself some distance above the water you will be able to see the activities much better; using binoculars or polarized sunglasses will enhance your view. Most of the activity among courting painted turtles is at or just below the surface of the water. Look for the smaller males to be swimming around the larger females; sometimes two or more males will be near a single female.

The courtship activities of a male entail trying to get the attention of the female. He will swim around her in a circle, keeping his head toward her. When directly in front, the male sweeps each of his long claws in alternation along the head and neck of the female. You may notice at this point that she dives underwater and swims away with powerful strokes to avoid the male. If she is receptive, however, she will reach out with her front feet and touch his, causing the male to turn and lead her away. Eventually she will slowly sink to the bottom where they will mate, the male holding onto her shell with his claws.

NEST-BUILDING AND EGG-LAYING

Within one or two months after mating, in May, June, or July, female painted turtles generally look for nesting sites, usually late in the afternoon. The nesting forays are often but not always associated with a soaking rainstorm during the day. Painted turtles are less likely than other turtles to travel long distances from water to deposit their eggs.

Typical nest sites are old gravel banks, mown fields, and sand banks. The nests are usually in open areas that get lots of sunlight and have some vegetation on the ground. The female digs the nest with her hind feet and rarely, if ever, looks around at what she is doing. Often she will dig several "false" nests before depositing her eggs in one.

A female painted turtle does such a good job of covering over the nest with soil that it is difficult to locate it even minutes after she has left. Still, many predators, including skunks, foxes, badgers, ground squirrels, and raccoons, dig up the eggs. In one study, most of the nests were found and destroyed within forty-eight hours. Recent observations indicate that some—as many as 50 percent—of the female painted turtles in a given population do not nest in any given year, but that a few might nest twice in a season.

## BEHAVIOR OF THE YOUNG

The survivability of eggs and hatchlings has not been studied in depth for this or other inland species of turtles, even though this is an important aspect of their life history. Some observers feel that very few eggs deposited by females in a given population survive for very long; predators or adverse weather conditions cause most of the loss.

The eggs hatch late in the summer, usually in late August or early September. The young painted turtles remain inside the nest cavity for varying lengths of time. In northern parts of their range, they may overwinter in their nest and do not emerge until the following spring. It remains to be seen just how widespread this behavior is and to what extent it occurs in other types of turtles as well.

Once they emerge, hatchling turtles must migrate to ponds or rivers. Their method of navigating and orienting is largely unstudied. Field research has shown that the hatchlings are strongly attracted to the brightest part of the night sky when they emerge and normally this is the area over the brightly reflective surfaces of lakes and ponds. In populated places, however, the bright areas may be over street and house lights, and the young can actually be drawn away from their ponds. A wide variety of predators, including frogs, snakes, wading birds, predatory fish, and alligators, will feed on the hatchlings and young turtles. (Only the largest carnivores, such as alligators, are likely to eat adult painted turtles.)

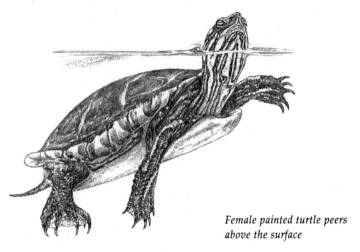

*Female painted turtle peers above the surface*

## BASKING

By far, basking is the most common behavior you will observe in this species. Many field researchers have looked closely at this activity and the costs and benefits to turtles who engage in basking. Individual painted turtles will climb onto rocks, logs, overhanging tree limbs, floating leaves, muskrat houses, beaver lodges and dams, beaches and sand banks, and even the backs of other turtles to expose themselves to the rays of the sun.

Basking sites are apparently very important to local turtles. You should expect to see the same places used regularly, though possibly by different individuals. It is usually the lack of good basking sites that seems to cause turtles to be crowded onto a few locations, stacking themselves up to four or five turtles deep. The characteristics of good basking sites include being fully exposed to the sun at most times of the day, having excellent views of the shoreline, not being too close to shore, and being of an appropriate size to accommodate the turtle comfortably.

Researchers have identified two different patterns of basking behavior in painted turtles. In some populations, painted turtles become active just after sunrise; they haul themselves onto basking sites, where they remain for up to five or six hours. The other pattern involves two distinct basking periods, one in the early morning and another in the late morning or early afternoon. In either case, morning basking is by far the most pronounced. Some turtles, however, can be found basking at almost any time of the day. Larger individuals also tend to bask for longer periods of time than smaller ones, though adults are often more wary than juveniles and will quickly slide off to the safety of the water.

FEEDING

After early-morning basking periods, painted turtles may spend some time foraging for food. Watch from bridges, lookout towers, or the crests of tall stream banks to see this clearly. Painted turtles eat a wide variety of plant and animal material, including dead and decaying carcasses. Some researchers have recorded painted turtles actually lunging into thick growths of underwater plants to scare out small animals that might be hiding there. If an insect, tadpole, fish, or other small animal moves, the turtle will actively pursue and attempt to capture it. Painted turtles also feed on snails, cattail seeds and stems, and long strings of algae.

Look for painted turtles feeding in areas where dense underwater vegetation grows to the surface. Often the turtles will feed for long periods of time and can be easily observed. Late in the afternoon, painted turtles may feed again, sometimes after another bout of basking.

Painted turtles become more or less inactive at night and sleep at the bottom of the pond. The few observations of sleeping painted turtles indicate that they do not burrow into the mud at night, but rest on the leaf litter, mud, or sand at the bottom.

ALGAE GROWTH ON TURTLES

At least five different species of algae have been found growing on the shells of painted turtles, and this coat of green is visible in some populations. The algae have no known function and most are lost when the turtles shed their outer layer of plates each year or so. Still, the presence of algae is widespread, and research may yet reveal more of a connection.

OVERWINTERING

More than many other freshwater species, painted turtles remain active for most of the year, even in cold parts of their range. When water temperatures do drop and ice begins to form, they head for deeper parts of ponds or lakes and bury themselves in soft mud on the bottom. In southern parts of their range, painted turtles may overwinter for just a month, while in very cold northern areas they may remain inactive for more than four months.

Painted turtles have been observed basking during winter thaws, when water temperatures are greater than 50° F, and even during the coldest periods they can occasionally be seen swimming beneath clear ice. They can be found and may be active every month of the year.

---

## Quick Reference Chart

**Length of Breeding Season:** March to June, occasionally into autumn

**Breeding Habitat:** In water, often in vegetated areas

**Nest Location:** In fields, banks, gravel pits, railroad beds, lawns, gardens, near house foundations

**Eggs Deposited:** Up to 20 (normally 4–8) eggs deposited from late May (South and West) to middle of July (North)

**Eggs Hatch:** In 2½–3 months; young may emerge in mid-August to late September; some overwinter in nest and emerge the following May

**Age at Sexual Maturity:** Males mature in 4–5 years, females in 5–6

**Lifespan of Adults:** At least 13 years, but presumed longer

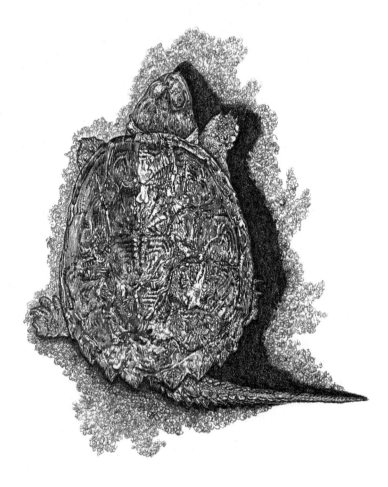

*Adult snapping turtle*

# SNAPPING TURTLE / *Chelydra serpentina*

ONE EARLY spring afternoon I found myself sitting in the sun at the edge of an active beaver pond in a wildlife sanctuary. A pair of Canada geese were patrolling the edges of a small island where their nest was located. Many songbirds could be heard near the pond and up on the nearby hillside. A few spring peepers were calling, and a couple of painted turtles were sunning on logs. Suddenly, a loud splashing caught my attention. It took several minutes of watching through binoculars to identify the cause of the commotion — two snapping turtles, locked together, tumbling over and over in the shallow water. I sat transfixed as they churned the water for minutes at a time. Then they would disengage, and one would slowly swim away, only to be followed closely by the other. Shortly they would come together again, and the two would roll and tumble once more. At one point the two rose vertically out of the water. They were belly to belly, with their necks straining and their front feet clasping each other. They were literally standing up on the bottom of the pond, then slowly they toppled. All this activity lasted for about forty-five minutes. Little attention was paid to it by other animals that were in and around the pond.

Throughout their range, snapping turtles are sought out and hunted for food or killed because they are believed to be responsible for everything from eliminating ducks in a pond to attacking bathers at the waterfront. Though these animals have been studied extensively, there seem to be more myths about them than about any other species in North America. Perhaps this is fitting. They are magnificent animals who are surviving in the twentieth century, unlike many other species of turtles.

## How to Recognize Snapping Turtles

### ADULTS

The main feature that distinguishes snapping turtles from other turtles is their ridiculously small bottom shell (plastron), which hardly protects them at all from the underside. Snapping turtles also have long tails, the tip of which can be wrapped around objects to hold them tight. The top surface of the tail has a series of large, triangular plates, giving the snapping turtle an appearance like some of the great dinosaurs.

This is one of the largest freshwater and salt-marsh turtles in North America. While most of the size estimates offered by excited outdoors people are exaggerated, snapping turtles can and do get large, both in physical dimensions and body weight. Their top shell (carapace) can reach a maximum length of twenty inches, and individuals have been accurately weighed at just above sixty pounds.

The top shell and skin color is generally dark gray, black, or brown. Often, a growth of algae covers the plates on the carapace. The tiny plastron is yellowish. Stinkpots also have small plastrons, but they have a high-domed carapace rather than the somewhat flat carapace of the snapping turtle.

The common snapping turtle is a member of the Chelydridae family, which includes only one other species in the United States, the alligator snapping turtle (*Macroclemmys temmincki*).

### THE SEXES

As with most turtles, males have longer tails than females. When the tail is straight, the cloacal opening is located beyond the margin of the top shell in males. In females, it does not reach past the shell edge.

Males tend to grow to slightly larger sizes than females, especially in carapace length and total weight.

EGGS AND NESTS

Snapping-turtle eggs are perfectly round and a bit smaller than a Ping-Pong ball — about an inch in diameter. Females can deposit up to eighty or more eggs, but the typical number in a nest is twenty to thirty.

Nests are dug in spring and early summer in open fields, gravel banks, railroad beds, earthen dikes, pond and lake margins, beaches, dunes, or even muskrat burrows.

At hatching, snapping turtles have a shell length of about one inch and their tail is often just as long.

## How to Find Snapping Turtles

**Habitat:** Marshes, large lakes, reservoirs, rivers
**Months of Activity:** Year-round (South); March to November (North)

*Range of the snapping turtle*

For the most part, snapping turtles are aquatic and are active at night, dawn, and dusk. Search for them with flashlights or lanterns from the edges of ponds and lakes or from a boat. However, some of their activities occur during the day and are easily observed.

There are few ponds, lakes, reservoirs, swamps, streams, or rivers in the eastern three-fourths of the country where snapping turtles do not live. In coastal areas they are known to inhabit salt marshes and even swim in oceans and bays. They are usually the most common and widespread of all turtles found in most states, and they have been introduced into many areas outside their natural range. This turtle is especially fond of shallow, marshy swamps where there is a soft mud bottom and lots of submerged and emergent plants.

During early morning hours, look for adults in lakes and ponds as they often rise to the surface of the water and extend their snouts and heads. On occasion they will climb out to sit on logs and tree trunks. During the breeding season (from spring to fall depending on latitude), territorial encounters and courtship activity will cause commotion on the water surface. A handy pair of binoculars will usually reveal the adult turtles.

Female snapping turtles are often encountered in early summer as they travel overland in search of suitable nesting sites. This is an unparalleled opportunity to watch some fascinating behaviors and interactions. If you stay a few yards behind a turtle, she is not likely to be disturbed at all by your presence.

## What You Can Observe

The classic vision of a snapping turtle is that of an ugly beast heaved up on its elephantlike legs, a loud hiss emerging from somewhere within, lunging forward with mouth agape and giving a hard, tenacious bite to anything placed in front of its mean snout. While snapping turtles can, and do, have an impressive appearance of ferocity, an understanding of their behavior leads to a much more balanced image.

About the only time snapping turtles leave the water is when they are moving to another pond or when a female is searching for a nest site. This is when they are most vulnerable to predation and, naturally, most eager to defend themselves.

Snapping turtles are designed perfectly for life on the bottom of shallow ponds. Their large carapace provides ample protection from danger coming from above, and since there is nothing that can attack them from under the mud, their tiny plastron is not a liability there. On land, however, snapping turtles are at a decided disadvantage. They are slow, somewhat awkward, and unable to pull their head and limbs inside their shell like most other turtles.

Their defense behaviors have evolved just like those of mammals and birds — if they are confronted and unable to escape, they bite. On land, they turn to face potential threats, often spinning around to maintain a head-on view. This is clearly defensive behavior, not aggression. They don't go looking for people to bite. In water, snapping turtles are decidedly shy and quickly swim away from disturbances caused by people.

## SPRING ACTIVITY

Snapping turtles are hardy animals that are active every month of the year in southern and coastal parts of their range. In very northern regions they become active in late winter or early spring. During heavy rainy periods, snapping turtles may be found crossing roads, basking in ponds, and courting.

Later in the spring, around the middle part of June, female snapping turtles will leave their ponds and search for nesting areas. This is the time that most people encounter them.

## TERRITORIAL BEHAVIOR

Physical encounters between adults are only occasionally observed but are very impressive to watch. Battles between males are usually associated with the breeding season. These encounters may cause cuts and bruises but have rarely been recorded as ending with the death of either of the combatants.

Individuals face each other in shallow water and lunge forward in a slow-motion, sumo-wrestlerlike encounter. They may hold tight to each other and even press their bottom shells together. As they scratch, kick, and sometimes bite at each other, the two, locked together in each other's grip, may roll over and over in the water. These interactions may go on for an hour or more. More detailed notes on observations are needed to understand fully the significance of these behaviors.

Courtship between males and females has been observed rarely in snapping turtles — a surprising fact in view of their abundance. A few field biologists have noted that the male swims above the female and grasps her shell with the claws of all four feet. They will remain in this position for many minutes, perhaps hours, as he maneuvers the base of his tail around and near hers. When actually copulating, the male may bite the female's head and neck, and she will retract her head and limbs. The female typically remains relatively passive.

## NEST-BUILDING AND EGG-LAYING

When ready to deposit her eggs, a female leaves her pond and heads overland. If you get the chance, follow her a short distance away and watch what she does. It may become apparent when she decides on a nest site; she may nose the ground and make a few scrapes with her hind feet. It is just as likely, however, that after a few attempts at digging she will stop and travel, sometimes for a long time, before attempting it again. When she finally settles on a spot where she will nest, you may note that she digs several nests before finally depositing her eggs. These "false" nests are dug by many species of turtles and may possibly function to confound potential egg predators in their search for the actual nest.

When ready to lay, the female positions the base of her tail above the nest cavity. One at a time the perfectly round eggs drop in and sometimes bounce a bit when they hit. When finished, the female will scoop sand back into the nest cavity and will sometimes tamp it down with her plastron.

## NEST PREDATORS

Once the nest is finished the female usually heads directly back to her pond. There is plenty to watch for at the nest site, however. A high percentage of nests (up to 100 percent in some years) are destroyed by predators, and though this may be difficult to observe, the results are easily seen. Most predation occurs within twenty-four hours of nest construction, though some nests are destroyed weeks later.

If you walk along a known nesting area for snapping turtles — railroad tracks, sand and gravel banks, or on the shoreline of ponds and lakes — you will easily see the remains of egg shells dug out by predators. Skunks are the main mammals responsible for this, but foxes, raccoons, and mink are known to dig up the eggs as well. Usually the entire complement of eggs is destroyed, but sometimes a few are left behind. Of course, the large number of eggs that females deposit during their lifetime are generally adequate to compensate for the numerous nest and hatchling predators, accidents, diseases, changes in habitat, or other things that befall the species.

## TEMPERATURE AND SEX DETERMINATION

The temperature at which snapping-turtle eggs are incubated determines what sex the turtles will be. Some remarkable details have emerged from field and laboratory studies of this phenomenon. For example, several researchers discovered that if all the eggs are kept at 58° F (at least for the early period of incubation), all the young will be females. Kept at 73° F, all the young become

*Newly hatched snapping turtle with egg tooth at tip of snout*

males. But if the temperature is raised to 77° F, once again all of the young become females.

More detailed studies have revealed that these temperatures need to be experienced by the growing embryos only during relatively short developmental stages. Changing the temperature earlier or later does not affect their sex. In natural nest sites, the eggs and embryos are subjected to widely fluctuating temperatures. The length of time the eggs take to reach certain temperatures is an added factor in determining the sex of the young. Furthermore, the temperature of the eggs near the surface of the ground is different from that of those deeper in the nest. This will produce nests that have varying ratios of males and females.

### BEHAVIOR OF THE YOUNG

Hatchlings break free from their eggs in August and September. In some places they will emerge from the nest within a few hours or days. In others, the group will remain in the nest all winter. Snapping-turtle hatchlings must migrate to an aquatic habitat that may be anywhere from a few feet to a quarter of a mile distant. Most of the young in a nest emerge within a few hours of each other, or certainly within a day. How they are able to navigate is unknown at present.

Once they do reach water, they tend to stay in very shallow areas. In fact, hatchlings are such poor swimmers that they have been known to drown in water half a foot deep when they were unable to find aquatic vegetation to hang onto. Most young snapping turtles are found in small brooks that adjoin lakes, marshes, and ponds where most of the adult population exists.

At about five or six years of age, most individuals become sexually mature and seek out mates. Others may require another year or two before reaching maturity.

### BASKING

While you will see snapping turtles perched on logs less frequently than other species, they do bask. Sometimes they will climb onto a fallen tree trunk or limb to sit, fully exposed, in the

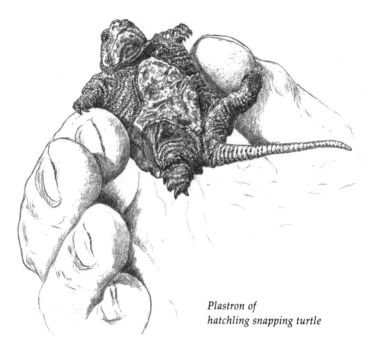

*Plastron of
hatchling snapping turtle*

sun. This has been called aerial or atmospheric basking. Almost as common, however, is aquatic basking, when snapping turtles lie still in water and expose most of their carapace above the surface. If you search the surface of the pond you will see the top part of the shell and the snout just out of the water. Lookout towers or high embankments make this type of observation much easier.

Basking increases the turtle's body temperature. This is important in digesting food and maintaining a temperature needed for movement.

### OTHER FACTS ABOUT SNAPPING TURTLES

Snapping turtles are hunted as food for the restaurant trade in many parts of the country, though in only a few states is this regulated. Not enough long-term studies have been done on snapping turtles to assess the effects of hunting, and some researchers are concerned about unregulated harvesting. One study in New York State also discovered that snapping turtles were able to survive with incredibly high doses of toxins in their body fat. When cooked, the soup meat still had elevated toxin levels. This may influence future plans for managing snapping-turtle populations.

OVERWINTERING

In the northern and mountainous parts of their range, adults and young tend to bury themselves in the mud of ponds and lakes to overwinter. They have been seen crawling along the bottom even in the coldest part of the year, however. It is likely that snapping turtles have a tolerance for low water temperatures and remain inactive for relatively short periods of time.

## Quick Reference Chart

**Length of Breeding Season:** March through June; occasionally into November

**Breeding Habitat:** Underwater in lakes, marshes, and reservoirs

**Nest Location:** Banks of marshes, gravel pits, sandy beaches, roadsides, railroad beds

**Eggs Deposited:** April to June

**Eggs Hatch:** In 3–4 months

**Age at Sexual Maturity:** About 5–7 years

**Lifespan of Adults:** At least 47 years; probably longer

*Adult stinkpot foraging for food*

# STINKPOT / *Sternotherus odoratus*

I WAS SITTING on the gravel edge of a woodland lake on a warm summer morning. As a small breeze rippled the surface of the clear water and waves lapped along the shore, I became transfixed by the activity of some of the small underwater inhabitants.

Several stands of underwater plants were separated by open areas a square yard wide, where schools of small fish darted about. Sometimes a fish or a red-spotted newt would approach and snap at one of the aquatic snails that grazed among the plant stems. The snail would compress its body and instantly pull its head and eye stalks inside its shell. A dragonfly larva, huddled close to the bottom near the plants, barely moved at all.

My focus on the tiny creatures allowed me to see an unbelievably small turtle whose shell was not much bigger than some of the gravel particles on the bottom. In fact, I had to stare for several seconds to believe that I was actually seeing a real turtle. It sat there, tiny black carapace barely containing its pointed snout and eyes. It was a very young stinkpot turtle, resting. I sat back and waited for something to happen. I sat for an hour and a half and the turtle didn't move.

Stinkpots only recently acquired their unlovely name. When I was growing up they were called musk turtles, and many people, including me, still prefer to call them by that name.

# How to Recognize Stinkpots

The most distinctive feature of stinkpots is a pair of yellow lines on each side of the head that run from the tip of the nose, back along the face, around the eye, and onto the neck. These are small turtles, their carapace reaching only three and a half to five and a half inches in length. The plastron is fairly small — too small, in fact, for the turtle to be able to withdraw all of its limbs inside. The forward part of the plastron of the adult is slightly movable, allowing the turtle some additional freedom of movement.

Stinkpots have a very high-domed top shell that is dark brown or blackish, sometimes showing a hint of tan or yellowish markings on each plate. Usually, however, individual turtles sport a fairly extensive shell coating of algae, making them even harder to find among underwater plants.

Mud turtles, in the genus *Kinosternon*, look similar to stinkpots in size and general shape, but both ends of their plastron are hinged and they do not have the yellow facial stripes.

The stinkpot is true to its name. Young ones especially emit a fairly strong, and some people think foul, odor when handled. Two glands adjacent to the bridge between the carapace and plastron that exude a yellowish liquid are responsible for producing the scent. The function of this odor is not known for sure, but it is suspected to be a predator deterrent or perhaps somehow involved with courtship.

The stinkpot is a member of the mud- and musk-turtle family, the Kinosternidae.

## DISTINGUISHING THE SEXES

Males and females are easily distinguished only if you get a close look at them or pick them up. Males have much thicker and longer tails that end in a sharp naillike point, and their cloacal opening extends beyond the margins of the carapace. Also, males have a deep notch at the rear end of their plastron.

In contrast, females have much shorter, slimmer tails that lack the hardened point. They also lack the notch on the plastron and have much smaller heads than the males.

EGGS AND NESTS

Female stinkpots show wide variations in their nesting behaviors. While some dig nests up to four inches deep, others seem simply to drop their eggs on the surface of the ground or barely cover those they deposit in a small hollow. Eggs are often deposited in rotting logs, muskrat lodges, or simply in leaf litter.

The clutch ranges from one to nine eggs in size, though four or five is the average number deposited by a female in northern areas and two or three for females in the South.

The eggs are smooth, almost glossy white, and elliptical, about an inch and a quarter long by three-quarters of an inch wide.

## How to Find Stinkpots

**Habitat:** Large ponds, lakes, reservoirs, slow rivers
**Months of Activity:** Year-round in the South; nearly so in the North

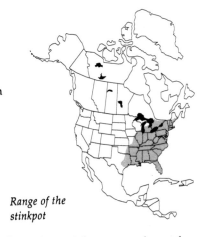

*Range of the
stinkpot*

The best time to look for stinkpots is at night, not too long after sunset, as they feed and move around the edges of ponds, lakes, and reservoirs. Obviously, the easiest ones to see are those closest to shore, and though they show some avoidance of a flashlight, they can be followed without too much disturbance. Calm nights, offering a still water surface, make looking into the water much easier. Various field researchers have discovered different activity patterns for this turtle. Overwhelmingly, however, stinkpots are nocturnal creatures that tend to stay within a relatively small area for years.

Because of their somber colors, coating of algae, and high-domed shells, stinkpots at rest are easy to confuse with rocks. Your best means of finding this species is to sit or stand quietly at the edge of the water and periodically shine a strong light into the water.

To find newly hatched young, you must be especially observant and fairly lucky. They tend to remain in shallow water where the bottom is composed of large pebbles and a fair amount of underwater vegetation. They may be found both day and night.

## What You Can Observe

### SPRING ACTIVITY

This is the main period for courtship behavior and mating in stinkpots, but little is known about their other activities and behaviors. For example, it is unclear exactly when adults and juvenile stinkpots become active again as water temperatures increase and what, if any, delay occurs before they resume feeding and growing.

### TERRITORIAL BEHAVIOR

Stinkpots are not known to display any sort of territorial behavior, though this has not been studied extensively. Several researchers have calculated the home range of stinkpots with somewhat varying results. Their information suggests that these turtles normally live within an area less than five acres in size, depending on the size, shape, and depth of their pond.

### COURTSHIP AND MATING

There have been several interesting observations of this generally springtime (and occasionally autumn) behavior in stinkpots. Apparently, in the spring males are fairly active in their pursuit of females. They have been seen to approach other turtles from behind and sniff their tails, a behavior that has been interpreted as an effort to determine the sex of the other turtle.

Males will pursue females and bite at their shell margins or even their head and neck. A receptive female will soon stop swimming and allow the male to overtake her and crawl onto her carapace. As they mate, the male holds onto her shell with all four feet and rests his head on hers. Males will seek out other females during the spring mating season and, at least on one occasion, a female was found to mate with more than one male.

### NEST-BUILDING AND EGG-LAYING

Some time from three weeks to two months after mating, a female stinkpot leaves the water in the late afternoon to search out suitable nesting sites. In the North, June is the month when females most commonly lay eggs, while in the South, May is more typical.

At least in a couple of southern locations, female stinkpots are known to nest and lay more than a single clutch of eggs in a season. There is no evidence that second, or suspected third, clutches contain fewer or smaller eggs than the first ones.

As in the case of snapping turtles, nest temperatures determine the sex of hatchling turtles. Unlike most turtles, however, where a single temperature threshold determines sex, female stinkpots tend to develop at two different temperatures — between 74° and 76° F. and between 78° and 82° F. Males develop when the eggs incubate at 77° F.

### BEHAVIOR OF THE YOUNG

Most stinkpots hatch within two to three months after the female deposits her eggs. Normally, the young emerge from the nest and migrate to a body of water late in summer or early autumn. Sometimes stinkpot hatchlings remain in the nest chamber all winter and emerge the following spring.

As mentioned, the young stinkpots are difficult to see, and consequently little is known of their early life. In captivity, they show a strong preference for eating aquatic insects and worms.

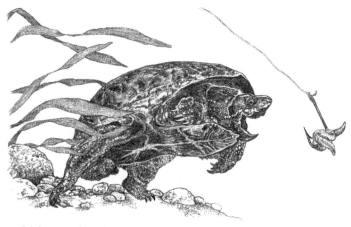

*Stinkpot reaching for an earthworm*

FEEDING

Adult and juvenile stinkpots that forage after sunset are relatively easy to follow as they walk along the bottom with their heads and necks fully extended. Often, they will investigate the spaces between large rocks and boulders and push their noses along the bottom. This has been described as a "peer-and-probe" feeding method. Stinkpots do not move particularly slowly when foraging, so you must keep your eye on them.

For the most part, stinkpots eat equal amounts of plant and animal food. Aquatic vegetation, insects, and small freshwater snails and clams are their main food items. Some populations only rarely catch and eat live prey, though others are known to stalk and hunt crayfish, leeches, tadpoles, and adult frogs. Young stinkpots appear to be more carnivorous than adults, relying on insects and carrion for their main food supply.

Thus, if you are lucky enough to be stationed near a decaying fish or other animal, it may be exceptionally easy to watch the turtles feed. Depending on the size and condition of the prey, stinkpots might have to hold on with their front feet and tear off pieces of the carcass before swallowing. It is impressive to see just how big the pieces of food are that this small turtle is able to swallow, its throat bulging with each gulp.

There are three times when you can expect to find this species out of the water. When females are looking for nest sites they clearly must be on land. This is usually in late spring in the southern part of their range and in early summer in the North. Occasional, random overland movements by stinkpots have also been observed and recorded by field biologists. These can occur anytime during the warmer months of the year and may indicate movement between nearby ponds.

Tree-basking also brings stinkpots out of water. When they do bask fully exposed (which is rare), stinkpots have been reported to climb onto the branches of fallen trees sometimes as much as six feet above the surface of the water. Though this behavior is often cited, few observations of it have been recorded.

PREDATORS AND PROBLEMS

One might expect that stinkpots, being small turtles, would have more predators than large species. This may be true, but too few in-depth field observations have been made to confirm it. The eggs of stinkpots are certainly eaten by raccoons, skunks, foxes, possibly other mammals (such as rats), probably insects (such as ants), and birds. Hatchling and juvenile stinkpots fall prey to many mammals, herons, snakes, fish, and frogs.

Adults are known to be injured by fish hooks when they are attracted to bait. Automobiles also kill some as they move from pond to pond, or when females leave to lay eggs.

ALGAE GROWTH ON SHELL

In most populations of stinkpots, a majority of the adults have varying amounts of algae growing on their top shells. At least nine different species of alga have been identified on stinkpot shells from several locations in its range. It is generally believed that the algae provide a superb camouflage for the turtles, but little is known about this fascinating interaction between plant and animal.

OVERWINTERING

Throughout their range, stinkpots tend to become inactive during the coldest months of the year. In northern parts of their range, they are rarely found between late October and early April. In the South, they become inactive only during the coldest parts of January and February.

There is little information on exact overwintering sites and behavior of stinkpots. They are known to use active and inactive muskrat lodges as winter dens. It is also presumed that they lodge themselves into debris at the bottom of ponds and lakes, though there is no evidence that they bury themselves much, if at all. In general, this aspect of stinkpot life is little studied and poorly understood.

## Quick Reference Chart

**Length of Breeding Season:** February to May (South); March to June (North)

**Breeding Habitat:** Ponds, lakes, slow-moving rivers

**Nest Location:** Banks of lakes, beaches, gravel pits, woodlands, roadside edges, rotting logs and stumps, leaf litter

**Eggs Deposited:** Typically 2–5 (up to 9) elliptical eggs in March through July (South) or May through June (North)

**Eggs Hatch:** Usually within 60–90 days; young may overwinter in the nest

**Age at Sexual Maturity:** 2–3 years for males; 3–4 years for females

**Lifespan of Adults:** At least 28 years; possibly up to 50

*Male (top) and two female spotted turtles*

# SPOTTED TURTLE / *Clemmys guttata*

Toward the end of March, when the snow has melted from all but the north-facing slopes and the brooks and streams are running full, I head out to a small pasture that lies at the bottom of a sloping hillside. There haven't been any cattle grazing here for some years, and the field is growing up into alders, birches, and aspen. Much of the meadow, especially near the dirt road where some friends and I sit in our automobile, is taken up by a shallow pond, thick with sedges, semiaquatic grasses, and a few skunk cabbages. This is the domain of our local population of spotted turtles, and we have come to expect them very early each spring. We try to follow their activities throughout the year, but as their meadow slowly dries with the onset of summer, we see fewer and fewer turtles. Only now, with a few redwings singing in the nearby cattails and the skunk cabbage fully open, can we have any assurance of finding these beautiful, elusive turtles.

Over the years we have seen and identified about twenty-five individuals, each recognizable by the color pattern and markings on its shell. Never, however, have we found anything but adults; no hatchlings or young animals have appeared. Someday we will, I'm sure, but for now we are content to watch the adults swim with their heads exposed above the surface. On sunny days early in April, we will watch first one, then another, and finally ten or twelve individuals crawl out of the water and sun themselves on a log or tussock sedge. Their shells glisten brilliantly when they first emerge, then dry to a chalky gray-black. When the spotted turtles bask in the sun, we can be pretty much assured that winter is over and that the trend will be warm and sunny.

## How to Recognize Spotted Turtles

### ADULTS

Adults are small, as turtles go, growing to a maximum shell length of only five inches. Spotted turtles are easily recognized by the distinct yellow polka dots on their dark carapace, head, neck, and legs. Hatchlings usually have a single yellow spot on each plate of their smooth carapace. Occasionally spotted turtles are found that have no spots at all. Instead they have a series of yellow or orange markings on the face.

The Blanding's turtle (*Emydoidea blandingi*) of north-central and northeastern regions has, in contrast, small yellow flecks on its shell, is much larger (up to ten inches), and has a bright yellow throat and neck. Newly hatched box turtles have a single yellow spot on each plate on the top shell, but they have a granular shell texture and few markings on their face.

Spotted turtles are in the genus *Clemmys,* the pond turtles. There are only four species in this group, three found in the East and one found along the West Coast. All are members of the large family Emydidae.

### DISTINGUISHING THE SEXES

Females usually have a light-colored lower jaw and orange-red eyes. Males have a black or dark-colored lower jaw and brown eyes. These characteristics are easily seen at a distance through binoculars and are suspected to be important in enabling spotted turtles to recognize the sexes.

### EGGS AND NESTS

Females usually dig nests in sandy or gravel areas in the open.

Nests average about two inches deep and two inches wide at the bottom. They are, however, filled in after laying, and the surface is often smoothed out.

The eggs are smooth, white, and elliptical — about an inch and a half long and three-quarters of an inch wide. Often there is a noticeable dent in these very flexible eggs immediately after being deposited. This apparently disappears during the period of incubation.

## How to Find Spotted Turtles

**Habitat:** Wet meadows, small ponds and marshes, slow sections of small rivers
**Months of Activity:** March through October

*Range of the
spotted turtle*

The best and most interesting time to watch this species is early in the spring, from March to May, before thick growths of wetland plants completely hide the animals from view and before they dig underground and spend the summer completely hidden.

Don't be misled by the general, but not always accurate, statement that all reptiles love heat and aren't active until outdoor temperatures increase dramatically. Spotted turtles are cold-loving animals that maintain appropriate body temperatures by basking or swimming. There is often ice on their small ponds when they are most active and visible.

Many people first see isolated individuals, especially females migrating to nesting sites. These individuals give a clue to a nearby pond or wet meadow, since turtles are not known to migrate great distances. You might have to wait until autumn rains or spring snowmelt fill the basin in the meadow or woodland edge, but it will be worth the wait. Once you have found a population, you can count on it to exist there for as long as the land is unchanged. Because of the small size of these animals, your spotted-turtle observations will be greatly enhanced by the use of binoculars or a spotting telescope. Their use will also allow you to keep your distance from the turtles, who sometimes are very nervous and swim to the bottom of the pond to hide when disturbed. Search a known or likely pond with binoculars, carefully looking for their tiny heads above the surface or for the edges of a shell that is tucked into vegetation on the banks.

Sketching the spot and head patterns of any animals you see will help you to keep track of individuals for many years.

## What You Can Observe

### SPRING ACTIVITY

In the early spring, both males and females spend a great deal of time basking. This can be accomplished singly or in groups and is done either on partially submerged logs, rocks, or tussocks of sedges, or on the shore line. You may notice two distinct reactions to humans in these basking turtles. Some, though their eyes are open and they seem awake and alert, will allow you to walk directly up to them without any hint of being excited. These may be photographed or looked at very closely. Others, perhaps most, won't let you get within a hundred yards before leaping off their basking sites and burrowing down into the plant debris and mud of the pond bottom.

If you scare them off their perches, find a spot where you can get a good look at where they were and sit down and wait. Within a few minutes you are likely to see several heads above the water's surface peering about in all directions. If you remain still enough, many of the turtles will haul out again and bask.

### TERRITORIAL BEHAVIOR

Spotted turtles are not suspected of being territorial. Indeed, several individuals will often bask together on the same log. There are occasional aggressive interactions between adults, but too few observations have been recorded to establish the exact relationships between turtles exhibiting this behavior.

Home-range size has been calculated for several populations of spotted turtles, with varying results. So far individual spotted turtles have been known to have home ranges of from one and a half to nineteen acres. The discrepancies are attributed to genetic variation among different populations, varying methods used to calculate home range, and varying amounts of time spent doing the research.

## COURTSHIP AND MATING

Males have been observed pursuing females in spring from March to May, even beneath thin ice that forms during cold snaps at this time of the year. An active, almost frantic, pursuit by the male is a noticeable part of the courtship of spotted turtles and may go on for nearly an hour. Several males may pursue a single female at the same time, biting each other in the process. Observers have seen the males reach out and bite the shell and hind legs of the female as she swims away. Occasionally the female may turn and face the one or more males following her.

Eventually, if she is ready, she will let a male catch up to her and grasp her upper shell with his four feet. He will maneuver to position his tail close to hers and they will mate. A mating male has been found to slide off the back of the female, but the pair continued to mate while their shells were perpendicular. It is unknown how many females a male will court successfully or if the female will mate with more than one male.

## NEST-BUILDING AND EGG-LAYING

Throughout their range, female spotted turtles mainly choose June as the month to leave their drying pools and nest. Most wandering spotted turtles seen at this time are accordingly females. Unfortunately, many cross highways and are killed before getting to the other side.

Females most often choose open sites in meadows, fields, or

along roadsides and typically begin digging their nests early in the evening. It is not known if spotted turtles make several attempts at nest-building or simply begin and construct a single nest.

If you follow a spotted turtle in June you may be lucky enough to see the nest-digging process. As is true of all turtles, the hind legs and feet are involved — usually alternately. This species digs a two- to two-and-a-half-inch-deep hole. It may take an hour or more to dig the nest. Once finished, the female takes a short rest before depositing her eggs.

Spotted turtles lay only a few eggs — an average of three or four. A few field reports indicate that the female actually positions each egg in the nest with her hind feet rather than letting the eggs just fall anywhere. When finished laying, the female will scoop the excavated earth back onto the eggs. But she doesn't stop there. Along with a few other species, spotted turtles are known to smooth over the covered nest by dragging their plastron over the site.

Many typical turtle-nest predators are nevertheless successful at finding the nests and eggs of this species. In addition, prolonged droughts during late summer and early autumn have been implicated in killing the developing turtles.

## BEHAVIOR OF THE YOUNG

In general, spotted turtles hatch in about eleven weeks. They emerge and head to the edges of grassy, wet meadow areas and bogs where they will find food and shelter. There is some evidence to suggest that the young may overwinter in the nest in some parts of their range but the extent of this is unknown.

Young spotted turtles are especially difficult to locate. They are tiny (about an inch long) and almost perfectly round. If they bask at all, they are well hidden by leaves.

Hatchlings are particularly carnivorous, hunting small land and water insects, worms, and snails.

## BASKING

Like other turtles that bask, spotteds alternate sitting in the sun

*Bottom view of three spotted turtles showing individual patterns.*
*Note short tail on female, left, and longer tail on male, middle*

with feeding. Both males and females bask about the same amount, but some observers report that females may spend more time basking in May. This has been noted in other turtle species of the same family and suggests that this behavior is associated with egg development.

No available information suggests any kind of dominance behavior among basking spotted turtles. It is not known if there are any associations between individuals or between the sexes, or any other social aspects of basking. Take some notes while you watch.

Generally, spotted turtles will bask more on cold, sunny days than on warm, cloudy ones, when they feed more often. Throughout the early spring spotted turtles alternate basking with hunting for snails, worms, slugs, and spiders. They disappear underwater late in the afternoon and spend the night at the bottom of the pond.

### SUMMER DORMANCY AND OVERWINTERING

People who have observed spotted turtles over long periods of time are impressed with the relatively few sightings of these animals late in the summer. Spotted turtles avoid extreme temperatures not only in winter but also in summer by burrowing into underwater vegetation or muskrat burrows. They may alternately enter cool streams and become inactive for days or even weeks. Individuals may dig small enclosures, called forms, where they remain for days at a time, inactive. On cool days in late summer or early autumn, spotted turtles may again appear at basking sites or swimming about their pond or marsh.

Some individuals, at least in some years, probably do not resume much activity between their summer dormancy and the time cold weather sets in. Some of these spotted turtles may remain inactive (not feeding, swimming, or generally moving about) from July to the following March or April. In these cases, it is difficult to tell when the animal's motivation changes from summer avoidance of heat to winter retreat from cold.

## Quick Reference Chart

**Length of Breeding Season:** March to May
**Breeding Habitat:** Shallow marshes, flooded fields, temporary ponds
**Nest Location:** Sandy, open areas, roadsides, meadows, fields
**Eggs Deposited:** 3–4 elliptical eggs, normally in June
**Eggs Hatch:** 2½–3 months
**Age at Sexual Maturity:** About 8–10 years
**Lifespan of Adults:** At least 26 years, probably up to 50

*Adult wood turtle*

# WOOD TURTLE / *Clemmys insculpta*

As a kid I was fortunate to have a wooded area nearby that had a small stream running through it. There were plenty of things to find in it, but the day I discovered my first wood turtle was especially memorable. As usual, I was wandering along the banks of the brook, looking for nothing in particular. There were raccoon tracks on the sandy, wet banks and water striders in the quiet pools of the stream. Little fish darted out from undercuts in the banks and disappeared into the current. I have always been drawn to the small animals that live in, on, and around the water, and this was the scale to which I had attuned myself.

It follows, then, that I was startled and jumped back when my eyes focused on a creature whose sheer bulk dwarfed everything else in the brook. An adult wood turtle perhaps nine inches long was swimming beneath a large boulder at one bend. It moved with powerful strokes of its four feet, with neck stretched far out in front of the shell. When the sunlight illuminated the turtle I could see it had orange-colored skin — a wonderful color for a streamside animal, I thought.

Wood turtles have crossed my path many times since then, though much less frequently than other species. One November not too long ago, a friend who had also been fascinated by wood turtles when he was young invited me to look for some where he used to find them. We knew they wouldn't be active but thought it might be fun to locate them while they were overwintering. There was no snow on the ground, but the air temperature was chilly. We followed the meanders of a tiny brook that wound its way through a young forest. The sunlight during the middle of the day allowed us to see clearly to the bottom of the brook. No doubt that is what helped us discover not one but two wood turtles.

They were resting on the gravel bottom of the brook, one on top of the other. We looked closely and discovered they were male and female. After recording some basic information, we continued along the brook and were not successful in finding any others. In fact, I haven't been that fortunate in finding wintering wood turtles since.

## How to Recognize Wood Turtles

### ADULTS

The burnt orange skin of the wood turtle is immediately noticeable, but its most beautiful and distinguishing feature is the texture of its top shell. True to the scientific name, the brown carapace appears sculpted, with each scute of the shell a separate, raised pyramid of concentric growth rings. This species, closely related to the spotted turtle, is a fairly large animal whose carapace length can reach nine inches.

The diamondback terrapin (*Malaclemmys terrapin*) of coastal salt marshes also has a sculpted carapace, but its habitat and its gray skin and shell color readily distinguish it from the wood turtle.

Wood turtles are members of the pond-turtle family, the Emydidae.

### DISTINGUISHING THE SEXES

Male wood turtles have a noticeably longer tail than do females. In large males, the concave bottom shell (plastron) is especially obvious; it is also shorter than the females'. Males have longer and more curved claws.

Female wood turtles have a short tail and their plastron is flat or even slightly convex. The rear margin of their plastron nearly reaches to the end of the carapace. They also have much smaller scales on the front part of their front legs — noticeable especially when the animal has withdrawn into its shell.

### EGGS AND NESTS

Typically, wood-turtle nests are found in sandy or soft loam sand areas, including gravel banks, roadsides, fields and meadows. They may be up to six inches deep, but are filled in and smoothed out on top by the female.

The elongated, white, and smooth-textured eggs are about an inch and a half long and an inch in diameter, though there is quite a bit of variation in egg sizes of different females from different parts of their range. Females may lay up to eighteen eggs, though six to eight eggs in a nest is typical. Larger females probably lay more eggs than smaller females.

### YOUNG

Newly hatched wood turtles are gray or brown, lacking the orange skin of the adults. The tail of the young is very long — usually equal to the length of their carapace.

## How to Find Wood Turtles

**Habitat:** Streams and small rivers and associated banks
**Months of Activity:** April to October

*Range of the wood turtle*

You will have your best chance of observing this turtle upon careful search of its preferred areas — slow-moving streams and rivers. They can often be discovered resting on banks or sitting underwater. Those disturbed near water are likely to dive into the stream quickly, so approach carefully. A good pair of binoculars will help to sight turtles before you get too close.

Wood turtles are for the most part active during the daylight hours, but females sometimes continue to nest after sunset. Individuals are usually found by midmorning resting or basking on the banks or on logs or rocks. By midday they are often foraging away from the water, feeding on a variety of plants and animals. Wood turtles are unusual members of their family in being able successfully to exploit both aquatic and terrestrial food sources.

## What You Can Observe

### SPRING ACTIVITY

In southern or coastal parts of their range, wood turtles become active in late March, but elsewhere it is usually mid- to late April and even May before they are regularly encountered. Males and females mate, normally in water, in the spring shortly after becoming active. They are also known to mate late in the autumn. The female migrates in late spring to locate a suitable nesting site.

### TERRITORIAL BEHAVIOR

Wood turtles remain relatively close to their streams and rivers, rarely getting more than a few hundred yards away from the banks. They have, therefore, relatively linear home ranges that tend to run up to a mile in length.

Males have been seen in aggressive encounters, chasing, biting, and butting, both during the mating season and at other times. Typically, one or both males make an "open mouth" gesture, snapping open and closing the mouth near the other's head. Sometimes, but not often, this accelerates into actual biting. Prolonged interactions are occasionally accompanied by audible hissing from one or both animals.

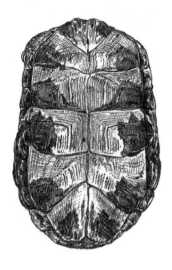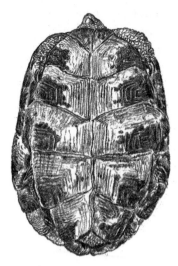

*Wood turtle, bottom view; male with concave plastron,
left; female with convex plastron, right*

COURTSHIP AND MATING

Very few observations of interactions between courting wood
turtles have been made under natural conditions, but what little is
known is intriguing. Apparently males and females approach each
other with their necks extended. Before they actually touch noses,
they droop their heads and swing them from side to side. They can
keep this up for nearly two hours. Courting adults have been
described as giving very audible whistles (again, rarely heard).
While these behaviors occur on land, all observations of actual
mating indicate that this takes place in water.

A male eventually will mount the female and hold her shell
with the strong claws of his feet. If sufficiently interested, the
female will extend her tail so they can mate. Mating may last for
fifteen minutes or more. It is supposed that males will continue to
search for a mate among other females and females may also mate
with other males.

Most accounts of nesting female wood turtles indicate that they wander in search of a nest site in late May or mid-June. As with some other species, female wood turtles often dig their nests during or just after a slight rainstorm. If you are lucky enough to find one beginning to nest, prepare for a long period of observation. From beginning to end, the process may take three or four hours.

Nest-digging can begin relatively early in the morning or late in the afternoon. I was able to watch one large female as she dug several "false" nests in a gravelly area that was covered with grasses and other small plants. She continued digging until after dark and then stopped her work and walked back to a nearby stream. Digging false nests may be a more common behavior than recorded. The function of this may be to confuse nest predators that are searching for buried eggs.

Females eventually dig their actual nest, using their hind feet only, and deposit their eggs inside. They carefully fill in the chamber and may tamp down the earth over the eggs before leaving.

Wood-turtle embryos show a surprising lack of response to incubation temperature. While most of their close relatives show a strong correlation between nest temperature and the sex of the young, wood turtles do not. If this proves to be true throughout their range, people interested in reptiles' evolutionary reproductive strategies will have found a fascinating animal to study.

### BEHAVIOR OF THE YOUNG

Little is known of the behaviors or activities of young wood turtles. After hatching, they make their way somehow to the shallows of streams and brooks. They probably feed mostly on invertebrates for the first two or three years of their life, then add more plant matter as they get older.

### BASKING

Basking in this species is well known and easily observed. Search for the turtles on the banks of streams and rivers or on logs or other suitable resting sites that emerge from the water. You might note that rarely will you find more than a single wood turtle at a time. They seem to lead rather solitary lives.

FEEDING

Wood turtles have a varied diet and feed both on land and in water. They consume about as much animal matter as plant and are especially fond of ripe fruits, berries, and mushrooms. Their prey includes such diverse groups of animals as fish, snails, slugs, insects, and tadpoles. Wood turtles have also been found feeding on the carcasses of dead animals. They are known to feed on the green leaves of various plants, particularly violets.

One of the most amazing observations of this species, first made in the 1930s, concerns a method of attracting earthworms. Wood turtles have been seen to stamp their front feet alternately in a regular fashion that has the effect of causing earthworms to surface from their underground burrows. The turtles are able to spot and catch them quickly and then normally move a few feet forward and begin the stamping behavior again. This feeding technique may be widespread but simply overlooked by impatient observers.

Consequently, if you find a wood turtle in midsummer, sit back and watch where it is going. You may find it delicately reaching up to pluck blackberries from a bush or stamping its feet to bring up earthworms.

OTHER FACTS ABOUT WOOD TURTLES

Many people over the years have remarked on the alertness and seeming intelligence of this species. In fact, researchers have run them through maze tests, and wood turtles have scored at least as high as white rats. Turtle biologist Archie Carr commented that this "had a rather uncomplimentary ring, though it was really pretty good for a turtle. And anyway," he added, "in a personality contest a wood turtle would win over a rat in a walk."

Captive wood turtles, kept in outdoor pens, have disappeared very quickly. They are good climbers and have been observed scaling chain-link fences without much trouble at all.

OVERWINTERING

Wood turtles usually overwinter in small streams or rivers. They may choose a muskrat burrow or lodge in the side of a streambank, or bury themselves beneath the mud and debris at the bottom, or simply rest on the gravel or mud streambed. Some observers have reported several wood turtles crowded together at the base of small dams or fallen logs in small streams.

## Quick Reference Chart

**Length of Breeding Season:** Two seasons: March to May and late September to November

**Breeding Habitat:** In streams and rivers and adjacent meadows and forests

**Nest Location:** Usually open areas in fields, meadows, roadsides, gravel banks

**Eggs Deposited:** Normally 7 or 8 (up to 18) elliptical, white eggs in May or June

**Eggs Hatch:** About 2½ months; young may overwinter in nest

**Age at Sexual Maturity:** Perhaps 14 years

**Lifespan of Adults:** Up to 60 years; probably more

*Female eastern box turtle in blackberries*

# EASTERN BOX TURTLE / *Terrapene carolina*

W<small>HILE WALKING</small> along the trail of a busy nature center I happened to spot a young red-tailed hawk sitting in an oak tree. The bird seemed awfully tame for a red-tail, and I inquired about it at the office. The bird had been injured some months earlier and had recently healed. It was released on the grounds so the staff could keep an eye on it and offer assistance if necessary. I went back outside and watched the bird, which seemed to be staring intently at the ground. Almost immediately it dove; in a few moments it was back up on the same branch, clutching something in its talons. I focused my binoculars and saw a small box turtle, tightly hidden inside its shell, of course, but strongly in the grasp of the bird. The hawk occasionally reached down to pick at the turtle with its beak, though I had difficulty seeing any detail. Whether the turtle proved too much of a puzzle for the young hawk or the bird was disturbed by other people moving nearby, it eventually dropped its prey and flew across the field. I ran over and picked up the box turtle, apparently unharmed by the experience.

Box turtles are well known throughout their range because they are widespread and, at least in a few places, common. They are also collected and sold as pets in many areas where they are not normally found. Many box turtles show up in areas outside their normal range when they are released or escape from captivity. Box turtles seem to embody the essence of turtles — slow moving and deliberate, passive, even displaying what amounts to a surprising bit of intelligence.

## How to Recognize Eastern Box Turtles

### ADULTS

The typically high-domed shape of the shell is one distinguishing characteristic of the box turtles found in North America. The main identifying feature of box turtles is the movable plastron that has a hinged seam. This allows the turtle not only to retreat inside its shell but to swing the bottom portions of the plastron tight against the carapace so that no soft parts are exposed. So tightly is the shell closed that a grass blade cannot be inserted between the shells in most free-ranging box turtles. Captive ones are often hopelessly overweight and unable to close their shells. The color pattern of the shell of eastern box turtles is beautiful and highly variable. Each plate of the carapace often has a radiating pattern of light yellow to orange lines or spots on a background color of mahogany or dark brown. Fully mature adults reach a maximum of eight inches in shell length.

Eastern box turtles are distinguished from western box turtles (*Terrapene ornata*) — with which they sometimes hybridize — by the presence in the eastern species of a low but obvious ridge along the midline of the carapace. Also, the plastron of the eastern box turtle lacks a pattern while the western one has radiating lines on the underside of its shell.

Box turtles are members of the Emydidae family of pond and freshwater turtles.

### DISTINGUISHING THE SEXES

Males can be distinguished from females by their concave plastron; that of females is flat or slightly convex. Males have much longer tails and the claws of their hind feet are short but noticeably curved. In addition, the vast majority (approaching 90 percent) of males have red irises, while the female's eye color is brown.

### EGGS AND NESTS

Female box turtles nest in hay fields, roadsides, cultivated gardens, lawns, beach dunes, and woodlands and around house foundations. Nests are three or four inches deep, but the earth over the site is usually tamped down and smooth.

Between three and eight (normally four or five) elliptically shaped eggs are deposited. Each of these is about an inch and a half long and just under an inch wide. They have a parchmentlike texture.

## How to Find Eastern Box Turtles

**Habitat:** Mainly terrestrial, in fields, meadows, forests, dunes; occasionally in ponds and marshes
**Months of Activity:** Year-round in southern and coastal areas; April to October in the North

*Range of the eastern box turtle*

The eastern box turtle is active during the daylight hours, though some have been known to move at night near house lights. During the day, the turtle appears to be much more active in the morning, especially after late-night rainstorms. They are found in a wide variety of places, including oak and hickory woodlands, grasslands, river-bottom land, and pastures. They are animals commonly of dry land but will soak in ponds and streams and even swim across them.

The color pattern of box turtles make them a challenge for you to find. There is still no substitute for looking and searching the ground in likely places, though you will probably find most of them by accident as they cross roads or come into your yard or garden. In fact, if the turtle is near your home, you might expect to be able to find and watch it for years.

## What You Can Observe

### SPRING ACTIVITY

Box turtles emerge from their underground burrows between late February (South) and late April (North). In extreme southern and coastal areas, eastern box turtles remain active throughout the year. If you discover an active individual, notice how alert it is, often stretching its neck and looking about for food or signs of danger. If you approach too close it is likely to withdraw and close its shell tightly. It will remain this way for many minutes before peering tentatively out to assess the situation. Retreat to a safe distance and remain still; the turtle will emerge and continue its activity.

As late afternoon approaches, box turtles typically construct a small, domelike space in leaf litter, grasses, ferns, or mosses where they spend the night. Called forms, these spaces are often used on more than one occasion over a period of weeks. They usually are simply a place where the turtle can wedge itself in for the night, but often the form is visible and identifiable for several days afterward.

### TERRITORIAL BEHAVIOR

Several field research studies have determined that eastern box turtles maintain relatively small home ranges and will live within that area for many years. These studies estimate home range sizes to be from eighty-two to three hundred yards in diameter, with females apparently having slightly larger ranges than males. Other studies indicate that their home ranges vary from two to about eleven acres. Where there are large populations of eastern box turtles, individuals show a high tolerance for others. Most of their home ranges overlap widely and often two or more turtles can be found sharing the same nighttime form. Box turtles displaced from their home areas have some ability to return from a quarter of a mile away.

It has recently been discovered that some individual box turtles may not remain in a given home range, but continue to travel through the areas occupied by other turtles. These "transients," as they are known, may be important mechanisms in maintaining a varied gene flow through populations, as these individuals are likely to mate (and have been observed mating) with more sedentary individuals.

There appears to be no social hierarchy or dominance displayed among free-ranging box turtles.

## COURTSHIP AND MATING

While box turtles allow others to cross their territories without paying too much attention most of the year, during the spring and summer breeding season males alter their behavior toward females. You may be lucky enough to witness the hour-long courtship that begins as a male approaches a female.

He will often circle her and nip at the edges of her shell. Occasionally he will climb on top of her shell or push and rotate her body. For the most part, the female remains relatively passive, or she may attempt to escape. If the female is sufficiently interested, however, she will open the rear end of her plastron slightly and the male will climb, from behind, on top of her shell and insert his hind-foot claws into the space between the carapace and plastron.

When ready to copulate the male pushes back and appears to stand upright on his hind feet. He may actually be resting the rim of his carapace on the ground, rather than using his feet for support. They will remain in this position for many minutes and often up to an hour or more. When finished, the two turtles may remain nearby for some time, or immediately leave the area in different directions. Males are known to search out and mate with other females. It is unclear if this is a common behavior for females.

## NEST-BUILDING AND EGG-LAYING

The female is able to produce fertilized eggs for up to four years after a single mating by means of a sperm storage system. Female box turtles ready to lay eggs seek out sandy areas in which to nest. You can easily watch them from a short distance away as they scratch the surface of the ground with their hind feet. Females often sniff the ground before they begin digging.

They will frequently make several false nests, digging the entire nest and refilling it before searching for another locale. All digging is done by the hind feet, each thrust scooping out a small amount of soil. Once the process of egg-laying begins, the females seem fairly oblivious to commotion around them. They deposit four to six eggs in a nest and often urinate on the sand as they repack it.

Most females begin to nest late in the afternoon, often following a light rainfall. Only rarely have they been observed nesting at night.

### EGG AND HATCHLING PREDATORS

The nests of box turtles are dug up and the eggs consumed by many animals. Skunks are the chief predator, but raccoons, foxes, and crows are known to do the same. Ants have been discovered invading the nest cavity and killing the embryos inside the eggs. In addition, snakes, frogs, hawks, herons, fish, otters, muskrat, and other vertebrates are known to feed on young box and other turtles.

### FEEDING

Box turtles eat a wide variety of plants and animals, both fresh and already dead. You may see them hunting beetles, slugs, or caterpillars. The turtles approach their prey by watching their movements and taking several steps to get within reach. The turtles stretch their necks deliberately (not rapidly) and reach down to grasp their food in their jaws. In season, they seem to seek out thick growths of blackberries, blueberries, and similar fruit, as well as mushrooms, including some that are toxic to humans. Observations of captive animals suggest that young box turtles show a strong preference for animal prey and gradually add more and more plants to their diet.

Box turtles often probe a selected food item with their snouts, apparently using their sense of smell. There is some speculation that this, combined with their ability to distinguish colors in about the same range as humans, enables them to reject unripe fruits and eat only ripe ones. Recently, field botanists have identified eastern box turtles as the only known agent for dispersing the seeds of the mayapple (*Podophyllum peltatum*). Squirrels and mice eat the seeds, rather than disperse them, while other mammals tend to avoid the plant because of its toxic properties. Box turtles, however, eat the ripe, fleshy fruits and eliminate the seeds, unchanged, some time later.

## AGE OF BOX TURTLES

Except for sea turtles and gopher tortoises, no other North American species of turtle is known to live as long as the eastern box turtle. Several people have made an effort to age individuals of this species accurately and have found that by carefully counting the annual growth rings on each of the plates of the shell a fair approximation of age can be made.

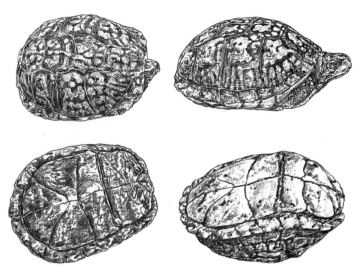

*Variation in box-turtle shell patterns*

Of course, these rings are difficult to read when there are more than twenty or thirty of them, so researchers have had to use other means of determining the age of centenarian box turtles. One method has been to verify marks etched into the shells by people. In the nineteenth century it was a common practice to carve dates, initials, and other markings onto the shells of turtles and release them. Several of these were found many years later and the turtle's minimum age estimated. At least one box turtle is known to have lived to 138 years, and several others made it to the century mark.

OVERWINTERING

As autumn approaches, box turtles become less active during the day, preferring to remain in their forms. The daytime temperature when this change in behavior occurs is between 60° F (in the South) and 69° F (in the North). When night temperatures during the autumn reach the mid-forties, box turtles move toward an overwintering location.

During the alternating warm and cold spells of late autumn, individual box turtles will emerge and settle into a new location. Some will do this half a dozen times or more, until all movement for the winter finally ceases. Wintering dens are often only two to eight inches beneath the surface of the ground. It is not surprising that a number of researchers report numerous box-turtle deaths at this time. Box turtles often use natural depressions in the ground and usually choose areas with a heavy covering of leaf litter to overwinter.

## Quick Reference Chart

**Length of Breeding Season:** Most of the spring, occasionally lasting into summer and autumn

**Breeding Habitat:** Forests, fields, meadows

**Nest Location:** Sandy areas in fields, meadows, lawns, gardens, agricultural fields, banks, dunes, roadsides

**Eggs Deposited:** Up to 8 eggs in May and June

**Eggs Hatch:** 2 – 3 months

**Age at Sexual Maturity:** Minimum of 4 or 5 years, probably much older

**Lifespan of Adults:** 50 to 75 years; over 100 years known

# Introducing Lizards

It has long been thought that lizards and snakes were closely related offshoots of a common ancestor, and they are normally placed in the same order, the Squamata. This is divided, commonly, into three separate groups (called suborders): the snakes (Serpentes), the ringed lizards (Amphisbaenia), and the lizards (Lacertilia). Sometimes the ringed lizards are classified as a separate family within the Lacertilia. Recent investigation of the fossil history and genetic makeup of lizards and snakes questions the proximity of the groups. In the near future, we may derive an altered, more accurate view of the Squamata.

Lizards appear to be the most successful group of all the reptiles, if one makes the assessment on the number of species alone. Throughout the world, there are about three thousand different species, many exhibiting unique adaptations for living in a wide variety of places. Some lizards swim in the oceans, others live in the soft desert sands; many have taken to vegetated desert ecosystems like no other animals on earth. Some lizards never climb out of trees, and some glide on extended winglike flaps of skin. Some are tiny animals, barely three inches long, while the greatest of all, the Komodo lizards, may grow to ten feet in length.

## LIZARDS ARE NOT SALAMANDERS

Throughout much of the United States there is general confusion of lizards and salamanders. Certainly, their similar body forms exacerbate this problem, but even in areas where only one group exists, each is commonly mistaken for the other.

On the other hand, even a casual glance at the animals will reveal dramatic differences. It does not take much experience to distinguish a lizard from a salamander. For the most part, lizards have scales covering their bodies, claws on their feet, and external ear openings. Salamanders have smooth, glandular skin, no claws, and no ear openings.

Both groups are often found in the same areas, since there are both dry-land and wetland, ground-dwelling and tree-climbing, hot-climate and cold-adapted, diurnal and nocturnal species of each.

### FOOD AND FEEDING ADAPTATIONS

Lizards have the front ends of both halves of the lower jaw solidly attached to each other, not permitting an extreme opening of their mouth as in snakes. Most lizards have small, cone-shaped teeth that are used for holding and sometimes killing prey. Some families of lizards have varying and useful tooth adaptations, such as broad molarlike teeth to crush plants or mollusks, sharp canines to tear into prey, or grooved teeth to conduct venom.

Lizards feed on a wide variety of items, from algae to large mammals. Some species of lizards have very narrow dietary ranges while others eat whatever may be available within certain wide limits.

### GROWTH AND SHEDDING

The growth rates of lizards are affected by many factors, including the amount and quality of food eaten, temperature, age, breeding status, and sex. Like snakes, lizards grow a new layer of skin beneath the old layer. Rarely, however, is a lizard's skin shed in a single, continuous piece; more commonly, patches of skin are lost at various times during a lizard's shedding period. Like other animals, the faster the lizard grows, the more often its skin is shed.

Many species of lizards can see very well, though others cannot. Because their eyes are on the sides of their heads, lizards may be able to see ahead, above, and far to the sides at the same time. In the insect-eating species, especially, the eyes are particularly sensitive to movements, which helps explain why it is difficult to get close to many of them.

Most lizards commonly exhibit tongue-flicking behaviors that give a clue to the importance of smell and taste in these animals. Lizards have nostrils, with which they take in odors, but, like snakes, this sense is enhanced by the tip of the tongue, which picks up small particles of odors. These particles are transferred to the roof of the mouth, where an organ similar to that found in snakes analyzes them and transmits information, via the olfactory system, to the brain.

Lizards hear quite well and respond to many sounds in their immediate vicinity. They can also pick up vibrations transmitted through the ground, rocks, or tree limbs. Except for a few tropical species, lizards make few or no sounds.

## COMMON FAMILIES OF LIZARDS

North America has a wide assemblage of lizards, especially in the southern and western parts of the region. There are about 115 species, divided very unevenly into eight different families. Two of the families include the most commonly observed lizard species in North America.

The Iguanid family includes about fifty North American species. All of them show fascinating behavioral displays that are easily observed. Males actively court females, defend territories (at least for a short time), and interact with rival males during daylight hours.

There are about fifteen species of skinks (family Scincidae) in North America, and these include some of the most frequently seen lizards. Active in the daytime, these smooth-skinned and brightly colored animals are fast moving and easily lose their tails.

The Gila monster family (the Helodermatidae) has only one genus and two species in the world. Both of them are venomous. The Gila monster, the only one of them found in North America, is a unique and exciting member of our fauna.

## LIZARD TAILS

The size, shape, coloration, and function of lizards' tails play a great role in the survival of individuals and perhaps in their evolution as well. The striking colors of the tails of many species (especially noticeable in the young) and the extreme length of the tail in others is a good clue to this importance.

One of the most amazing features about a lizard tail is the ease with which the animal parts with it. Not all lizards easily lose their tails, but many North American species, at the slightest pressure, will leave behind a wiggling, animated target for a predator to ponder. The survival value of this may seem obvious; while the predator is dazzled by the tail, the lizard scurries off to safety, to live, and perhaps breed, another day. However, little field research has been conducted on the survival and social welfare of these tailless lizards and the success they have in the future.

Lizards also use their tails to store fats, presumably to survive winters and long stretches of weather too poor to forage in. During long periods of semistarvation, the tail will shrink to minute proportions. It enlarges again after the animal has taken in sufficient nourishment.

It is likely that the long tails of many species aid their balance as they run along tree branches or scamper over rock walls. Tails are also used in visual displays, as can be assumed by the bold markings and erect position in which they are held in during various interactions.

## CONSERVATION OF LIZARDS

Lizards in many parts of the world have lost local populations due to development projects. Some types of forest management, extensive mining, clear-cutting, and road building no doubt take their toll. Pesticides and herbicides probably have both direct and indirect effects upon lizards, though few studies have been done to validate this assumption.

It is surprising, then, that so few states feel there is a need to protect lizards. Perhaps this is because they are often small and assumed abundant. Most species, in fact, seem to be doing well enough on their own. A few, like the Gila monster in Arizona, do receive protection by state laws since they are unique animals and have been heavily collected as pets and curiosities in the past. Several other states protect some of their lizards in various ways as well. More accurate field studies are needed to assess population changes over time, especially on the edges of species ranges.

### LIZARD TERMINOLOGY

Lizards have a head, neck, body, and tail, and most have four legs with five toes on each foot. The common opening for excreting wastes and for reproduction is the *cloaca,* or vent; it can be seen as a slit that runs perpendicular to the length of the body, at the base of the tail. During the breeding season, the cloacal area of males is sometimes enlarged due to the development of the sex organ (called the *hemipenes*), which is usually hidden inside the base of the tail until needed.

The *scales* covering the various sections of a lizard's body have been given names by biologists who use their numbers and shape to distinguish species and sexes. The scales of some lizards are smooth, while those of others are ridged. The scales may all lie very close to the body surface, giving the animal a smooth, shiny look, or they may be overlapping, like the shingles on a roof, making the lizard look rough.

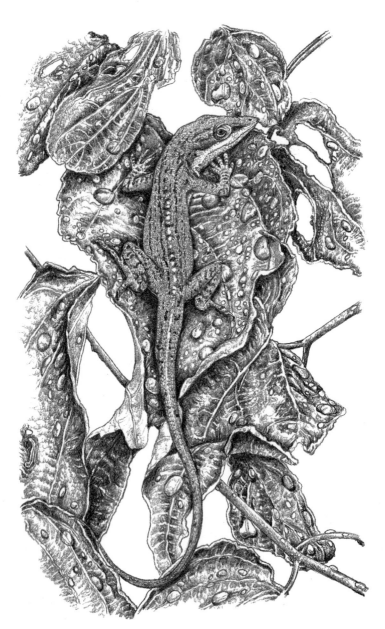

*Green anole resting after rainstorm*

# GREEN ANOLE / *Anolis carolinensis*

IN THE SHADE of a picnic grove, some friends and I were eating lunch one sunny afternoon. The tall pine trees all but darkened the ground beneath them, and the only vegetation springing up from the ground were saw palmettos. The edge of the picnic area, however, where a small opening in the forest had been made, was lush with vegetation. It was here that we saw several green anoles.

It took us a while to notice the lizards, since we weren't really looking for them. Finally their short, quick movements caught our eye, and we followed several of them from the comfort of our benches. We were close enough to have a good view of them, though they sometimes went behind a tree trunk or scampered along the ground behind a shrub.

We were most impressed with the territorial display of one large male who invariably saw other anoles long before we did. He began to bob his head up and down, slightly at first, and then a bit more vigorously. This continued for several seconds, until he lifted his head higher and expanded his brightly colored throat pouch.

The intruding lizard sometimes gave a bit of a head-bobbing movement, but we didn't notice any other action. Often, the large male would leap from branch to branch, or occasionally run along the ground toward the intruder. We always saw the intruder turn and escape. The large male took up the chase, at least for a short distance. We suspected that this male was defending a relatively complex, three-dimensional territory in this tangle of trees, shrubs, and vines. Long after lunch was over we stayed to watch the lizards.

The green anole commonly finds itself in faraway places because so many are captured and sold in the pet trade as "chameleons," only to escape far outside their normal range. Generally, most of these die with the onset of cold weather, or due to their inability to set up a territory and find enough food.

## How to Recognize Green Anoles

### ADULTS

These are medium-sized lizards that can grow to eight inches in length, most of which is taken up by the tail. Anoles can change color, from bright green to dark brown, often within a few seconds. There is no pattern on the body or tail of the green anole. Green-anole males have a large pink or red (or in some populations a green) throat fan or pouch.

The tips of anoles' toes are oversized on all four feet. These tips, along with their claws, enable anoles to climb all but the smoothest surfaces easily.

Other types of anoles, all introduced into the United States, either never turn green, have a different color throat fan, show a stripe or other pattern on the back, or have rings on their tails. (Several exotic species have become established in southern Florida and possibly southern California.)

Green anoles are members of the large and varied iguana family, the Iguanidae. The largest genus in this family, *Anolis*, also has the largest number of lizard species in the world, with over two hundred known. Most members of this genus are tropical, with the green anole being the most northerly member.

### DISTINGUISHING THE SEXES

Male green anoles possess a large throat fan, visible as a fold of skin beneath their head when it is not extended. Males tend to grow to larger sizes than females.

Females may show a slight folding of the throat skin, but it is not as protrusible as the males'. Females rarely grow longer than six inches.

EGGS AND YOUNG AT BIRTH

Green-anole females lay one or two eggs at a time. Each of these is only about a quarter of an inch long and three-sixteenths of an inch wide. They are off-white in color, with a smooth, rubbery texture.

No nest is built by this lizard. Eggs are simply left beneath leaf litter, rotting logs, rock piles, or other similar locations. Newborn anoles are miniature replicas of the adults, only an inch and a half in total length.

## How to Find Green Anoles

**Habitat:** Forests, edges of fields, cypress domes, hammocks
**Months of Activity:** Year-round (South); March to November (North)

*Range of the green anole*

This is one of the more successful lizards of North America, surviving in many types of ecological communities and thriving even in suburban and urban areas. Look for them in pine and oak forests, dry or wet grasslands, deciduous woodlands, cypress swamps, mangrove tangles, parks, and gardens.

Anoles are day-active lizards. They may be difficult to spot when they are resting or perched, elongated, on the trunk of a sapling. Carefully search the leaves, branches, and trunks of various plants. Individual lizards often bask less than six feet from the ground; however, they can get into treetops sixty feet or so in the air.

The best way to encounter these lizards is simply to walk along areas with shrubs or tall grasses and keep attuned to any quick movements that occur, perhaps caused by your disturbance of the landscape. Once you spot an anole, move back a few feet and make yourself comfortable. In a few minutes, the lizards will resume whatever behaviors they had been engaged in just before you arrived.

A final way to locate green anoles is to go out at night, and with the aid of a flashlight carefully search leaves, branches, air plants, the eaves of buildings, or other likely, exposed locations. These lizards do not typically tuck themselves into small crevices behind bark or leaves to sleep, but remain out in the open. When the light hits their bodies, anoles seem to glow a ghostly yellow-white, and this reflected light is visible at quite a distance.

## What You Can Observe

### SPRING ACTIVITY

Since green anoles are found mostly in a wide band around and through the gulf states, they remain active during much of the year. Along the south coast of Florida and Texas, for example, individuals can be found every day of the year. Their activities in the spring are similar to those of the rest of the year. In the mountains of North Carolina, near the northern extent of their range, anoles are active at least from the first week of March to the first week of November. Warming air and ground temperatures induce the animals to stir in the springtime.

Anoles seem to be strictly daytime animals, becoming active a little after sunrise and settling into a nighttime roost before sunset. Lizards seem to use some of the same overnight roosts on succeeding evenings. Researchers have estimated that the preferred body temperature for at least one population of green anoles was about 95° F (34° C).

### TERRITORIAL BEHAVIOR

Both male and female adult green anoles set up and maintain

territories that they defend from other anoles. They use both visual displays and aggressive behavior to accomplish this. The size of these territories varies with the density of the population and presumably with the quality of the habitat. Territories can range from a couple of square feet to a circular area one hundred feet or more in diameter. Most territories include a complex tangle of shrubs, vines, and trees. There is some overlap with territories of adjacent individuals, and young animals may be tolerated, at least occasionally, within the boundaries.

Head-bobbing is a common display of green anoles. This is done on a vertical surface, such as a tree trunk, or a horizontal surface, such as a branch or the ground. A lizard will often straighten its legs, thereby lifting its body off the substrate. It then will snap its head up in a quick motion and drop it down immediately. An anole may repeat this activity vigorously a dozen times or more. Typically, though, a lizard will bob its head only once or twice, then remain attentive for the action or reaction of nearby lizards.

Often associated with head-bobbing is the extension of the throat fan, or *dewlap*. Males have a bright red dewlap with a yellow margin visible for several yards. Its extension is a signal to nearby males as well as females, much the same way as the bright shoulder patches of male redwing blackbirds function. It indicates a male who has established a territory.

### COURTSHIP AND MATING

Both the male and female exhibit numerous visual displays and other behaviors during courtship. Through much of their range green anoles court and breed from early spring to early autumn, providing ample time to look for and watch these behaviors.

Normally, a male in his territory will advance toward a female who is nearby. It is unclear at what distance a male anole can spot another member of the same species and distinguish its sex, but it is certainly several feet. With every few steps, or leaps, toward the female, the male will stop and bob his head and extend his throat pouch. He may also perform push-ups, flexing and straightening his front legs.

*Displaying
male anoles*

If she is not ready to mate, the female may either turn and escape from the male's territory or hide behind a tree. She might also hold her position and allow him to approach, or she may move a short distance away, but stay visible. At some point, you might see a female whip her tail several times. This is usually indicative of a lack of interest in mating.

A female who is ready to mate will remain relatively still until the male reaches her. She will then point her snout downward and arch her neck and expose the skin on her neck to the male. On some occasions, the female will actually display her neck during the initial head-bobbing and throat display of the male and perhaps even approach him.

A male will usually move alongside and grasp the female's neck in his jaws. He will then wrap one or two legs around the female's body and intertwine his tail around hers in order to copulate. Mating may last about twenty minutes.

It is unclear how many times females may mate in a given season. They are known to be able to store sperm for weeks or months; it is thus possible that a single mating may be adequate to fertilize their eggs over the entire season.

### BREEDING

Female green anole, unlike most other lizards, do not have a single nesting period in a given year. Instead, they lay only one or two eggs after each mating, and then continue to seek out males and deposit eggs from late spring to early autumn.

Little information is available concerning the frequency of egg deposition in free-ranging females, but estimates based on indoor enclosure experiments give some clues. Variations do occur and are attributed to female size, but mature females typically lay one egg, and sometimes two, every eight to ten days for the length of the breeding season. In some cases, this season may last about eighteen weeks, allowing a female to lay as many as fifteen eggs in a single year.

Females either make a small depression in leaves, moss, or earth to form a nest of sorts, or almost randomly drop their eggs in and under all sorts of items without any prior consideration of the spot. Eggs have been found (sometimes several in one place) in air plants, holes in tree limbs, leaf litter on the forest floor, brush piles, and rotting logs, and under or next to rocks.

### CARE OF EGGS

After depositing their eggs, female green anoles have been seen to turn and push with their snouts until the eggs are buried in leaves or beneath objects. Further maternal behavior has been observed in animals maintained in captivity and includes some interesting activities. Females have been seen rolling an egg some distance and for many minutes and, following this, may rapidly wave their front legs. Though these behaviors have not yet been recorded in natural situations, they may function to increase the survival ability of the eggs if the female ultimately pushes them into a better location or actually covers them with material.

### LIFE OF YOUNG ANOLES

The incubation period for green-anole eggs is about a month and a half. At hatching, the young are about one and a half inches long. They are completely independent and begin foraging for insects, spiders, and other small prey.

Young green anoles grow very quickly, and some of those that hatch early in the year may nearly double their size by September. Biologists have found a sexual difference in growth rate; by about two months of age, males can be about four inches in length, while females are not quite three. By the time they are a year old, males can be almost two inches longer than females.

Both male and female green anoles become sexually mature when they reach a total length of about five and a half inches. In some quickly growing males, this can occur within a couple of months, and they may even court and mate females in the same breeding season as that in which they were born.

### FOOD AND FEEDING

This lizard eats a wide variety of small insects and other invertebrate prey. Lizards begin hunting about midmorning after a period of basking. During the heat of summer days, anoles stop feeding and rest in the shade, and resume hunting later in the afternoon.

Like other predators, anoles effect a selective pressure on prey species who might, in turn, evolve certain behaviors or characteristics to increase their own chances of survival. Entomologists have investigated whether the bright coloration of some poisonous members of the true bug family might be a signal to predators, like green anoles. Tests show that anoles will taste but spit out these toxic bugs and then will avoid even tasting them, or any other similar-looking bugs, again.

### SHEDDING

Like all reptiles, green anoles shed their skin. Typically, patches of the white skin come off at varying times. Young and adult anoles have been seen eating this shed skin, though the extent of this behavior is not known.

### PARACHUTING

In their active pursuit of each other, green anoles sometimes lose their footing or launch themselves out into space to escape larger males or predators. Even if they fall dozens of feet, the lizards usually land and bounce on the forest floor without noticeably harming themselves; they usually scamper to the nearest tree trunk and begin climbing again.

It has been postulated that the speed of their fall through the air is reduced by the enlarged toes on their feet. These relatively wide, flat surfaces may, in fact, serve to catch the air and brake the fall rate of the animal, allowing for a more gentle decline and less damaging arrival.

## TAIL FUNCTION

Like many lizards, green anoles may lose most of their tail during encounters with predators. Since their tail is usually twice as long as the body itself, it is likely that this may be the part of the lizard that is grabbed. A break-off point on the tail allows the lizard to lose this appendage and scamper off to safety. Anoles will begin to grow another tail, but it rarely gets as long as the original.

Losing their tail may be a disadvantage to the lizards, who seem to use it for balance and possibly as a way to size up territorial rivals. It is not surprising, then, that tail autonomy does not appear to be taken to an extreme in this species. It takes quite a bit of effort for them to lose their tails, and when they do, the tail does not twitch as vigorously as it does in other species.

## OVERWINTERING

In northern parts of their range and during cold snaps elsewhere, green anoles take refuge for days or even weeks at a time. They are known to move into and down natural crevices in rock walls and to seek refuge in dense vegetation both in trees and on the ground.

---

### Quick Reference Chart

**Length of Breeding Season:** Late spring to early autumn
**Eggs Deposited:** 1 or 2 elliptical eggs, deposited every 8–10 days from late spring to early autumn in moist earth or bromeliads
**Eggs Hatch:** 6–7 weeks
**Age and Size at Sexual Maturity:** Both sexes mature at about 5½ inches in total length; may be as young as 3 months
**Lifespan of Adults:** Probably less than 2 years in natural situations

---

*Five-lined skink hunting on the forest floor*

# FIVE-LINED SKINK / *Eumeces fasciatus*

On a canoe trip through Georgia's Okefenokee swamp, we stopped at a small cypress-and-pine island. The Spanish moss dripped from the trees. We saw a barred owl perched next to the trunk of a large cypress. The sounds of birds and the sight of butterflies added a lovely mix to the sights of the black water and golden tickseed sunflowers that grew in lush stands.

We pulled the canoe next to the shore and retrieved our lunches. It was a warm and sunny spring morning, and we had been anxious to get out and see what was about. There were many things that caught our attention, including several young raccoons that seemed to appear out of nowhere. They had seen canoeists before, obviously, and had successfully begged for food enough times that they were trying it again. We resisted.

As one of them came up from behind a tree that was close to us, a brilliant flash of blue blazed on the trunk. The raccoon may not have noticed, but it had frightened a young five-lined skink who had scampered around the base of the tree when we arrived. Now, with a more pressing danger approaching it at ground level, it had returned, in a hurry, to our side of the tree and thus presented us with a magnificent view. The raccoon moved nearer, and the lizard jumped to the ground and scurried away.

The five-lined skink has one of the most extensive ranges of any North American lizard. Consequently, they are frequently found, even in backyards, around houses, and in vacant lots. They are swift, agile animals that are alert and constantly flicking out their tongues to pick up scents. Because they are active in the daytime, they are one of the most often seen lizards within their range.

## How to Recognize Five-Lined Skinks

### ADULTS

This is a medium-sized lizard that grows to about eight inches in total length. Most individuals really do have five light-colored stripes running the length of their body from their neck to tail tip. Older skinks, however, have a dark brown or blackish body, and the stripes may be almost completely obscured. Adult males who show only a hint of stripes generally have an orange or reddish hue to the face.

There are several other species of skinks found throughout the country, all of whom have smooth, shiny skin, some with stripes. Either there will be fewer than five stripes, or the stripes will not reach onto the tail, or the animal will be larger than the five-lined.

The five-lined is a member of the skink family, the Scincidae.

### DISTINGUISHING THE SEXES

As adults, males tend to lose the striped pattern, which the females retain. In the breeding season, male five-lined skinks develop an orange-red coloration on the face and head that can be quite intense.

### EGGS AND YOUNG AT BIRTH

Females deposit up to fifteen eggs in a small cavity dug into leaf litter, rotting logs, or loose soil. There is no covering on the nest, normally, but the female does remain with the eggs.

When first deposited, the creamy white eggs are about half an inch long and about three-eighths of an inch wide. Just before they are ready to hatch, the eggs may have swelled to three-quarters of an inch long and half an inch wide. They do not adhere to each other.

Newly hatched five-lined skinks are attractive, brilliantly marked animals that seem to glow. Their stripes are especially vibrant, but the hallmark of the young is their brilliant blue tail. This can be particularly striking when the lizard sits on a dark log or greenery.

## How to Find Five-Lined Skinks

**Habitat:** Terrestrial, particularly found in moist, humid forests
**Months of Activity:** February to November (South); April to October (North)

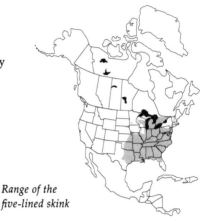

*Range of the
five-lined skink*

These are active, darting, diurnal lizards that are easily frightened if you approach too closely. It takes a little bit of experience to find them before they see you and scurry to safety; if you see one disappear into a rotting log, sit back and wait it out. Before too long it will probably poke its head out and eventually resume its activities.

Five-lined skinks are woodland animals, especially common in moist, humid forests. Their territories often include basking logs or rocks where sunlight penetrates to the forest floor or close to it. Look for them on sunny days in spots where they will be exposed and basking.

For the most part, five-lined skinks are ground-dwelling animals, searching for food and patrolling their territories on the forest floor. They will climb into shrubs and trees, however, and in some parts of the animal's range in Texas, populations are essentially arboreal.

# What You Can Observe

Adults become active as early as mid-February in the South or as late as May in northern parts and higher elevations of their range. Individuals set up home ranges and territories and investigate other individuals through a series of visual displays, aggressive actions, and tongue-flicking behaviors. A male may rub his cloaca on the substrate and then rush at another lizard, with his mouth wide open. If the other lizard returns the same behavior, a territorial fight may ensue. If instead the other lizard scurries off, the original male may chase it for a few feet, then stop and return to searching the area for more skinks.

Skinks become active when full sunlight reaches their home range, which can be mid- to late morning in some locations. They feed by actively searching out likely hiding places for insect and other invertebrate prey.

## TERRITORIAL BEHAVIOR

During the breeding season especially, male five-lined skinks set up territories that may be several yards in diameter. They actively pursue and chase other males who come in or near their territories and often grapple with them. The maintenance of territories wanes as summer approaches.

Five-lined skinks appear to be rather sedentary animals, living most of their lives in relatively small areas. The home ranges include areas for basking, hiding, feeding, and nesting. Home ranges broadly overlap for most of the year and sometimes many individuals can be seen in and around the same immediate location. One researcher found that numerous five-lined skinks shared a rock pile that was only seventy by thirty feet in size. Within four years, over two hundred individual skinks were found at this one spot.

## COURTSHIP AND MATING

Courtship and mating may take place late in the winter in southern parts of the range and not until April or May in the

North. Courtship is generally brief in this species, with males actively investigating any other skink that comes close enough.

When a female is approached, she may either retreat and leave the male's territory or remain still and let him continue his courtship. There may be some head-bobbing, chin-rubbing, and scratching before the male attempts to bring his body alongside hers. The female may then point her snout to the ground, and allow the male to grasp her neck in his jaws.

The male wraps his tail around hers and lifts her tail, or she may lift it on her own. They will copulate in this position for up to ten minutes. Afterward, the female leaves the male's territory.

*Female five-lined skink with eggs*

BREEDING

Females do not build their nests or lay their eggs for about a month after mating. Nest-building may begin as early as April or May in the South or as late as mid-July in the North.

Nest sites include areas in hollow, rotting logs and stumps, beneath boards or rocks, within and under forest-floor leaf litter, or in moist soil. The nest is a simple excavation of material that the female scrapes away with her feet or a natural indentation enlarged by movements with her body.

Up to eighteen eggs are deposited in a relatively tight cluster, and the female immediately takes up a position curled around them. Close observations of this brooding behavior has revealed some interesting aspects of female five-lined skink behavior. Periodically, for example, the female rolls each of her eggs. She will remain with them until they hatch, but has little or no interest in the newly hatched young. A day or two after the eggs hatch, the female leaves the young and does not return.

### LIFE OF YOUNG FIVE-LINED SKINKS

As is typical with most lizard species, young five-lined skinks maintain smaller home ranges than adults. You may expect to see the same animal regularly in the same location.

In some parts of their range, growth and maturity of skinks are slower than in other small, fast-moving lizards. It may take, for example, up to three years for an individual to become sexually mature, which they do when they grow to a snout-to-vent length of two and a half inches or so.

### FOOD AND FEEDING

Part of the reason for this lizard's success in the United States and Canada is the wide variety of foods that it consumes. It eats many small invertebrates, from insects and earthworms to spiders and millipedes. Large adult five-lined skinks are also known to eat other lizards, small frogs, and even young nestling mammals, such as mice.

### TAIL FUNCTION

Both adult and juvenile skinks readily lose the greater part of their tails when grasped by a predator. More than in many other lizards, this severed tail piece thrashes violently about for many minutes. The belief is that this attracts the predator's attention and allows the lizard to slink away to safety.

The brilliant blue color of the juvenile's tail may, in fact, enhance the attractiveness of this less vital part of its body. Not only its length, which is almost the same as that of the body, but the much brighter coloration is likely to direct a predator's attack to that end of the animal.

Because of a unique arrangement of vertebrae, muscles, and blood vessels, healing takes place almost instantly. There are rarely more than a few drops of blood lost when the tail is severed, and a new tail begins to grow relatively quickly.

## PHEROMONE DETECTION

You are likely to see any skink you discover more or less regularly flick its tongue in and out and press its nose to the ground or tree trunk. Lab researchers have found that skinks are able to discriminate very subtle odors left behind by other lizards. In fact, adults are usually attracted to odors given off by other members of the same species and thus follow a trail to them or attempt to get closer. This may be of particular consequence in the winter. It is possible that some individuals locate winter dens by picking up the odors of others who are already there.

## OVERWINTERING

Throughout their range, five-lined skinks spend the coldest part of the winter underground or at least not exposed at the surface. They may appear during warm spells in the South, but they normally do not emerge until April or even into May in the far North.

Den sites include rotting logs and tree stumps, small mammal burrows, wood and sawdust piles, rock piles, and natural crevices in rock walls. Skinks may overwinter singly or in small groups. Up to eight individuals have been found together in underground burrows in late autumn and winter.

---

## Quick Reference Chart

**Length of Breeding Season:** April to May
**Eggs Deposited:** Up to 18 oval eggs placed in a small nest chamber in moist earth or leaf litter from late May (South) to early July (North and West)
**Eggs Hatch:** In about 1½ months
**Age and Size at Sexual Maturity:** 1–3 years; 3½–4 inches
**Lifespan of Adults:** At least 6 years

---

*Pair of Gila monsters*

# GILA MONSTER / *Heloderma suspectum*

WE WERE all tucked into a van and excited about entering Saguaro National Monument in Arizona one early morning in July. By 7:30 A.M. the air temperature was already 80° F and the sky was clear and blue. Slowly, we drove past the entrance station, eyeing the tops of saguaro cacti for perched birds and looking for anything that might be sitting in the shade of the great cacti.

Several Gambel's quail scurried past a paloverde, and a couple of round-tailed ground squirrels scratched for seeds. A red-tailed hawk sat in the distance and a black-tailed jackrabbit crouched in a dry stream gully. We were headed to a short walking trail and knew we would get to see these and more species once we got underway. But we never did make the trail.

As we rounded a small curve in the road and began to ascend a hill, a large Gila monster stepped into our path. The driver stood on the brakes, and we poured out of the van. For most of us, it was the first time we had seen one of these animals. Even for those who had, it was still a magnificent sight.

The big lizard did not seem to be in a particular hurry, though it kept watching us. Periodically, it would protrude its thick, blue-black tongue and slowly wave it up and down. Our comments at the time revolved around the overall size of the animal, in addition to its large feet and thick, sausage-shaped tail.

257

Gila monsters are legendary because they are poisonous, brilliantly (almost gaudily) colored, and large. This one was bright orange and black and nearly two feet long. It certainly captured our attention. We stayed near it for almost an hour before both it and we retreated to cooler locations.

## How to Recognize Gila Monsters

### ADULTS

This large, thick-bodied, fat-tailed lizard is easily distinguished by its beadlike scales and the bright orange (or pinkish) and black markings all over its body. The face and forward part of the head are entirely black, though the rear half of the top of the head is patterned.

Gila monsters come in two different color patterns, which seem to be geographically separated. One set has a pattern of four black bands on an orange or pinkish body and five black bands on the tail. The width of the black bands is about equal to the width of the bright-colored spaces between them, giving the whole animal a rather candy-striped appearance. The other color form is reticulated; a complex intermixing of orange or pink infuses the black bands, giving the animal a broken pattern of light and dark markings.

Gila monsters are one of two members that make up the entire Helodermatidae family.

### DISTINGUISHING THE SEXES

Outward signs that distinguish the sexes of Gila monsters are difficult to see. The best clue is that the males have a much wider and larger head than the females. At the same time, females tend to have wider bodies than males, but this is even more difficult to see without a great deal of experience.

### EGGS AND YOUNG AT BIRTH

Females deposit up to a dozen glossy white eggs that are about two and a half inches long and just under an inch and a quarter wide. The shell is soft and pliable.

Females place their eggs in an underground nest, though it is not clear whether they use one of their own burrows or a specially dug compartment in an entirely different area. Nests are within a female's home range, however, on the desert floor or on the slopes of adjacent mountains.

Upon hatching, young Gila monsters are about six and a half inches long and have an especially bright pattern. The young may or may not retain this pattern into adulthood.

## How to Find Gila Monsters

**Habitat:** Mountain slopes, desert areas with shrubs and small trees
**Months of Activity:** Year-round in southern parts of range; April to November in the North

*Range of the
Gila monster*

It has been estimated that Gila monsters remain in underground burrows most of the year and most of their lives, spending as much as 98 percent of their time below the surface or at the entrance of their dens. Dens are normally natural crevices in the ground or burrows excavated by ground squirrels or tortoises.

Since they are active early in the morning and late in the afternoon, these are the best times to be outside looking. For all their size and brilliant coloration, Gila monsters can be terribly difficult to find. They are not particularly uncommon animals, but their color pattern helps to conceal them in the dappled light beneath trees, cacti, and shrubs. You must keep alert to see the difference in texture or color that signals their presence.

Slowly driving along roads through desert and scrub grasslands may also afford a chance view of this lizard. Once you do find a Gila monster, you might expect to see not only this one again in the same region, but others as well.

## What You Can Observe

### SPRING ACTIVITY

Field observations of Gila monsters indicate that the bulk of their aboveground activities for the year occur between March and early June. It is at this time, shortly after they emerge from over-wintering, that they are most active, feed heavily, and mate. They are most active when their body temperature is between 72° F and 93° F.

During spring, Gila monsters spend up to several midday hours foraging on the ground. As the season progresses, this activity is divided between two periods, early in the day and late in the afternoon. Gila monsters have been seen to forage in April and May between 8 and 11 A.M. and again between 4:30 and 6:30 in the afternoon. In June and July, these times shift an hour or two away from the heat of midafternoon, with most activity occurring in the morning.

### TERRITORIAL BEHAVIOR

Most Gila monsters remain within an estimated home range that is less than three-quarters of a mile in diameter. There have been few studies on populations of Gila monsters, and it is not clear if home range size varies with the density of the population.

For most of the year there seems to be no territorial behavior in these lizards, as ranges of both males and females broadly overlap. Observations of encounters between individual Gila monsters reveal little or no attention to each other, other than engaging in some additional tongue-flicking.

Surprisingly, two or more adult Gila monsters may even share the same burrow for weeks at a time. Individuals freely move into and out of these dens and may return to them irregularly, with no

*Gila monster pattern variations*

apparent aggressive interaction with the current resident or residents.

At least for a short period of time in the spring, however, male Gila monsters may, in fact, become highly territorial and aggressive toward each other. Interactions between them can be forceful and long lasting, with individuals, in extreme cases, locked in combat for many hours. Males approach each other and bob their heads vigorously up and down. They also extend and relax their legs, giving the appearance of doing push-ups. Both of these behaviors are given with various amounts of speed and energy.

These visual displays may rapidly lead to physical combat if one male or the other does not leave. Sometimes the interactions will be rather brief, with hardly a bite or two exchanged. But they can also escalate to the point where the two clasp each other with their limbs, continually bite each other, and roll and tumble over and over. Gila monsters are apparently immune to their own species' venom so that death is not usually the outcome of these bouts, though individuals may be scraped and cut deeply.

Courtship and mating occurs between late April and mid-June throughout most of their range. A pair of Gila monsters may have, in fact, spent the winter together in an underground burrow, or they may take up a short residence together for some time in the spring.

Courtship in Gila monsters begins when a male approaches a female and begins tongue-flicking. A receptive female (receptivity being indicated by her stationary posture) will remain still while the male circles and continues to flick his tongue. He may also rub his chin on her head, neck, or body. Field observers report that the female may respond by flicking her tongue as well. Eventually, the male attempts to align his body lengthwise next to hers. If the female is ready to mate she will lift her tail, allowing the male to wrap his tail and legs around her. They will copulate in this position for several minutes or up to an hour.

BREEDING

Relatively little is known of this aspect of the Gila monster's life history. Females become relatively inactive and spend even more time underground. They dig their nests (which are nothing more than depressions scraped on the ground) and lay their three to twelve eggs about the same time the midsummer rains reach the Southwest, in July and August. Five is the average number of eggs in Arizona nests. After laying her eggs, the female leaves the area.

There is much conflicting information about the incubation period of Gila-monster eggs. This may be due to the lack, until relatively recently, of detailed field research on this species. New observations indicate that the eggs overwinter in the nest site and hatch the following May, some ten months or so after deposition. There is no evidence that the female cares for the eggs in any way.

LIFE OF YOUNG GILA MONSTERS

At birth, the young are about six and a half inches long and weigh almost a quarter of an ounce. They are fully equipped with venom and seem to defend themselves ably when accosted. Biologists studying bites by newborn animals indicate that the venom is quite potent.

Little is known about the behaviors and activities of young Gila monsters. They are known to eat a great deal, at least when the opportunity presents itself. In one study, juveniles consumed food equal to half of their own body weight. There is no information available on the size and age at which Gila monsters reach sexual maturity.

FOOD AND FEEDING

Many types of animals seem to be part of the diet of these carnivorous lizards. Nestling mammals and birds' eggs have been listed by many researchers as being by far the most important foods for the Gila monster. Though there are written accounts of Gila monsters climbing trees and shrubs, most of their predation is accomplished on the ground.

Mammal prey include various rodents, rabbits, and hares. They are known to eat round-tailed ground squirrels and desert cottontail young, as well as numerous mice and other rodents.

A bird species commonly reported as serving as prey for Gila monsters is the Gambel's quail, whose range in North America is nearly identical to that of the lizard. These common birds nest on the ground and lay an average of eight to twelve eggs. In one study, researchers discovered that when Gila monsters encountered a bird's nest they ate varying amounts, but never all, of the eggs in the nest, and they never returned to a nest to feed. On the average, nearly half of the eggs in the nests were undisturbed. Gila monsters sometimes eat small eggs whole but usually break them apart and lap up their contents.

TAIL FUNCTION

Most feeding on either eggs or live young occurs in the late spring and early summer. It is believed by some that the lizards can get enough food during these two or three months to last them the entire year. The Gila monster's ability to store water and fat in its thick tail gives some credence to this.

## TOXIC PROPERTIES OF GILA MONSTERS

As one of only two poisonous lizards in the world, much attention has focused on the type of toxins Gila monsters carry, the mechanics of the venom system, and its use by the lizards.

Rather than have a single pair of hollow fangs on the upper jaw, as most poisonous snakes do, almost all the Gila monster's teeth are grooved. The venom glands open to the base of the teeth on the bottom jaw. The venom simply oozes out of the glands and runs down the grooves of the teeth. While the system may not be as efficient as that of rattlesnakes, the lizards compensate by holding tightly to prey and working the venom into the wounds made by the teeth over an extended period.

Data on the toxic properties of Gila-monster venom vary with the researcher. Suffice it to say that a bite can be a potentially serious medical problem even for humans. Everyone agrees, however, that it takes a fair amount of ignorance or just plain bad luck to get one to bite. Left alone, Gila monsters do not look to bite people or other large mammals. If grabbed, or accidentally stepped on, however, they may quickly snap and bite.

## OVERWINTERING

Over much of their range, Gila monsters tend to retreat to underground dens in the winter. Even in the deepest part of winter, however, strong sunny days may entice them from their burrows to bask in the sun for several minutes to several hours. These dens can be found in rocky outcrops on the slopes of nearby mountains. The dens, or ones close by, are also often used by various species of rattlesnakes and desert tortoises.

The winter dens are apparently used year after year by the same individual. Sometimes two Gila monsters, often a male and a female, will share the same winter den and will mate the following spring.

Midwinter body temperatures of Gila monsters can be as low as 55° F, a temperature that might induce them to emerge and sun themselves nearby.

---

## Quick Reference Chart

**Length of Breeding Season:** May to early July
**Eggs Deposited:** 5–12 eggs deposited in depressions or underground chambers
**Eggs Hatch:** The following April or June, some 10 months after being laid
**Age and Size at Sexual Maturity:** Unknown
**Lifespan of Adults:** Up to at least 20 years

---

*Regal horned lizard resting on desert pavement*

# REGAL HORNED LIZARD / *Phrynosoma solare*

We PLANNED to head out early, just before dawn, to hike through the desert to the base of the hills and back before the heat of the day. By eight in the morning, the air was still and hot and most of the bird song had died. Most of us were enjoying the walk immensely and continued searching out various plants and insects.

When we got to the entrance of a small canyon we spread ourselves out and sat under the welcome shade of tall trees. The conversation turned to the topic of desert reptiles, and someone remarked that they had hoped to see a horned lizard. We made that our goal for the return trip and after a rest began to retrace our steps.

The task seemed impossible; there were countless places a small lizard could hide. Some people scoured the gravelly edges of arroyos, while others peeked in at the bases of mesquite trees and saguaros. Just after noontime, one of my friends announced that he had found one.

Though we stood around him, it took quite a bit of searching to see the lizard. When it finally came into view, we were amazed, as usual, at being able to find one of these incredible animals whose color and texture seem to match the desert pavement so well. We got down on the ground and stared at a beautiful, adult regal horned lizard. The reptile seemed perfectly content to hold its position, flattened against the earth; only its eyes moved, following the people on either side of its head.

## How to Recognize Regal Horned Lizards

### ADULTS

Because of their flattened, toadlike shape and dinosaurlike spikes on their heads, horned lizards are instantly recognizable. They can grow to a total length of about five and a half inches. Overall, it is tan or reddish-brown, though there is much variation in color. The body has many raised, sharp-edged scales, giving the lizard a spiny appearance.

The spikes on the back of its head are all in contact with one another at their bases. The spikes are the largest in the center of the back and progressively smaller as they continue as a fringe along both sides of the head to the snout. There is also a single row of softer, smaller spikes on the sides of the body.

Other horned lizards have widely separated head spikes, only two or four head spikes, an obvious light-colored stripe running down the back, or two rows of lateral fringes, or they lack fringes altogether.

Horned lizards are in the iguana family, the Iguanidae. This large family includes about 650 species, most of which are found in the Western Hemisphere. Most lizards in the United States belong to this family. There are about thirteen different species of horned lizards in North and Central America; about seven of them enter the United States.

### DISTINGUISHING THE SEXES

There are subtle ways to distinguish the sexes of horned lizards, though they require handling the animals. Males generally have a row of pores opening from slightly enlarged scales running the length of the thigh on their hind legs. Females may have these also, but they are very small and difficult to see.

When filled with developing eggs, female horned lizards show a widening of the body, and the shape of the eggs can be seen through the skin.

Females lay a clutch of seven to thirty-three eggs. The eggs are about three-quarters of an inch in length and almost half an inch wide, making them almost circular.

Nests of regal horned lizards are dug into soft earth, often near desert plants, and are about five to seven inches deep. There is sometimes evidence of the nest site in the form of loosely packed soil, but they are difficult to locate, since the female covers them over with soil.

Upon hatching, regal horned lizards are small and grayish and have soft horns. They are about two inches in length.

## How to Find Regal Horned Lizards

**Habitat:** Desert floor to mountain slopes; occasionally juniper and oak forests
**Months of Activity:** March to November

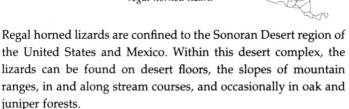

*Range of the regal horned lizard*

Regal horned lizards are confined to the Sonoran Desert region of the United States and Mexico. Within this desert complex, the lizards can be found on desert floors, the slopes of mountain ranges, in and along stream courses, and occasionally in oak and juniper forests.

One of the best ways to find these lizards is to search the area immediately around an ant mound. Though they do not eat ants exclusively, this is such a major part of their diet that most of them take up residence nearby.

Because these lizards are so well camouflaged, you must step very carefully in your search. Binoculars might help in some situations, but you will probably be more successful if you simply scrutinize the immediate area around the ant mound. Sometimes, most of the lizard will be buried beneath the soil, leaving only its head exposed to the surface. They are especially difficult to find then.

Regal horned lizards, like all of their close relatives, are day-active animals that often spend early mornings sunning themselves. This is an especially good time to look for them. In some areas the lizards will crawl out onto roadways, often with disastrous results, but if you are out before other motorists, this is a good place to look for them.

## What You Can Observe

### SPRING ACTIVITY

For the most part, courtship and mating occur from early spring to at least midsummer, though it is not clear what the exact extent of this behavior is for regal horned lizards. Individuals and pairs may begin courting shortly after emerging from their winter dens in March. Others set up territories near ant mounds and begin to feed for several weeks before breeding.

### TERRITORIAL BEHAVIOR

Horned lizards, as a group, seem to be tolerant of other members of their species. Individuals do live within a certain home-range area, but there is no particular part of it that is actively defended. Home ranges of regal horned lizards overlap widely, and several individuals might be found relatively close to one another.

Females roam much smaller areas than males, and juveniles are even more restricted. Adult males' home ranges are within an area sixty yards in diameter. Females usually stay within an area half that size, while juveniles may remain within three square yards around an ant mound.

Because their home ranges overlap so much, regal horned lizards rather frequently encounter their neighbors. Usually they greet each other with a head-bobbing behavior that is repeated several times for up to a minute or so. The animals may walk toward each other or simply scurry in varying directions. Sometimes one of the lizards will turn and face away from the other and raise its tail straight into the air. The other horned lizard may approach and investigate its vent area and base of the tail. It is unclear how common this behavior is and in what context it is performed. It may be related to sex recognition.

## COURTSHIP AND MATING

Females enter the home ranges of males rather frequently in both spring and summer. Males typically begin a courtship involving the head-bobbing movements commonly used when approaching any horned lizard. One or both may then appear to do push-ups with the front legs alternately straightened and relaxed.

A receptive female holds her position and allows the male to approach closely. The male may continue bobbing his head while aligning his body next to hers, head to head. The female, like other members of the Iguanidae family, may point her snout to the ground and expose her neck to the male.

This may be a signal or simply a posture that enables the male to grab her neck in his jaws. He will then attempt to twist his tail around hers, trying to get their vents in close proximity. Because of their odd body shape, their mating posture looks a bit more awkward than those of other lizards. The pair may copulate for twenty minutes or more.

A male is likely to court and breed with any number of receptive females who enter his home range, though it is not clear what the extent of this is. It is unknown if a female will mate with more than one male, but this is not suspected to be likely.

## BREEDING

After mating, the female tends to move away from the male's home range. Over the next few days or even weeks, a female begins to search her immediate surroundings for a suitable nest site. During this time, the eggs inside her body are being subjected to the heat and warmth of the sun whenever the female basks. This may, in fact, allow development of the embryos to proceed even while they are retained inside the body of the female.

A female may begin construction of several nests, only to abandon them and move on to another location. Eventually, she begins to excavate a chamber in the soil, using her front feet. As the opening enlarges, she digs deeper and may use her hind feet to help push away material already excavated.

The nest may become a tunnel up to fourteen inches deep, with an enlarged chamber at the end. Here she will begin to deposit her white, soft-shelled eggs. Females have been seen rolling each egg after it is deposited, coating it with soil. Most nests that have been excavated show that all the eggs are coated with soil and look like small, brown spheres.

When finished, the female returns to the surface and refills the nest cavity. Individuals are known to tamp down the earth with their feet and bodies, and they may continue to scratch and loosen the earth in an area several feet around the nest. The function of this behavior is not clear.

It is not known if female regal horned lizards deposit more than one clutch of eggs in a season, but since it is known in other species with more northerly distributions, it seems likely.

LIFE OF YOUNG REGAL HORNED LIZARDS

Typically, not all of the eggs hatch. In at least one observation, over 80 percent of the eggs successfully hatched. Those that don't succumb to damage, disease, fungus, or other factors.

Incubation is estimated to be between four and five weeks, with the young hatching in late July. They emerge by digging at the top and sides of the nest chamber, eventually breaking through the surface of the ground. Hatchling horned lizards may linger in and around the nest site for some time before dispersing. They have been seen to congregate near ant mounds and remain there for many weeks.

Both male and female regal horned lizards take one to two years to reach sexual maturity.

FOOD AND FEEDING

As with most horned lizards, ants, particularly harvester ants, form a major part of the diet of this species. They are so important that many individuals set up their home ranges very close to anthills. The lizards probably do eat other insects and perhaps other invertebrates but certainly not in the same concentration as they do ants.

When feeding, regal horned lizards simply approach an ant colony and reach down and pick up individual ants with the tongue. Some lizards station themselves adjacent to a column of marching ants and casually feed as they pass by. The lizards do most of their feeding in the morning before ground temperatures get too high.

*Horned lizard
hunting ants*

### TAIL FUNCTION

The very short tail of regal horned lizards functions mostly as a fat-storage organ. The tail does not snap off when grabbed by a predator. In some cases, when a horned lizard is flipped onto its back the tail may be used to help right itself.

### BASKING

Juvenile regal horned lizards often bask right on or near ant mounds. Adults seem to prefer to retreat some distance away and use rocks in the vicinity of small shrubs and leaf litter.

Horned lizards bask only in full sunlight and are rarely fully exposed on the surface of the ground in other weather conditions. They are not normally active at all on windy days with cool temperatures, but they are often seen in the summer after brief but strong thunderstorms.

### OVERWINTERING

During the coldest months of the year, as well as during the driest and hottest, regal horned lizards remain underground to a depth of a foot or more. They enter mammal burrows, dig their own dens, or find natural crevices. The lizards can begin to disappear by late October and may not be commonly seen again until April. There is plenty of variation in this, however, and prolonged warm periods into the fall and in early spring can extend the active period for this species.

## Quick Reference Chart

**Length of Breeding Season:** Late spring to early summer

**Eggs Deposited:** Up to 33 small, oval eggs in an underground nest chamber

**Eggs Hatch:** In about 4–5 weeks

**Age and Size at Sexual Maturity:** Estimated to be 2 years for both males and females; adults are then over 3 inches in length

**Lifespan of Adults:** At least 9 years

# Introducing Crocodilians

Few other animals are as well known as the American alligator. It is a major attraction for families who vacation within the species' range, where they are actually common sights in backyards in suburban areas. The American crocodile, on the other hand, found only on the extreme southern coast of Florida, is rarely seen. Both are members of a declining group of reptiles, called the crocodilians, that have managed to survive for the past 200 million years or so, unlike their close relatives the dinosaurs.

The crocodilians comprise at least three different families and about twenty-two species. All members of this group have strong, muscular tails that are flattened from side to side. They have five toes on the front, unwebbed feet, and four toes on the hind, webbed ones. Males have a single copulatory organ and (like their other close relatives, the birds) lack a urinary bladder.

All crocodilians have a four-chambered heart, quite a bit of cerebral cortex, and teeth that are set into their jaws. They have bony cores to some of the platelike scales imbedded in their skin and a clear membrane that covers their eyes when underwater. Evolutionarily, the group has specialized in living on the edges of tropical swamps and marshes. Some were (and some still are) primarily marine animals, while others prefer freshwater habitats. All of them are essentially aquatic and function as major predators in the ecological communities of which they are a part.

Although the American alligator and the American crocodile are related, there are distinct differences between them. The alligator's snout is broad and rounded, while the crocodile's is long and pointed. Crocodiles are more or less confined to saltwater areas, alligators to freshwater wetlands.

## FOOD AND FEEDING ADAPTATIONS

The configuration of the bones of the roof of their mouth enables crocodilians to continue to breathe while eating or when partially submerged. The enlarged snout of alligators and crocodiles gives them a flat profile with only the eyes and nostrils protruding. Because of this they may remain hidden beneath water with little more than their nostrils and eyes above the surface while they wait for prey.

Alligators actively hunt by slowly advancing and quickly lunging. Small prey are simply swallowed whole, with several gulps. Large mammals and birds are carried to deeper water and held beneath the surface. Occasionally a crocodilian will rotate its body while holding onto the limb of a large animal in an effort to dislodge parts of it to eat.

Often alligators and crocodiles will guard or even carry dead prey around for several days before it decays enough to be easily consumed.

## COMMON FAMILIES OF CROCODILIANS

There are three groups of crocodilians in the world, comprising twenty-two species. A single species, the gharial of eastern India and Nepal, is the sole member of the family Gavialidae. Seven species of alligators and caimans make up the family Alligatoridae. These are found in North and South America and in eastern China. The final family, the Crocodylidae, includes fourteen species of crocodiles found in tropical areas throughout the world. Only one species, the American crocodile, reaches North America.

## CONSERVATION

Nearly all the species of alligators and crocodiles in the world are declining or in danger of becoming extinct. Historically they were killed for their skins and because they presented a potential hazard to people. More recently, wetland drainage has also been a major factor in the decline of most species.

Recent, successful management of American alligator populations appears to show that some species of crocodilians can be at least maintained, if not replenished to their former numbers. Conservation groups around the world are monitoring the dwindling numbers of crocodilians and are working hard to provide suitable refuges for them.

### CROCODILIAN TERMINOLOGY

Alligators and other members of this group have distinct head, body, and tail sections. The head includes protruding nostrils and bulging eyes, both more or less on the same plane. When its body and tail are submerged, the animal can see and breathe by keeping only its eyes and nose above the surface. All crocodilians have five toes on their front feet and four webbed toes on their hind ones. Crocodilians do not use their webbed feet for swimming. Instead, the splayed-out toes enable the animal to stay on the surface of the mucky bottoms of their swamps and marshes. The powerful tail is the main source of propulsion. In addition, it can be used to knock prey off their feet and into the water where it can be grabbed more easily.

On the surface of their skin, crocodilians have large plates, called *scutes.* Imbedded in some of the larger ones on the back are bones that provide protection. The skin on the underside of the crocodilians is very smooth and soft.

*American alligator*

# AMERICAN ALLIGATOR /
*Alligator mississippiensis*

IN A POND adjacent to a busy walking trail, an American alligator began thrashing about with enough vigor to attract a small crowd of onlookers. Though several egrets, ibis, and herons were only a few yards away, they paid only occasional attention to the big reptile. The rest of us were transfixed. An eight-foot-long male was scouring out a winter refuge; we were watching a "gator hole" in the making.

Though I had found and watched alligators numerous times before, this activity was particularly interesting in part because alligators often lie in seeming lethargy for long periods of time, and this one was in almost constant motion. Secondly, this particular activity of alligators has a biological importance beyond the individual's desire to gain deeper water. The excavation it was making would persist through the long winter drought of the southern states, holding enough water perhaps to keep hundreds of other species of aquatic animals alive. Collectively, the hundreds of thousands of alligator holes throughout the range of this species must play a significant role in the life histories of many others.

We watched the alligator continue its activity for several hours. During that time, several of the wading birds came to feed on the fish that were already in the pool. They were clearly aware of the alligator's nearby presence and always walked into the willows when it moved too close. None of us could predict just what, if anything, the alligator would do if the birds came within reach. But they never did, and the reptile continued to use its snout and front legs only to widen the ten-foot-wide pool. Few other reptiles, or even other vertebrate animals, make such large-scale changes in the landscape.

Many people, including those who have never seen one in natural areas, are intrigued by alligators. Partly this is due to the great number of tales and stories of steamy swamps and bayous. In addition, the alligator's appearance evokes the age of those most famous of all reptiles, the dinosaurs. Indeed, alligators and their close relatives have an ancient lineage stretching back to the beginning of the great age of reptiles. One of the most fascinating biological questions that remains unanswered today revolves around the fact that the dinosaurs in all their variety and glory became extinct, while alligators have survived into modern times.

American alligators are in the order Crocodilia, the crocodiles and alligators. The name alligator is derived from two Spanish words, *el lagarto*, meaning "the lizard."

## How to Recognize American Alligators

### ADULTS

In North America, adult alligators, commonly reaching eight to ten feet in length, can be confused only with the very rare American crocodile (*Crocodylus acutus*). The wider snout, hidden lower teeth (when the mouth is closed), and overall dark coloration will help identify the alligator. The American crocodile is light gray or green in color. It shows teeth from both upper and lower jaws when the mouth is closed.

### DISTINGUISHING THE SEXES

Males grow to greater total lengths than females, but otherwise it is difficult to tell the sexes apart.

American-alligator eggs are white and have a brittle shell. They are elliptical in shape and about three inches long. They are deposited in a large nest made of twigs, leaves, and underwater plants. Young American alligators, which are about nine inches long at birth, might be confused with large lizards. But the small alligators have a double row of protruding scales on the back of the tail that join to form a single row, very large claws on their feet, and a longitudinal cloaca (the vent is transverse in other reptiles). Also, alligators are confined to wetland areas, though they may make occasional overland movements.

## How to Find Alligators

**Habitat:** Freshwater and coastal wetlands; rivers, swamps, canals
**Months of Activity:** Year-round (South); warmer months (North)

*Range of the American alligator*

At present, American alligators are found in only nine states: Alabama, Arkansas, Florida, Georgia, Mississippi, North Carolina, Oklahoma, South Carolina, and Texas. Confined to wetlands, canals, and major rivers, alligator populations, which had been decimated by the 1960s, have recovered in a few of the more southerly locales. Few, however, survive outside of publicly protected land.

Throughout this range, alligators attract much attention and local "gator holes" are easily found by asking residents. At state, local, and national parks throughout the southeastern United States, resident staff can point you in the right direction. Almost any canal, lake, pond, and swamp in the deep South will have a local population of alligators as well.

Alligators are easily found during the daytime, especially on sunny mornings. Look for the fully exposed adults and especially the young basking on logs, shore lines, or each other. You must look carefully to discover them in water, however. From a distance, floating alligators look like logs, and, when mostly submerged, only their protruding eyes and nostrils are above the surface. A pair of binoculars will help. Up until recently, alligator hunters and poachers would shine a lantern over a pond at night to see the coal-red eye-shine of the alligators as they floated on the water. (Today, licensed hunters search for alligators in the daytime in restricted areas.)

## What You Can Observe

### SPRING ACTIVITY

In northern areas of their range, American alligators become active in late March or early April. They spend a good deal of time basking on sunny days. Most of the courtship and mating behavior of the species also takes place in April and May throughout their range.

Young alligators seem to be more active during the spring, alternating basking with swimming to new areas of ponds and marshes.

### TERRITORIAL BEHAVIOR

Alligators tend to be solitary animals that may or may not be territorial. There has been shown to be a dominance hierarchy when several individuals are in close proximity due to decreased water levels or other factors. Larger adults displace smaller ones at preferred basking sites or feeding areas. The feeding activity of an individual alligator often attracts nearby animals, and larger ones may be successful in taking all or part of the prey.

Displaced alligators have returned from more than thirty-five miles away. Males are known to travel within a breeding territory of fifty to one hundred acres. Adult females tend to remain within a half mile of the nest site for most of their adult lives. All individuals move in response to water levels, and this alternately disperses and congregates the alligators in a given region.

VOCALIZATIONS

Males produce a dramatic, bellowing roar that is one of the true sounds of the wilderness. At a distance, it sounds like an electric generator starting or the rumbling of thunder. Heard nearby, the roar is surprising in its loudness and similar to the sound produced by male lions. Females also roar, though the sound is softer and travels less of a distance. During the spring breeding season, females often roar immediately after a nearby male vocalizes. When bellowing, alligators keep their mouth shut, the sound being produced by vibrating the throat. Both sexes also produce a variety of hisses and grunts, perhaps to communicate with each other or to indicate a defensive attitude to intruders.

Newly hatched alligators and young produce a high-pitched, grunting whimper. They make this sound when the female is nearby, but most often it is heard when she is out of sight or the young are hidden from her, or when they are attacked by predators. Females clearly respond to this call and will move in the direction of the sound, often very quickly.

Alligators also produce sounds by using other parts of their bodies. The most common of these is when an individual raises both its head and tail out of water. The alligator then rapidly opens its mouth, causing its lower jaw to drop onto the surface of the water. A loud popping sound is produced. This is most often heard during the breeding season.

COURTSHIP AND MATING

Most observations of these behaviors have involved captive or semitame populations of alligators. The onset of courtship and actual copulation appears, at least in some areas of the alligator's range, to be dependent upon a number of environmental factors such as air and water temperature and water level. Females seem to take the initiative in courting, and they tend to approach males who may be living alone in a particular pool or stretch of river. At other times, females move freely through a group of alligators, eventually stopping close to a particular male. Some researchers have found that the female will remain in the vicinity of a male for several days before they mate. Few vocalizations are given during this time by either sex, though the role of several scent glands that alligators have is unstudied at this time.

Just before copulation, both adults enter the water and float at the surface with their heads close to each other and bodies up to forty-five degrees apart. The male remains stationary while the female, keeping her head near his, moves her body around in a circular motion. Eventually, she lies alongside the male and arches her tail upward. The male responds by lifting his tail and copulating with her for several minutes. It is unknown how many times a pair will copulate, or just how long a female remains in the male's vicinity. Eventually, however, she leaves the area. While the male can mate with other females, it is unknown if the female will court other males.

### NEST-BUILDING AND EGG-LAYING

Female alligators search for and set up a nesting territory about two months after mating. The nest site is located in shallow, freshwater wetlands with an abundance of floating and emergent plants. She begins to build a large nest, constructed of mud, aquatic or semiaquatic vegetation such as cattails and other grasses, and various species of willows, sedges, and shrubs. Some of this material is uprooted underwater and pushed up onto a bank or scraped toward a high spot in the marsh. Nests can be constructed in either location.

She uses her jaws, feet, and tail to gather and place the nest material. In two or three days, the nest mound can become over a yard in height and several yards in diameter at the base. Once constructed, the female will climb to the top and scrape out a depression, using her hind feet. Often, she will move down off the nest to gather more mud and vegetation and carry it back in her mouth. She packs this in to fill the original cavity, then excavates another depression in the new material.

It is in this second cavity that she deposits her eggs, one at a time and about a minute apart. Larger females tend to lay more eggs than smaller females; the range found in natural clutches is fifteen to eighty-eight eggs. After the female finishes depositing all her eggs, she scoops up with her mouth some of the twigs, mud, and soft vegetation from the side of the nest and places it on top of the eggs. She continues to mound the top of the nest and eventually shapes it into a cone with scraping and dragging movements of her body and legs.

The nest material acts as compost to warm and heat the eggs in the nest chamber. The steady heat produced by the rotting plant material can be cooler than outside air temperatures in the day and warmer at night. The egg chamber's average temperature in one study was 83° F (28° C), while the air temperature went up to 87° F (31° C). Humidity inside the egg chamber is usually at or above 90 percent.

SEX DETERMINATION OF YOUNG

The temperature at which the eggs are incubated determines the sex of the young alligator. It has been found that nest temperatures less than 85° F produce all females while temperatures above 91° F result in all males. Furthermore, researchers have found that there is only a short period of time when this determination takes place—usually within the second and third week of incubation. Further temperature fluctuations do not alter the sex of the young.

CARE OF NEST AND YOUNG

One of the more fascinating aspects of alligator behavior is the female's care of her young, which takes place in several ways only relatively recently discovered. While the eggs are incubating, the female is often stationed nearby. This is variable, however, since some populations of alligators have high nest-abandonment rates.

The presence of a female is very likely a deterrent to many egg predators, such as black bears and raccoons. Research in Georgia's

*Hatchling basking on female alligator's head*

Okefenokee Swamp National Wildlife Refuge showed that while 88 percent of unguarded nests were destroyed by egg predators, only 17 percent of those attended by females were disturbed.

During the incubation period, the hard, outer layer of the egg is attacked by bacteria, causing the shell to crack and loosen. There is some evidence that suggests that this bacterial action is a vital step in the hatching process. Laboratory research on alligator eggs incubated in sterile environments showed that some of the embryos and ready-to-hatch young suffocated inside the bacteria-free and uncracked outer shell.

Toward the end of the two-month incubation period the alligators begin to hatch. The young are equipped with an egg tooth on the tip of their snout, used to shred the rubbery inner layer of the egg and escape from the egg. Once inside the nest chamber, the young emit their characteristic high-pitched grunt.

In cases where a female has not attended the nest site, the young hatch out of their eggs and then must dig out of the egg chamber and surrounding vegetation. Normally they then crawl down the outside of the nest mound and enter the shallow water nearby. In some instances, however, the nest material may be so compacted that the young are unable to escape. In other species of crocodilians, the young must have help by the female to leave the nest; some researchers suggest that this may be more important than previously thought in alligators.

Where the female is in attendance, she occasionally responds to the young's sounds with her own grunting vocalization. Most frequently, the female's response to the sound inside the egg chamber is to scrape open the top of the nest with her front and hind feet. When the nest chamber is uncovered, newly hatched young may emerge. Others are in various stages of escape from their own eggs. It is at this point that the most remarkable behaviors occur.

Field researchers have watched females reach into the nest chamber and carefully lift the young and even still-hatching eggs with their mouths. The young appear to orient toward the female's snout, and she tends to scoop them up from the side of her mouth, rather than in front. Some of the young are tossed back into the throat pouch, and they may walk toward the edges of the female's mouth. The young, eight to ten inches in length, are carried to the water's edge between the teeth of the upper and lower jaws and released.

Nearly hatched eggs and young with egg fragments on them are occasionally brought to the water and held while the female gently swirls water through her mouth cavity to loosen attached debris and egg shell. She may take only a single young or egg at a time to the water, or she may lift two or more. There is still some debate as to the significance of female alligators' transporting their young from the nest to the water. Not all nests are attended by females, and not all females appear to engage in this behavior. More field research into natural alligator nests will increase our understanding of this behavior.

FEEDING

Alligators are entirely carnivorous. The young begin feeding on small aquatic and terrestrial insects, mollusks, fish, frogs, and other inhabitants found in their immediate area. Adults feed on a wide variety of vertebrates and invertebrates, including birds, mammals, reptiles, fish, amphibians, and snails. In some seasons the large apple snail (*Pomecea* species) supplies a surprisingly large percentage of the diet of adult alligators in some parts of southern Florida. Most of their feeding is done at night, though alligators can and will take prey anytime of the day. There are three methods of prey capture in alligators: opportunistic feeding, active hunting, and passive hunting.

Sudden lunges and attacks from an otherwise surface-floating and obvious alligator are typical of an opportunistic feeding attempt. In these cases, the alligator, lying still for many minutes, is either unseen or forgotten by birds, fish, or mammals. When they approach closely enough, the alligator makes a sudden rush or a quick snap with its jaws. The effort seems to pay off for the alligator only some of the time, but little energy is wasted in the effort.

Keep your eye on any animal that is approaching a seemingly lethargic alligator. Passively hunting alligators remain partly hidden and motionless and wait for potential prey to come close enough to attack. Some alligators may choose particular places to lay in wait—such as the outfall of a culvert, an isolated watering hole, or a well-used trail.

In active hunting, alligators scout for food and choose an appropriate prey item. How this decision is made is unknown, but the alligator will stalk and deliberately approach the prey. Stalking is often done with just the top of the head on the surface of the water or even just the eyes breaking the surface. When it is within a dozen feet or so of the intended prey, alligators often submerge completely and make their final attack underwater. They will pursue prey up onto land, at least for short distances.

Small prey is simply swallowed whole, sometimes after being mouthed and bitten. Larger prey, such as turtles, muskrats, larger fish, or snakes, requires the alligator to bite down and crush the bones or shells of the animal first before swallowing. This may take from several minutes to several hours. Occasionally the alligator will return to a favored feeding site before swallowing its prey.

The largest prey, including deer and other larger mammals, large birds, or even other alligators, are grabbed and dragged to deeper water where they drown. If the prey is exceptionally large, the alligator may simply drag it around for several days and guard it until the skin and meat begin to putrefy. Then the alligator may tear off sections of the carcass, grabbing onto a limb, for example, and rotating its body until the limb works free. Alligators will also eat carrion, though it is unknown how important this is as a food source.

## BASKING

Lying exposed on a bank, a log, or even another alligator is the most obvious method alligators use to regulate their body temperatures. Researchers have found that alligators can live between a body temperature range of 79° F (26° C) and 98° F (37° C), but that they prefer to be between 90° and 95° F. To maintain this optimum range, alligators make use of the different heat retention abilities of water and air and the heating capacity of sunlight. On sunny days, alligators will leave the water and crawl up to a basking site, typically by 10 A.M. Individuals may keep their tail or limbs dangling in the water or emerge completely out of water.

Often, alligators move and adjust their basking positions to take advantage of both open and shaded areas. It is speculated that various parts of their bodies heat and cool at different rates. You can observe a sunning alligator with its head in the shade and the rest of its body fully exposed to the sun.

Alligators will return to the water late in the afternoon and stay there all night. On overcast, cool, or rainy days, alligators may not emerge onto land at all, especially if the water temperature is higher than the air temperature.

## OVERWINTERING

From December to March, many people living in northern states vacation in the Southeast and here encounter their first alligators. As local residents can relate, this is the most quiet time for the alligators, and it is not surprising that so many tourists come away with the idea that these reptiles are slow, lethargic animals. During warm periods in the winter, however, alligators can be observed feeding, sunning, interacting with other alligators, and exhibiting other behaviors as well. Patience and long observation periods will help ensure a successful experience.

As winter approaches and water temperatures drop, alligators become dormant and remain so for several weeks at a time. They normally lie on the bottom of wetlands. Sometimes they may enter underwater burrows or dens.

# Quick Reference Chart

*Life Cycle*

**Length of Breeding Season:** March (onset) to July (mating)

**Eggs Deposited:** 25–60 hard-shelled eggs deposited in huge nests on riverbanks or high ground in the body of water, from July to August

**Eggs Hatch:** September (South) to October (North)

**Age at Maturity:** At least 6 years for males and up to 8 years for females

**Lifespan of Adults:** Probably 25–40 years

*Vocalizations*

**Bellowing roar:** Given by both male and female, mostly during the breeding season

**Hissing:** Produced by adults when threatened or approached too closely

**High-pitched grunts:** Made by young and female to communicate their location to each other; females follow the sounds made by the hatchlings and young to locate them

# Introducing Snakes

Some people are afraid of snakes. This seems a bit silly to those of us who delight in a chance encounter with a wild snake. We watch one bask in the springtime sunlight or gracefully work its way along the tips of tree branches with such care and attention that its weight seems not to bend the bough in the slightest. We marvel at the designs and patterns of a snake who matches its surroundings so well that it is remarkable we ever see it at all.

Many people consider snakes mysterious. Certainly there are ample fables and stories involving snakes, especially rattlesnakes, but even to pragmatic researchers and biologists snakes are relatively unknown animals. Their fossil history is shrouded in mystery; there is little evidence for the general belief that snakes evolved from lizards at least 150 million years ago, and some evidence suggests that both lizards and snakes evolved from a still earlier ancestor.

Snakes and lizards are currently united in the same family, the Squamata, though there is some question as to how appropriate this is. The two groups differ in many ways, the most visible being the lack of legs in snakes (present in most lizards). Snakes also lack eyelids and external ear openings.

There are just over 2,100 different species of snakes in the world today. They live in a variety of places, from high mountains to shallow oceans. Most snakes have evolved relatively narrow eco-

295

logical requirements, and each species can be expected in only one particular type of place, such as grasslands, wetlands, mangrove forests, temperate forests, wet deserts, or canyons. There really are no snakes in Ireland, nor are there any in Iceland, New Zealand, or Antarctica. Some snakes have wide ranges and inhabit several ecological communities. Others are extremely rare and have very limited geographic ranges.

Modern field biologists are just beginning to understand some of the complexities of the life history and behavior of American snakes. Recent advances in technology now make it possible to follow snakes into their winter dens and record all sorts of information. Still, there is no substitute for getting out into woods, hills, fields, and wetlands to sit and watch what snakes are doing. More and more people are doing this, and their collective observations continually offer new insights into the lives of snakes.

### WATCHING SNAKES

There is rarely any reason to approach snakes, especially poisonous ones, closely, and I generally find using binoculars is the best and most effective method of observing them. This not only keeps me out of the way but perhaps allows the snake to behave in a more normal manner. There is no reason for a nonprofessional to handle a rattlesnake, or any other venomous snake for that matter. They, like all snakes, are delicate, and there is evidence that developing embryos can be damaged and the adults left with permanent internal injuries from handling. It's best to approach snake-watching like you do bird- and mammal-watching: keep your distance and enjoy the event.

### LIFE WITHOUT LIMBS

The fluid movements of a snake are fascinating to watch and a feat of no small proportion. One can sit and watch a snake swim through a field a hundred times and never be able to explain how it is accomplished. Detailed analysis of slow motion and X-ray photography of snakes indicates that snakes use two basic methods to move themselves.

The most common, as seen in most North American snakes, is called *lateral undulation*. In this method, the snake pushes off the ground or vegetation from several points of its body at the same time, propelling it forward. Actually, all snakes can accomplish this motion, especially when swimming, crossing branches, or moving over a rocky surface.

The second method of moving is described as *rectilinear motion*. This involves pulling the belly scales forward across an immovable part of the ground. Then, with a series of complex muscle, rib, and backbone adjustments, the snake's skin and body are pulled along in the same direction. Most large, heavy-bodied snakes use this method, and some small, stocky species as well. One unique variation of this movement is called *sidewinding*, found in some rattlesnakes and a number of other snakes in the world. Here, parts of the body are lifted off the ground and moved forward and sideways at the same time. This may be a more efficient method of locomotion on sand; it also enables the snake to lift part of its body off the hot surface of the ground.

FOOD AND FEEDING

Snakes have numerous adaptations for finding, subduing, and eating their prey. All snakes are carnivorous; some species have a wide variation in their diet while others are much more restricted. There are three ways that snakes get their food: by catching and swallowing it immediately, by catching and constricting the prey until it is dead or nearly so, and by employing a toxin that kills or immobilizes an animal.

Snakes generally have six rows of teeth, two on the top jaws (one on each side), two on the bottom jaws (one on each side), and two on the roof of the mouth. The teeth generally are sharp and curve backward, but microscopic examination of snakes throughout the world shows that there are numerous variations that allow certain teeth (or rows of them) different functions, including holding, moving, or poisoning prey.

Venom glands have evolved in various species and produce toxins that are sent, via ducts, to the base of specialized teeth (called *fangs*) that in many snakes are hollow. Some, such as the rattlesnakes and copperheads, have such large fangs that they are attached to movable bones allowing them to be folded back to the roof of the mouth when the jaws are closed.

## GROWTH AND SHEDDING

Snakes grow throughout their lives, though adults add very little length after they become mature. To grow they must replace their outer layer of skin in a process of shedding, or *ecdysis*. The entire process takes several days to a week or more to complete. A new outer layer of skin must first begin to form beneath the old one. Then, fluid from the lymphatic system spreads between these two layers, separating the old from the new. Snakes have no eyelids, but do have clear scales over their eyes, and the lymphatic fluid gives their eyes a gray or bluish cast and clouds the snake's vision during this period.

Within a few days the fluid is reabsorbed, and the snake begins to expand and contract its body and head. Eventually it rubs its nose or head on rocks, bark, or other rough material, and the moist, pliable old skin begins to peel and get lodged. The snake then simply crawls forward, turning the shed skin inside out and leaving it behind.

It was believed that snakes shed their skins at irregular intervals throughout the year, but recent field observations may indicate otherwise. Certainly, shedding is a function of growth, and young snakes typically grow faster than adults and therefore shed their skins more often. Because each species and family of snakes has a unique number of scales in a pattern on their bodies, shed skins can be easily identified.

## COMMON FAMILIES OF NORTH AMERICAN SNAKES

There are about 115 species of snakes native to North America. The vast majority of them belong to two families, the pit vipers (Viperidae) and the common snakes (Colubridae). The Viperidae includes about seventeen species of rattlesnakes, the copperheads, and water moccasins. The hallmark of the group is temperature-sensitive pit organs, one on each side of their head, located between the eye and nostril.

The Colubridae is a very large, diverse, and confusing group of animals. The diversity found in this family is so immense that many researchers are trying to sort out in a more detailed fashion the relationships within the over 1,700 species found throughout the world. In the United States and Canada there are about ninety-two members of this family, some possessing venom glands and fangs, while others are constrictors. Some lay eggs; others give birth to live young. There is no single characteristic defining this family.

## SNAKE SENSES

A snake's tongue is not used for manipulating food, as it is in many animals, but functions as a highly evolved smelling and tasting organ. The two tips of the forked tongue emerge from and disappear into the snake's mouth through a tiny opening in the front. A snake's general state of activity or excitement can often be determined by the rate at which it flicks its tongue.

The tongue tips pick up molecules of taste and odor that waft through the air and transfer them to a pair of cavities (called the *Jacobson's organ*) at the roof of the mouth. These cavities open into the nasal cavity of the snake, and it is here that the molecules are analyzed and information about them transferred to the brain.

All snakes can see, though the acuity of their vision is not clearly known. Snakes do have a very wide field of vision, being able to take in an angle of about 150 degrees. This gives them the ability to see prey and predators in front of them and to their sides as well.

Hearing in snakes is generally believed to be limited, at best, to sensing vibrations from the ground or fallen trees or rocks. Some researchers question this, even suggesting that snakes can hear airborne sounds. Convincing evidence is lacking and detailed research needs to be done before we can fully understand this sense in snakes.

One family of snakes (Viperidae) possesses pit organs, large depressions found between the eye and nostril that offer a unique way to sense the world. Able to detect very small differences in temperature from one to several feet away, a pit viper can tell the location of a frog or mouse and be able to strike at it accurately even in total darkness. Movement of the prey is easily followed by the pit organs alone.

## CONSERVATION OF SNAKES

There is little doubt that snakes in many parts of the world have been persecuted by people for centuries. It is surprising that so many appear to be doing as well as they are.

It is not surprising, however, that some populations have become extinct in certain areas and others are declining precipitously. The reasons for these declines include capture and killing of snakes for food and leather, collection for pets, and destruction of their habitat. Conservationists note, however, that the little information that is available, even concerning common species, makes it difficult to make clear statements about the decline and disappearance of snakes. More field work is needed.

## SNAKE TERMINOLOGY

A snake's body is divided into a head, body (or trunk), and tail sections. Snakes do have a short neck between the head and body and can turn their head somewhat at that point. The tail begins where the vent or *cloaca* opening is found. There are, of course, no legs, external ears, or eyelids on snakes.

The body of a snake is covered with skin, much of which has scales or *scutes* imbedded in and covering the outer layer. These scales can come in various shapes and can be either *keeled* (with a raised ridge down the center) or *smooth* (without the ridge).

Most of the scales on the head of a snake are either large or have unique shapes. The single scales on the belly of a snake are usually quite wide and are called *ventrals* or *ventral scales.* Beneath the tail are either one or two enlarged scales known as the *subcaudals* or *subcaudal scales.* The large scale covering the cloaca is called the *anal plate.*

The body of a snake is often patterned with colors that form distinctive shapes. Snakes can have rings running around their body, stripes that run the length of their body, blotches, spots, or saddles that cross some or all of the top of their bodies.

The pupils in the eyes of snakes may appear to be rounded or vertical. Often a snake with vertical pupils in daylight may have rounded ones in dim light.

*Alert common garter snake*

# COMMON GARTER SNAKE /
*Thamnophis sirtalis*

ONE SPRING AFTERNOON I found myself with a group of a dozen other people on a walk at a local wildlife sanctuary. We were there to look particularly at some of the plant and animal life found around a small fire pond, dug by hand in the 1930s. Over the years, the pond had developed into an attractive breeding site for several amphibians, numerous aquatic insects, wood ducks, and many other animals. When we reached the sunny, sloping side someone noticed a garter snake slipping underneath the leaf litter. We decided to sit down and watch what it would do.

In a short time the snake emerged from under the leaves and moved forward slightly. It appeared alert, with its head and neck raised several inches off the ground. It began to flick its tongue in and out of its mouth, not particularly rapidly, but slowly and deliberately. We sat perfectly still at first, not wanting to frighten it. Eventually, though, we began to relax a bit, and some stretched out completely to get a ground-level view of the garter snake.

After twenty minutes or so, a small patch of sunlight reached the snake, and it arranged itself into a loose coil. The garter snake allowed us to get within several inches of it and didn't move at all. One person slowly reached out and stroked its back, and it continued to remain perfectly still. After a few more minutes, when discussion of the life history of the garter snake waned, we carefully moved back and walked away. When we left, the snake was still in the same position in the sunlight.

## How to Recognize Garter Snakes

### ADULTS

This common and widespread species is immediately recognizable by the yellowish stripe that runs down the center of its back and two yellow stripes along the sides, running the length of the body. There is much variation, however, and some populations of common garter snakes lack the central stripe on the back, show only faint side stripes, or both.

The ground color can be black, tan, greenish, or red, and the stripes can be yellow, tan, or orange. Garter snakes have a red tongue with a black tip. Each scale on the body has an obvious ridge running down the center of it. These snakes can grow to a maximum length of just over four feet, but most are much smaller than this.

There are about a dozen different species of garter snakes in North America, and while some are very individualized, most require careful observation to distinguish them. The closely related ribbon snake (*Thamnophis sauritus*) is similarly striped, but has a very slim body and a glossy yellow central stripe.

The common garter snake is in the Colubridae family. With all its various patterns and forms, the common garter snake has one of the most extensive ranges of any reptile in the New World, and it reaches further north than any other snake.

### DISTINGUISHING THE SEXES

Females have much shorter tails than males and when ready to give birth appear to be very massive, further accentuating the shortness of the tail. Females tend to be longer, sometimes by far, than males.

Even in newborn garter snakes, the relative diameters of the end of the body and beginning of the tail are good clues to tell the sexes apart. Males have a very smooth transition of body width, ending in an even taper of body and tail base. Females show a slight but obvious bulge and constriction where the body and tail base meet. These differences are due to both of the male's sex organs' being inverted into the body cavity and to the presence of particularly large scent glands in the base of the female's tail.

### YOUNG GARTER SNAKES

Born alive, garter snakelings emerge within a transparent sac out of which they must work their way. They are seven to nine inches long and are identical to the adults in pattern and color.

## How to Find Garter Snakes

**Habitat:** Terrestrial; in fields, forests, suburban yards, especially near wetlands
**Months of Activity:** Year-round in southern and coastal areas; March to October in the North

*Range of the
common garter snake*

Garter snakes appear to be particularly visible and approachable early in the spring, especially April and May. At this time they have recently emerged from underground retreats and are looking for mates. They also sun themselves frequently and will remain in the same location for days at a time. Often there will be several individuals in close proximity.

On the first warm days of spring pay close attention to grassy slopes, roadsides, fields, railroad beds, or open places in woodlands. When startled, these snakes usually don't go very far; instead they just withdraw their head and neck under the cover of leaves or tree roots. Often, they will simply stay where they are and will allow unprecedented approach. If they do take cover, simply sit and wait for them to emerge, which they will do shortly if the sun is still warm.

Later in the summer, when they have taken up their warm-season residence, garter snakes display relatively regular activity patterns. If you find one in the hedges or by the birdbath at a given hour, look for it again on another day at the same time. Generally garter snakes begin clear mornings by sunning themselves on the tops of low bushes or on exposed surfaces of the ground. After an hour or two they forage for food. If they are successful, they then hide themselves to keep out of sight of predators.

At any time, you may actively look for garter snakes. They often take refuge beneath logs, boards, pieces of metal, or other debris. Some of these locations may be especially important to the snake as places not only to hide from danger but also to soak up moisture, maintain correct body temperature, or look for food.

## What You Can Observe

### SPRING ACTIVITY

When they first emerge in the spring, garter snakes in most populations tend to linger in or near their wintering dens. These dens need not be more elaborate than a woodchuck burrow or a crack in a house foundation, but in some areas they include underground caves or hillside crevices.

Adult males appear to emerge first, and in some places up to several hundred individuals may be observed. At least in some areas, females tend to emerge singly and over a longer period of time than the males. When they reach the surface, females are actively pursued by males, often several or even dozens at a time.

### TERRITORIAL BEHAVIOR

Garter snake populations that have been studied show a relatively high tolerance for overlapping home ranges. Most snakes remain within a home range less than two acres in diameter.

If you see a number of garter snakes traveling together in April or May, or in a writhing mass of bodies, you may have happened on one of the most amazing courtship rituals in the reptile world. Often a single female, much larger than the males, is the center of attraction. Sometimes called *mating balls,* there may be as many as a hundred or more garter snakes intertwined in a writhing mass.

Females at the center of an aggregation may try to avoid mating with any of the males or simply take some time deciding on which one to mate with, though little is known about how a female garter snake chooses from so many potential mates. The male continually rubs his chin on the head, back, and sides of the female. You will note that there is much tongue-flicking behavior in the male, and he attempts repeatedly to align his body next to the female's.

When the female is ready to mate she stops her forward movement and slightly raises the rear part of her body and base of her tail, exposing her cloaca. The nearest male in the best position and body alignment will evert his sex organs and the two will mate. Once they are coupled, the other males are likely to leave almost immediately and search out new females. At least in some populations, male garter snakes are known to insert a substance into the female's cloaca that repels other males.

The successful male may court other females, but females will mate only once and immediately begin to migrate away from the den area.

### MALE-FEMALE MIMICS

Biologists have discovered that one mating strategy of the males, who clearly must compete for the few females that appear at any given time, is to try to confuse rivals by mimicking a female. Some males are able to produce pheromones that are similar to the ones females produce to attract courting males. While rival males are attending to the mimic, he is probably able to spend his time courting and mating with a real female.

It is not known if female garter snakes fast while their young develop inside their bodies. In some snakes, the growth of their embryos somehow inhibits the female's feeding response. When ready to give birth, late in summer (some five months after mating), female garter snakes take refuge under some form of cover. The female makes obvious labored movements and contractions of her body while giving birth, eventually expelling the young, one, two, and sometimes three at a time. The female sometimes lingers with the young for several days, though this does not imply that any maternal care is offered.

## LIFE OF YOUNG GARTER SNAKES

If you actively turn logs, boards, and other material in a search for garter snakes in late summer or early autumn, you are likely to notice that more than one, and often up to half a dozen, young garter snakes will be under the same cover. Newborn garter snakes are known to gather together, at least in small groups, for several weeks. The social and behavioral functions of these aggregations are debated.

## FOOD AND FEEDING

To eat, garter snakes simply grab their prey and work it into the mouth and throat. There is no constricting beforehand, and it is not surprising, therefore, that you will rarely find garter snakes attacking anything more formidable than frogs or nestling birds. In fact, one way to locate garter snakes is to follow the distress calls of captured frogs.

Occasionally a fairly large number of garter snakes will linger in one area when food becomes concentrated. This species has been known to hunt around pond margins when the tadpoles of several species of frogs are transforming. At this time the amphibians are at their most vulnerable stage.

Though garter snakes across North America collectively feed on a variety of food items, local and regional populations may have strong likes and dislikes. Both newborn and adult snakes may

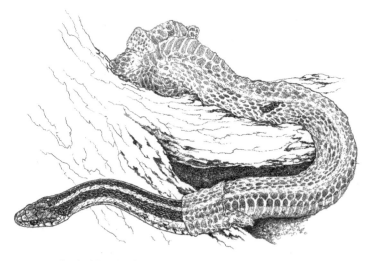

*Garter snake shedding its skin*

show these tendencies. Garter-snake populations are also known to shift their diets from year to year, depending more on one type of food than others when it becomes seasonally available.

Garter snakes eat earthworms, various insects, frogs, salamanders, birds, and small mammals. They are active daytime hunters with a particular fondness for, and ability to locate, earthworms, even underground. Laboratory investigations have found that earthworms produce a chemical substance in their skin that is easily detected by garter snakes, who also find it extremely attractive. Researchers testing garter snakes in mazes and other devices can direct their movements by leaving an earthworm scent trail.

### OTHER FACTS ABOUT GARTER SNAKES

This species has the largest range and distribution of any snake in the New World. It reaches almost to the Arctic Circle in Canada's Northwest Territories and south into Mexico, excepting desert regions. Because of the garter snake's abundance, willingness to live near people, and relatively small size, it is probably the one snake collected by fascinated children more than any other. Consequently, many people are familiar with the foul-smelling fluid that excited garter snakes expel. This probably comes into play when the snakes are attacked by natural predators and may serve to make the snake distasteful.

While the garter snake has no fangs, there has been at least one case of a serious reaction to its bite and also that of other so-called nonpoisonous snakes. The simple solution is to leave them alone and watch from a short distance away.

OVERWINTERING

By autumn garter snakes begin to migrate back to their wintering dens, though it is not known if they go to the same one year after year or choose different ones as the opportunity arises. Some locations, with either minimal den sites or perhaps for social reasons, harbor hundreds to thousands of garter snakes. At other locales, garter snakes overwinter as individuals or in small groups.

They winter inside houses, quarries, mammal burrows, rock outcrops, and other places that maintain above-freezing temperatures. In northern parts of their range, garter snakes can be active for only four or five months, while in southern areas they may be active year-round. Garter snakes appear to be able to withstand some freezing temperatures in winter without exhibiting any stress or damage, though it is not known how widespread this is or what mechanisms allow it to occur.

# Quick Reference Chart

**Length of Breeding Season:** In spring, immediately upon emergence from winter dens

**Young Born:** 7–85 young born alive from mid-August to late September

**Gestation Period:** About 5 months

**Age and Size at Sexual Maturity:** 2 years, for both male and female; about a foot in total length

**Lifespan of Adults:** At least 8 years

*Northern water snake*

# NORTHERN WATER SNAKE / *Nerodia sipedon*

O<small>NE SUMMER'S</small> evening a friend and I walked along a narrow causeway that separated the main part of a reservoir from a natural pond filled with all sorts of plants and animals. The evening was warm and fireflies dotted the landscape. There were male bullfrogs and a few green frogs vocalizing from various quarters as we quietly walked along. We had brought flashlights with us to look for frogs and other nocturnal animals and were excited when we spotted a northern water snake gliding along the surface of the pond.

This was not a particularly large individual, perhaps a foot and a half long. It stopped, then moved ahead sporadically; it didn't seem to be bothered by the light. For a short time the snake swam with its head raised just slightly above the water. Then, it would stop, put its whole head below the surface, and search through some of the thick aquatic vegetation that grew in dense stands in the shallows. We felt sure that this snake was hunting for food, although we were not able to see it capture anything in the half hour that we watched.

Very different observations are usually made of water snakes throughout their range during the daytime. In the sunlight, water snakes are usually found sunning themselves on the banks of ponds, lakes, canals, and streams. Often they remain still—at least until they are approached too closely. Then, they seem to explode with energy, wildly thrashing about until they reach the water and disappear to safety underneath.

Because of their large size and preference for aquatic habitats, water snakes throughout their range are commonly misidentified as venomous water moccasins and, unfortunately, often killed.

## How to Recognize Northern Water Snakes

ADULTS

This is a stout, water-loving animal with numerous saddles and crossbands running across its body, alternating with spots and blotches on the sides. The bands on the neck are particularly dark in northern water snakes, and most of the bands are wider than the spaces between them. The color pattern of old water snakes is often very obscure, giving them an overall dark brown or black color. There are some populations, on islands in Lake Erie, for example, that show no pattern at all.

Underneath, this snake shows a beautiful design of yellow, black, or reddish half-moon shapes on the sides of the belly scales. The scales on the back and sides have strong ridges running down their centers, giving some water snakes a rough-looking body.

There are about seven different species of water snakes, and most are best distinguished by their ranges. The dark neck bands and brilliant colors underneath, however, will usually identify the northern species from most of the others.

Water snakes are forever confused with the venomous water moccasins (*Agkistrodon piscivorous*), even in areas far outside the range of the latter species. There can be some confusion, as both snakes are heavy bodied, present a fearsome appearance when cornered, and live in aquatic areas. Keeping your distance when watching these snakes is the best way to be sure of your safety.

The northern water snakes are in the family Colubridae, the common snakes, who make up the largest and most diverse group of snakes in the world. Members of this family are the most common snakes on every continent with snakes, except for Australia, where the cobra and coral-snake family is more prevalent.

Female northern water snakes grow larger than males and, interestingly, they also seem to outnumber them, at least in some populations studied. In addition, at most sizes and ages females are heavier than males. As is typical with many snakes, females have much shorter tails than do males; this is more apparent in water snakes than in other species.

## YOUNG WATER SNAKES

Newborn and young northern water snakes often show a brilliant pattern of reddish brown saddles on a gray, tan, or brown background color. Their pattern is especially vibrant compared to the adults, and seems to have evolved for allowing the snake to be concealed in semiaquatic vegetation. At birth, water snakes range from about six inches to nearly a foot in length.

## How to Find Northern Water Snakes

**Habitat:** Semiaquatic; edges of lakes, ponds, marshes, bogs, rivers, reservoirs
**Months of Activity:** Year-round in southern and coastal areas; April to October in the North

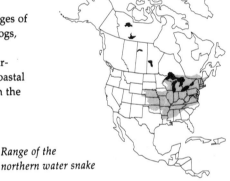

*Range of the northern water snake*

These animals are normally found in freshwater ponds, rivers, lakes, reservoirs, and marshes. They can be surprisingly common; a walk on a sunny afternoon might reveal several or more individuals. During the warm parts of the days, you can expect to find northern water snakes sunning themselves on stone walls, beaver lodges, dried cattail stems, causeways, or the overhanging branches of small trees and shrubs, or in the most shallow areas of the water. Young water snakes, like all small animals, are particularly difficult to locate because of their size and secretive behavior. Look for them amid the plants along the edge of the water.

Sometimes, but less often than most other species, water-snake adults and young can be discovered beneath logs, rocks, boards, or similar hiding places. Usually it is best simply to scan the banks of a local freshwater lake with binoculars or walk slowly and carefully along pond or stream margins to spot them.

Since this species can be active both day and night, try your hand at finding and watching them after dark. Obviously you'll need a flashlight, and some boots might be helpful. Scan the areas just off shore that have thick mats of underwater and emerging plants. These are good feeding areas and likely places to spot this species. Water snakes appear to have a much more vibrant pattern in water than they do on land because when their skin dries, dust, soil, and other debris obscure its luster. Swimming water snakes can appear glossy and bright; they are delightful to watch. If you disturb a water snake it is likely to make a quick dive to the bottom to lie beneath some debris or hide between large rocks. If you are patient, it will resurface and may allow you to watch.

There are some populations of northern water snakes that have taken up a coastal existence in some of the saltmarshes of the Southeast. To survive in any but the lowest salinities, snakes must have various methods of regulating the flow of water and salt into and out of their bodies.

## What You Can Observe

### SPRING ACTIVITY

Much of a northern water snake's time before courtship and mating is spent sunning and basking. Males actually feed very little from the time of spring emergence to just after the courtship season, and females may feed only occasionally.

Five to fifty water snakes may congregate shortly after emerging from their overwintering sites. This interesting social behavior may have much to do with subsequent mating behaviors.

There appears to be no territorial defense by male or female northern water snakes during any time of the year. Indeed, especially in the spring and fall, water snakes are often found in groups, even coiled together at basking sites.

Various field observers have reported the home range of water snakes, with widely varying figures. This variation is due to different methods used to study free-ranging snakes and the natural differences that individual snakes and populations display. Throughout their period of activity, water snakes may move hundreds of yards in short periods, then remain in a given place for days at a time. Though they may move over an area several acres in diameter, they may use only one or two small parts within that range most of the time.

## COURTSHIP AND MATING

These behaviors have rarely been observed in natural situations and even less frequently by someone with a notebook. Here is an area in which any aspiring herpetologist can help to advance basic knowledge of one of the most common and widespread snakes in the United States. Most information already on hand comes from captive animals or chance encounters in the field. Observations generally have begun when the snakes are already mating or are just about to.

Courtship and mating occurs from April to June, depending on the latitude, and seems to be concentrated in late May and early June. Courtship begins when a male crawls alongside a female and rubs his body along hers, sometimes quite vigorously. The male may rub his chin on her head, neck, or body at the same time.

Two or more males may attempt to mate with a single female simultaneously. To attempt mating, a male water snake will twist and coil his tail around the female's body and tail, trying to get their cloacae aligned. Normally, only one male will actually copulate with a female, but other males may either continue to court the female or perhaps attempt to dislodge the successful male.

During this time the female and the attending male or males

may move slowly forward, enter water, and return to land without changing any of their relative positions. At least on one observed occasion the unsuccessful males eventually moved away from a mating pair, who continued their activities on the surface of the water. While mating, the male was actually out of water, perched on the much larger female's back. After a couple of minutes, the two parted and moved off in opposite directions. It is not known if a female mates with more than one male in any given season, though males probably mate multiple times.

## BREEDING

Female northern water snakes apparently reproduce every year, although this has not been established with certainty. Most females mature by the time they are three years old, but some two-year-olds who have grown quickly will also mate and produce young.

There is a strong correlation between the size of the female and the size and number of young she will produce in late August or September, some four to six months after mating. Between twelve and sixty young are born alive, normally one at a time. The female lifts her tail as each one emerges. Before long, the young crawl away. The female pays little or no subsequent attention to them.

## LIFE OF YOUNG WATER SNAKES

Northern water snakes range in length from six to twelve inches at birth. They are stout and have a brilliant pattern.

Little is known of the life of young water snakes. Newborns grow at a much faster rate than older juveniles and adults, perhaps adding two or more inches of growth during their first season.

## FOOD AND FEEDING

You may find water snakes searching for food both day and night. One clue to this behavior is a frequent movement of the snake's head beneath the surface of the water. They often will keep their body on the surface and push their head through un-

*Color patterns of newborn and juvenile water snakes*

derwater plants or investigate spaces near large rocks, submerged logs, or undercut banks.

Water snakes have been known to herd small fish or tadpoles with their bodies to the edges of a bank in order to concentrate them into a smaller area and have a better chance of catching some. If they are successful in finding prey, water snakes will either swallow it immediately or haul themselves back out on land before eating. This variation may have something to do with the relative size of the snake and its prey, how fast or maneuverable the prey is, or other factors still to be determined. Water snakes are known to feed on amphibians, fish, reptiles, mammals, and birds. Their most frequent food items are frogs (adults and tadpoles), small fish, and salamanders.

### WATER-SNAKE PREDATORS AND MORTALITY

Many vertebrates are known to eat northern water snakes. They include herons, egrets, hawks, raccoons, skunks, and foxes. Gulls also feed upon water snakes, and channel catfish are known to scavenge dead animals. Black racers have been found eating water snakes; snapping turtles take some as well. Large frogs undoubtedly feed on newborn water snakes.

*Young water snake with black-nosed dace*

Without question, people are a major cause of individual mortality of water snakes, especially near urban or heavily visited rural swimming and fishing locations. Individuals are killed directly by automobiles and by other means. Indirectly, water-snake numbers decline as shoreline areas are increasingly built upon for home and recreational use.

### BASKING

Sunning, by far, is the most common activity you are likely to see northern water snakes performing. Snakes in general bask in several different postures; these may have an effect on how efficiently and quickly they can raise their body temperature. Some snakes bask in elongated, oval coils, while others are more tightly wrapped and circular in aspect. The former allows for better cooling, while the latter allows for maximum heat buildup and retention.

By moving slightly throughout the day, northern water snakes keep their body temperature at a fairly even level, no matter what the air temperature is. Don't assume that if a snake isn't moving it isn't doing anything. Small and subtle changes in position or orientation can mean important variations in the comfort, alertness, and intention of the animal.

Water snakes spend varying amounts of time according to season basking in exposed locations. Snakes bask most of the day in spring, shift to basking just in the morning by early summer, and by late summer bask only in the early morning.

### UNEQUAL SEX RATIOS AND SURVIVAL RATES

In at least one thorough study of a water-snake population, there was shown to be an unequal sex ratio; females outnumbered males. In other detailed studies on the causes of mortality in water snakes, it was shown that while both sexes suffer equally overall, the death of males occurs much more often during the spring mating season, due in part to their being much more active and rarely feeding during this time. Female mortality is more likely during the summer, after they give birth.

### OVERWINTERING

Water snakes normally overwinter during the coldest months underwater, in the mud at a pond bottom, or inside the lodges of muskrats or beavers. However, some are known to migrate uphill to overwinter in rocky outcrops where they have access to underground fissures. Estimates that up to 40 percent of the northern water snakes in Michigan do not survive the winter have been reported.

---

## Quick Reference Chart

**Length of Breeding Season:** From April to June; most commonly in late May and early June

**Young Born:** Up to 60 young born alive, from mid-August to late September

**Gestation Period:** About 2 months, depending on temperature

**Age and Size at Sexual Maturity:** In males, about 2 years, females about 3; both about 1½–2 feet in total length

**Lifespan of Adults:** Estimated to be at least 7 years

---

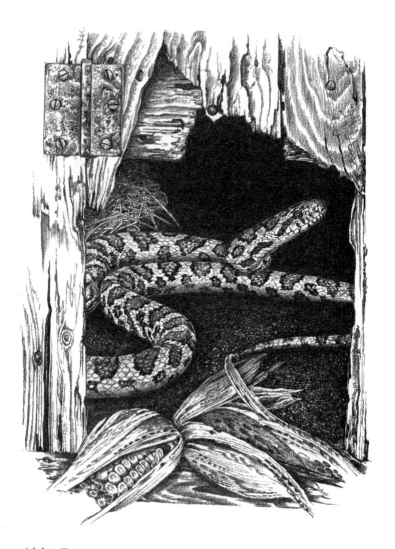

*Adult milk snake*

# MILK SNAKE / *Lampropeltis triangulum*

On a sunny April afternoon I was lured by the warm temperatures and bright sunlight to a nearby hilltop, home to several species of amphibians and reptiles. Anxious to try to find some of them, by late morning I found myself sitting at the base of a basalt column a hundred feet tall that overlooked a small red-maple swamp at the base of the mountain. I could hear a strong chorus of spring peepers drifting up from the temporary ponds within the swamp.

After taking this short break, I wandered over to a site where timber rattlesnakes and northern copperheads den and from which they normally emerge at about this time. I looked carefully in all the places where I had seen them before. A red-tailed hawk dropped out of the sky and landed in a tall oak not far from me. I tried not to move.

The bird didn't stay long, but I got the impression from the way it was scanning the talus slope that it might have been looking for snakes as well. I continued making my way along the edge of the loose rocks and entered the forest again. Blueberry buds were just beginning to open and, as I bent down to stare at one closely, a beautiful scene came into view.

Here, peering out from the thick layer of oak and hickory leaves, were the head and neck of an adult milk snake. It obviously had seen me long before I saw it, but the snake remained perfectly still. I stopped in midstoop and tried to take in every detail of its glossy head. My impression was that it must have recently shed its skin to be so shiny; its genus name means "shiny shield," obviously referring to what I saw.

I slowly inched myself back to a comfortable observation point. Carefully I searched for any other snakes and then quietly settled in to watch the milk snake. When I looked up, however, it was not in sight. Within a few seconds I heard the leaves rustling. I got a brief glimpse of its body through the leaves as it slid out of sight.

## How to Recognize Milk Snakes

### ADULTS

Milk snakes are brightly colored, smooth-scaled snakes that exhibit an almost bewildering series of variations over their range. Local and regional populations appear to maintain stable colors and patterns, but differences are so great from one end of their range to another that at least nine different subspecies are recognized, all with distinctive names such as scarlet king snake, red milk snake, and eastern milk snake.

Common color forms include a gray or tan base color with numerous black-bordered copper or red blotches on the back, alternating with similar, though smaller, marks on the sides. Another common pattern in milk snakes is bright, wide red (or orange) bands divided by narrow, black-bordered yellow bands.

The tremendous variation found among the milk snakes may cause some confusion when trying to tell them apart from closely related king snakes. Take into account the milk snake's range, its overall bright colors (some king snakes are basically black), and its lack of stripes (found only on some king snakes).

Milk snakes are commonly mistaken for venomous species. Some populations look very similar to copperheads (which have brown or tan bodies with chestnut saddles), while others resemble coral snakes (which have red and yellow bands touching each other, rather than separated by black as in the milk snake).

Milk snakes are members of the common snake family, the Colubridae. The genus *Lampropeltis,* comprising the king snakes, includes about nine species found from Canada to northern Venezuela, of which the milk snake is one. All king snakes are glossy, smooth animals that have highly variable patterns and feed primarily on rodents, lizards, birds, and snakes.

## DISTINGUISHING THE SEXES

Males tend to grow longer than females. Measurements indicate that females rarely grow to more than three and a half feet, while males commonly grow to four and beyond. Males also tend to have longer tails that taper more gradually from the body. Females have shorter tails and show a slight but obvious constriction near the cloaca.

## EGGS AND YOUNG

Three to twenty oval-shaped eggs are deposited beneath boards or logs, or in sawdust piles, wood chips, compost, or sand. The eggs, about an inch and three-quarters long by three-quarters of an inch wide, are smooth and white and sometimes adhere to each other, possibly due to body fluids extruded with them.

Several females may lay their eggs in the same location, with all the eggs clustered together. While there is no indication of a nest's being built, the actions of the female may produce a small chamber in which the eggs will be deposited.

Newly hatched milk snakes are particularly attractive, their color pattern bright and vibrant. At hatching, normally in August or September, they are seven to ten inches long. A tiny egg tooth on the tip of their snout enables the young to slice out of the egg.

## How to Find Milk Snakes

**Habitat:** Terrestrial; deciduous
forests, semiarid grasslands,
pine forests, rocky slopes,
coastal dunes, suburban yards,
and rural farm buildings
**Months of Activity:** Year-
round (South and desert areas);
mid-April to October (North
and higher elevations)

*Range of the
milk snake*

Milk snakes are woodland animals, though they can also be found
in fields, meadows, and power-line cuts and around buildings,
even in relatively urban areas. They frequent deciduous forests,
southern pine plantations, bog forests of the far North, sand
plains, and dunes. They are also known to be found in central
prairies, hummocks, and rocky hillsides. Milk snakes range into
northern South America, where they live in and around tropical
rain forests.

Foraging milk snakes are rarely encountered during the daytime, and even then they are so well camouflaged that the chance
of seeing one is small at best. At night, they hunt for small rodents
or lizards in many different places. You might sit quietly in an old
shed or around barns, brush piles, or other mounds of debris
where rodents abound. Use a flashlight to search along the walls,
corners, and holes in the wood for the snakes.

An active method of locating milk snakes is to go to any likely
area and start turning over boards and logs. Rummaging through
abandoned buildings can be productive. Some coastal islands can
have astonishing numbers of milk snakes on them.

## What You Can Observe

SPRING ACTIVITY

In the northern regions and upper elevations of their range, milk snakes emerge in the spring perhaps a bit later than other species. It may be mid- to late April before any are noticed at all, though in the South and in tropical areas milk snakes are active every month of the year.

Milk snakes do not appear to bask as openly as other species of snakes. They commonly remain in leaf litter that is exposed to the sun, though the snakes themselves are particularly difficult to see.

### TERRITORIAL BEHAVIOR

There is no indication that milk snakes maintain and defend territories from other individuals of the same species. The home range of individual snakes is not known, but it is expected to be several acres.

### COURTSHIP AND MATING

For several weeks after emerging from their dens, milk snakes search out mates. Once a pair is in close range, the male tries to crawl alongside the female and occasionally wraps a loose coil around her body. The male will crawl over and under the female and attempt to lift her tail off the ground.

When the female is ready to mate she lifts her tail off the ground. In the final phase of courtship, a male milk snake may reach over and grasp the head or neck of the female in his mouth and maintain a hold on her for the length of time the two are actually copulating. Whether milk snakes exhibit this behavior regularly is not known.

### BREEDING

Female milk snakes are known to gather together at communal egg-laying sites early in the summer. Often several clutches will be deposited within a few inches of each other. The significance of this behavior is unclear. It may simply be due to a lack of suitable egg-laying sites.

Most eggs are deposited in late June or early July. It is believed that a female lays only a single clutch of eggs in a year, but it is not known if she reproduces annually or requires two years to produce

*Female milk snake with recently deposited eggs*

a new clutch of eggs. It is suspected that larger females deposit more and larger eggs than smaller females, though this has not been looked at closely.

### LIFE OF YOUNG SNAKES

Milk snakes hatch in August or September, about three to four months after the eggs are deposited. Almost nothing is known of the early life of young milk snakes. They can be found in a variety of habitats, including pond and bog margins. How often they feed, if at all, before their first winter is unknown. In northern areas the newborn milk snakes may have all they can do to locate a suitable den site before winter sets in and consequently have little or no opportunity to feed.

### TAIL-VIBRATING

A common behavior of milk snakes is the rapid vibration of the tip of the tail when confronted by a potential predator or other threats. Some field biologists speculate that the sound produced, because of its similarity to that of a rattlesnake, may in fact cause predators to pause, at least long enough for the milk snake to escape to safety. Others suggest that the sound is more similar to that of fast-chirping insects and thus may lure potential prey closer to the milk snake, who can then ambush it. Unfortunately, there are too few long-term field observations of this behavior for any statement to be more than conjecture.

FOOD AND FEEDING

Throughout their range, milk snakes show a strong preference for small mammals, especially rodents such as chipmunks and mice. They are also known to prey upon birds, lizards, slugs, birds' eggs, small fish, beetles, other insects, snakes, and snake eggs.

Like most members of its genus, milk snakes seem to have some natural immunity to North American pit-viper venoms. While all king snakes are known to eat rattlesnakes and copperheads, milk snakes are less known for this behavior. However, there is no reason to believe that some individuals, found where the poisonous snakes exist, don't eat them as well. The list of other snakes that milk snakes are known to consume is large, and includes water, garter, brown, green, worm, and ringneck snakes, in addition to copperheads and timber rattlesnakes.

Milk snakes kill their prey by constriction, often wrapping several tight coils around them. The length of time involved in subduing prey is highly variable. No doubt this sometimes results in either the prey's escaping or even in serious damage to the snake during the encounter.

OTHER FACTS ABOUT MILK SNAKES

As noted, the wide variation in the patterns of milk snakes results in their commonly being misidentified as copperheads in some parts of their range while in others they are mistaken for coral snakes. The milk snake's patterns are clearly similar to those of these other two species; mimicry seems to be a likely and obvious explanation. There are many harmless species of snakes that

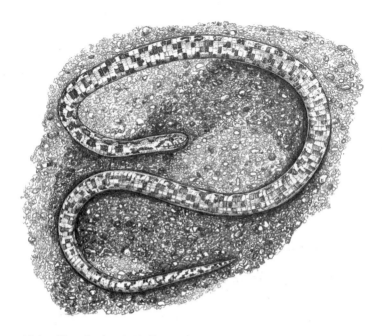

*Adult milk snake showing belly pattern*

appear, even under careful scrutiny, nearly identical to a local venomous snake. But there are few snakes in the world, other than milk snakes, who have such a wide range and variable pattern as to be able to match two different models.

### OVERWINTERING

In upland areas, milk snakes have been seen to migrate in September and October up mountainsides, where they then linger around the rocky crevices they prefer for den sites. In these areas they are sometimes found with copperheads, racers, rattlesnakes, and other species. In southern, western, and lowland places, milk snakes may simply enter mammal burrows, limestone crevices, or turtle dens to spend the coldest part of the winter.

Overall, milk snakes are not known to be particularly communal. Rarely are more than a few individuals found close to one another.

## Quick Reference Chart

**Length of Breeding Season:** Late April to May

**Eggs Deposited:** Up to 20 elliptical eggs deposited, sometimes communally, in June and July

**Eggs Hatch:** Incubation about 2 months; hatching in August or September

**Age and Size at Sexual Maturity:** About 3 years; about 1½–2 feet in length

**Lifespan of Adults:** At least 7 years; perhaps up to 10 or 15 years

*Adult hognose snake, hood inflated*

# EASTERN HOGNOSE SNAKE /

*Heterodon platyrhinos*

Sᴇᴠᴇʀᴀʟ ɪɴᴄɪᴅᴇɴᴛs come immediately to mind when conversation turns to hognose snakes. Once a couple of friends of mine rushed to my house to tell me, with great excitement, about a hognose they had just seen. It was the first one that either of them had ever seen, and they eagerly reported all the details of the encounter, including the textbook bluffing and playing-dead behaviors. Their enthusiasm is reminiscent of most people's encounters with a hognose snake—nobody leaves unimpressed.

So it was for me while staring out the kitchen window one warm, late spring afternoon. A slight movement caught my eye. There was a brilliantly patterned adult hognose snake slowly moving around the house. I went out to watch more closely. The three-foot-long snake continued to crawl about the foundation, its thick, black tongue flicking intermittently. Occasionally it lifted its head several inches out of the grass. On the couple of instances when I approached too closely, it would lift its head, suck in air, hiss audibly, and sometimes spread the skin at the base of its head and neck into a wide, impressive hood.

Not too many weeks later, someone stopped by with a small coffee can wanting to know if the snake inside was dangerous. When I peeked in, I was pleased to see a newborn hognose, because young ones seem particularly difficult to find. When I lifted it out, it went through most of the behaviors that the species is so well known for. Though I have had a number of encounters with this and closely related species, I never fail to enjoy them.

## How to Recognize Eastern Hognose Snakes

ADULTS

One key characteristic to look for in these relatively thick-bodied snakes is the pointed snout that turns upward at the tip. There are three species of hognose snakes in North America, all of which have fairly wide heads and upturned noses. The color of individual hognose snakes is variable, and this makes distinguishing them from other types of snakes a bit difficult. Eastern hognose snakes can be solid black, gray, or brilliant yellow-green with dark blotches and spots on their back and sides. Snakes with a pattern normally show a series of up to thirty large dark spots running down the length of the back. These alternate with a row of similar-sized spots along the sides. All hognose snakes have strongly keeled scales, normally quite visible from a short distance.

Hognose defense behavior, which includes hissing, flattening the neck, and lifting the forward part of the body off the ground, will be ample to identify them. Throughout their range, hognoses are among the few snakes that actually hiss.

The southern hognose (*Heterodon simus*), found in the south-eastern part of the United States, has a distinguishing series of large spots running down the center of its back, alternating with much smaller spots on either side. The western hognose (*Heterodon nascius*) of the west-central part of the continent, also has large spots down the midline of the body. On their sides, however, western hognose snakes have two rows of alternating spots.

Adult eastern hognose snakes can grow to be almost four feet in total length, though most encountered are just over two feet long. The eastern hognose is in the family Colubridae, the nonvenomous snakes, which includes nearly two-thirds of all the known species of snakes in the world.

## DISTINGUISHING THE SEXES

Female hognose snakes can have very robust bodies and short, tiny tails compared to males. Females also tend to grow to a longer total length than do males. In many hognose-snake populations studied there seems to be a slight, but noticeable, preponderance of males. This does not appear to be due to differences in mortality of the sexes or to their ability to be found, but to an actual population bias in favor of males.

## EGGS AND YOUNG

An enormous range in the number of eggs deposited by a single female has been reported, from four to sixty. Typically, clutches contain from fifteen to thiry-five elliptical, thin-shelled, and whitish eggs. Each egg is about one and an eighth by three quarters of an inch, though there is much variation in egg size throughout the range of the species. The eggs are deposited under logs or rocks, in loose soil, or in rotting vegetation.

The six-to-eight-inch young are stout-looking, with an obvious, turned-up nose. Most have a distinct pattern of bands and marks on the back and sides.

## How to Find Hognose Snakes

**Habitat:** Terrestrial; sandy areas, woodlands, and fields
**Months of Activity:** Year-round (South and coastal areas); from mid- to late April to late September or October (North)

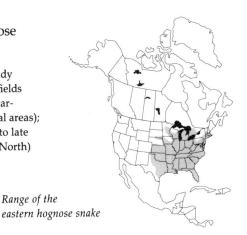

*Range of the
eastern hognose snake*

Hognose snakes are active during the warmer parts of the year in any given locality. They have been seen as early as the end of

*Eastern Hognose Snake*  /  335

March in some southerly locations but not until the end of April in the North. They generally begin to disappear in the autumn, but in the gulf states some hognose snakes may be active throughout the year.

The clear preference for sandy soils is an important clue in your search for hognose snakes. You can find them in such diverse areas as dry oak woodlands, red-pine plantations, sand dunes, grasslands, coastal woodlands, and open beaches. They have even been observed swimming in the surf.

Different populations of hognose snakes seem to be active at different times of the day. Accounts indicate that this species can be day-active, nocturnal, or crepuscular (active at dawn or dusk). During the cooler spring and autumn hognose snakes are most active late in the morning, while during hot summers they move only early in the morning and again late in the afternoon. Their preferred body temperature ranges from 85° to 88° F.

## What You Can Observe

### SPRING ACTIVITY

Little is known about the behaviors and daily movements of the eastern hognose over much of its range. Details of their seasonal movements and many other facets of their daily lives are still relatively unstudied. It is believed that males search out females shortly after emerging in the spring, as mating has been observed in early spring.

### TERRITORIAL BEHAVIOR

Little is known about this aspect of the lives of hognose snakes. It is likely that individuals remain within a given home range, but the extent of this is unstudied. Occasionally, several individuals are found close to each other, giving the impression that other hognose snakes are tolerated and perhaps that home ranges broadly overlap.

## COURTSHIP AND MATING

Courtship and mating in hognose snakes has been described only in vague terms. Actual mating occurs in April and May, and very likely again in the autumn. Female hognoses, like most snakes, are able to store sperm for weeks or months before fertilizing their eggs. This enables females to produce viable young later in the season in response to poor environmental conditions (such as food scarcity or cold temperatures).

## BREEDING

Female hognose snakes lay their eggs in June (in the southern parts of their range) and July or August (in the North). Females deposit their entire clutch in a single location. Though they have pliable and somewhat wet shells, the eggs do not adhere to each other as they do in some snakes. Females do not build a nest, but several observations of captive snakes indicate that hognose snakes may excavate a small depression in sand. Except for one or two observations, female hognose snakes do not seem to remain with their eggs.

*Black color form
of eastern hognose snake*

Young hatch from the end of July to early September, from thirty-nine days to two months after the eggs are deposited. Hatchlings must slash their way out of the egg with the egg tooth on the tip of the snout. Close observations have been made only on captive eggs and young, but it seems to take the young a long time (from many minutes to several days) to work themselves completely free of the egg.

Eventually, their entire body emerges from the wilted remains of the egg. The young are then entirely on their own. Immediately upon hatching, young hognose snakes can admirably perform the entire set of visual and auditory displays that are so well known in adults.

## FOOD AND FEEDING

Hognose snakes are relatively slow-moving animals, and the few field observations of them feeding in natural conditions indicate that their approach to prey is no exception. Fast-moving prey generally can escape from a hognose relatively easily. However, the mild toxin and stealth of a hognose compensate for this shortcoming in speed.

It is widely known that the hognose is a specialist in eating toads; it has evolved at least a couple of adaptations that help it excel at this. Toads, of course, have plenty of defenses themselves, including two in particular that work well for most other predators. The first is behavioral—most toads can inflate their bodies widely, making them impossible to swallow for many potential predators. The second defense is chemical—the warts on the backs of toads are glands containing fairly powerful toxins that make the toads bad-tasting at best, deadly at worst.

Most observations suggest that the hognose snake takes care of the first problem with a pair of enlarged teeth at the rear of the mouth, used to puncture the inflated frog's skin, lungs, or both. Critical laboratory observations do not necessarily show this to be true, however, except in rare cases. Typically, a toad remains inflated until the snake completely swallows it, or the power of the snake's jaws alone is enough to deflate the toad.

Hognose snakes also secrete a mild venom from glands near the enlarged teeth. This venom can actually subdue the prey, or it may somehow counteract the toxins produced by the toads.

Hognose snakes do eat animals other than toads, such as lizards, other snakes, birds, and small mammals. The few food studies that have been done on eastern hognose snakes, however, indicate a clear preference for toads. Prey is not constricted, but simply grabbed and swallowed.

### VISUAL AND AUDITORY DISPLAYS

Since most snakes, by far, see you long before you see them, your first encounter (as well as most of the subsequent ones) is likely to cause the hognose to go into some phase of its defensive behaviors. There are several stages to this, each more amazing to witness than the one just completed.

By taking in air, the hognose is able to inflate its body and become much larger in diameter than it appeared just a few seconds earlier. This helps it present an imposing figure, especially since the animal is quite stout anyway. Often, hognose snakes will

*Portraits of a hognose snake*

follow this behavior with one or more loud hisses, audible several yards away. For potential predators, such as foxes or raccoons, this might be enough to cause them at least to pause in their attack.

While all snakes can lift their heads up off the ground, the hognose seems to take this to an impressive extreme, in spite of its thick, heavy-bodied appearance. It can lift its head several inches to a foot or so in the air, bringing it eye to eye with many potential predators. Following this the snake spreads the skin on its neck, giving an observer the impression that its head is several times the diameter that it was a few moments earlier.

Further hognose defensive behaviors include mouth-gaping and lunging the head and neck forward in a mock or actual bite. The snake's actions seem directed at frightening away the potential predator, since they rarely make contact.

Lingering presence of a predator may cause the snake to continue its array of behaviors. When all else fails, the snake may actually wave its head, neck, and the part of its body above the ground for a few moments, let its tongue droop down from its mouth, and then collapse upside down into a loose, limp coil. The snake will remain in this position for many minutes, certainly as long as the danger is still nearby. Eventually, it may turn its head, apparently to look about, and, if all seems safe, will right itself and go on its way.

### OTHER FACTS ABOUT HOGNOSE SNAKES

Some of the earliest reports of hognose snakes sent back to Europe by colonial naturalists indicated that this was another poisonous species found in America. No doubt the defensive behaviors of this snake misled people then as now. But some early descriptions detailed varying, and sometimes quite serious, reactions from a hognose bite, not unlike those from known venomous snakes.

Close examination of the anatomy of hognose snakes reveals that they do indeed possess a mild toxin that can induce a reaction in people, other mammals, and other animals. The gland that supplies the venom sends its contents directly to the sheath surrounding the base of enlarged teeth at the rear of the mouth. These elongated teeth are not hollow, but the toxin flows down them and into a puncture they cause.

OVERWINTERING

Hognose snakes begin to move to overwintering sites from early September (in the North) to late October or November (in the South). During warm periods in winter, hognose snakes have been found out and active in some of the gulf states and perhaps also in interior states.

There seems to be no marked concentration of hognose snakes at overwintering den sites. Sites may simply be beneath debris (in southern areas), or the snakes may seek out deeper crevices.

---

## Quick Reference Chart

**Length of Breeding Season:** April and May
**Eggs Deposited:** 4–60 (typically 15–35) elliptical eggs deposited in loose bark or soil, in June and July
**Eggs Hatch:** Incubation between 40 and 60 days, hatching mostly in August
**Age and Size at Sexual Maturity:** 3 years for both sexes; 1–2 feet in length
**Lifespan of Adults:** At least 5 years

*Pair of adult black racers*

# BLACK RACER / *Coluber constrictor*

O<small>N A HOT</small> summer afternoon a friend and I were walking along a trail that wound through a thick growth of honeysuckle shrubs and poison ivy. We could feel the coolness of the ocean just past the next dune. Greenhead flies were not bothering us too badly so we slowly sauntered along.

Because of the time of day we didn't really expect to see or hear too many things, though male yellowthroats were calling and a bobwhite whistled from the distant pitch pines. Shortly we heard a loud squawking from the shrubs; some of the sounds we recognized as those of catbirds. We moved closer and could see the branches waving wildly about. It was difficult to see more until we crouched down for a better angle.

First two, then a third, and finally a fourth catbird were dashing in and out of the shrubbery. The object of their attention was an adult black racer. We did not see a nest but assumed that was the reason the snake was there. The catbirds, obviously distressed, were flying within inches of the snake, flaring their tails and wings and vocalizing. The snake moved very slowly, its head and neck extended to examine several branches before proceeding further. It seemed relatively unperturbed by the birds. On a couple of occasions, one or two catbirds actually grabbed the skin of the snake and pulled.

Eventually the racer moved down out of the shrub and disappeared into the poison ivy. The birds kept up with it for a few yards before dispersing over the field.

## How to Recognize Black Racers

### ADULTS

These are strikingly beautiful snakes with glossy, smooth-textured scales. They seem to shine in the sunlight, and at the right angle a lovely iridescence can be seen. Racers in the East tend to be solid black in color, while western racers are tan, greenish, or have a yellow hue. Beneath, most racers are light gray. Most have extensive white markings on their lips and chins. They can grow to be about six feet in total length, although most encountered are at least two feet shorter.

Racers look similar to other large, dark snakes. The presence of faint but distinguishable ridges on the central back scales of the black ratsnake (*Elaphe obsoleta*) will distinguish them. Indigo snakes (*Drymarchon corais*) are much larger, more stout, and usually have a tinge of red on their heads and throats.

### DISTINGUISHING THE SEXES

Females tend to grow to greater total lengths than males in any given population. Their tails are shorter than the males' and have a somewhat obvious indentation at the base. In several locales studied, males are more numerous than females.

### EGGS

Up to twenty-five elliptically shaped eggs are normally buried inside rotting logs, compost piles, or wood chips, or beneath rocks and logs. Eastern racers tend to have more eggs per clutch (about eighteen, on the average) than do western (about six).

The whitish eggs have a distinct roughness caused by small nodules on the surface. They are about an inch and a quarter long and almost an inch wide. The eggs are very pliable at first and then become fairly brittle.

Newborn racers are about a foot long at hatching and radically different in color and pattern from the adults. Rather than having a solid, relatively unmarked body, young racers are boldly patterned with wide blotches running the length of the back and smaller markings on the side. Their basic color is gray; the markings are brown or red. Typically, they have a gray, unmarked tail. By their third year, when they have reached two and a half feet in length, the juvenile pattern fades and the adult coloration becomes obvious.

## How to Find Black Racers

**Habitat:** Terrestrial; most common in open forests, near pastures; also prairies, overgrown fields, dunes, rocky hillsides
**Months of Activity:** Year-round (South and coastal areas); March and April to October and November (central plains and North)

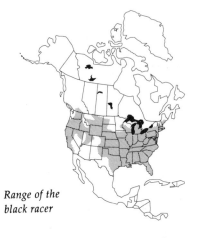

*Range of the black racer*

Racers appear to be very much diurnal animals, sunning themselves on rocks, shrubs, or pavement quite early in the morning. It is easiest to find them in early spring before they have dispersed from their denning areas. Here they linger for several days, at least, and may be found sunning, moving, and perhaps mating.

Use binoculars to scan any likely locations. Racers have good eyesight and often remain perfectly still while waiting for you to pass. If you blunder too close to one you are likely to get an idea of the origin of their common name. With incredibly swift and powerful movements, a racer can seemingly glide over the roughest terrain and disappear into an underground crevice before it is possible to get much more than a quick glimpse of it.

If this occurs, simply sit down and make yourself comfortable. Commonly, the snake will reappear, often within just a few minutes, to look around. It is hard not to imagine that the racer is searching for signs of you or other potential danger, and this attention from a snake is somewhat refreshing.

Another way to find racers is by driving slowly along roads that bisect their preferred habitats. Many racers are killed along highways where they either cross or linger to bask early in the morning.

## What You Can Observe

### SPRING ACTIVITY

Racers begin to appear on the surface near their wintering sites in late March in southern and western areas or from early April to early May in the North.

Don't be surprised if you come across a racer in the spring who does not scurry away at your approach. Many people have had the experience of encountering a racer that not only stands its ground but may even advance a few yards in a person's direction. This activity may be associated with spring courtship and mating and is possibly a method used by the snake to drive intruders out of its immediate area.

### TERRITORIAL BEHAVIOR

Most racers migrate away from their den sites within several weeks of emerging. Distances traveled vary, but some have been found two to three miles away, where they set up summer feeding territories. Males tend to set up summer areas farther away from dens than do females.

The size of the home range varies considerably in individual racers. It can be as much as seven and a half acres or as small as a fifth of an acre. In addition, many snakes change their summer patterns and leave intermittently to establish new home ranges, or may not appear to stay in any one area for a given length of time. Racer home ranges widely overlap. There does not appear to be any defense of their area against other racers.

*Adult black racer in typical sunning posture*

Field studies have confirmed that at least some black racers will return to the same summer territories that they occupied the previous year. How they find these locations and what mechanisms they use for navigating are unknown at present.

### COURTSHIP AND MATING

Young and nonbreeding females apparently do not linger at the den sites when they emerge in the spring, but rather move right along to summer territories. Males seek out and follow the pheromone scent left by mature females as they emerge. Adult racers probably mate within the first several weeks after emerging since they disperse to summer ranges shortly afterward.

Males attempt to lie alongside the female and crawl over and under her. At least one observer has seen the male biting the female's neck just prior to mating. When ready, the female will allow the male to lift the base of her tail and copulate. Little is known about how often males will mate or if females will mate with other males. Racers appear to mate only in the spring.

Females who are filled with developing eggs tend to remain in much smaller home ranges than young females. There is some evidence that they will aggregate with other females also ready to deposit eggs. Racers throughout their range begin egg-laying in early summer, some four weeks to two months after mating. At least in some areas, female racers seek out small mammal burrows in which to deposit their eggs. Typically, these are found in old fields and meadows, especially near stone walls, abandoned buildings, and brush piles, where there is an abundance of mammals. Other females deposit their eggs in depressions under logs or stones, or within leaf litter. Up to twenty-five eggs are extruded one at a time until the entire clutch is deposited.

Females may linger around the eggs for a day or two, but they provide no care. Due to drying conditions, damage, and predation, one study suggested that half of the eggs are destroyed during the incubation period. Those embryos that do survive hatch in August or September.

## LIFE OF YOUNG RACERS

Like many snakes born late in the summer or early autumn, newly hatched black racers must find their way to den sites on

*Juvenile pattern of black racer*

their own. Typically, young animals reach the dens days or even weeks after the adults. Since the young have been found to follow the scent trails of adult racers, this is one possible explanation for how they find their way without any previous experience.

FOOD AND FEEDING

Young black racers eat a variety of prey, including insects such as crickets and grasshoppers. They will investigate dead animals carefully with the tongue before eating them. When confronting live, mobile prey, black racers seem to be stimulated to attack by the movement of the prey and will move forward, often with jerking motions. Of course, some prey animals, including mammals, reptiles, and insects, will often run short distances and freeze. When confronted with this, racers, especially young animals, seem not to be able to locate the animals and exhibit rather random, searching movements. If they bump into the prey and get it moving again, they will continue their advance and strike. Racers actually appear to be more successful in capturing moving prey.

In some parts of their range, racers consume a large number of other reptiles, including snakes. In fact they are known to eat rattlesnakes and copperheads, though the extent of this is not well documented. The fact that these snakes are commonly found in close range of one another and often share the same den sites suggests that the racer's predation on other snakes is relatively limited.

OTHER FACTS ABOUT BLACK RACERS

When cornered, racers typically try to escape and will do their utmost to disappear from view. They often climb into shrubs or small trees to escape or hunt. When they are suddenly approached or their escape route is cut off, however, racers will defend themselves by raising the forward part of their body off the ground. This is accompanied by vigorous striking movements, often with the mouth wide open, and a rapid tail vibration.

The sound of the tail slapping against dried leaves, rocks, or even their own bodies is quite audible and very reminiscent of the sound made by rattlesnakes. The fact that racers are often found in places that rattlesnakes exist is probably no coincidence, but much more detailed field observation must be made to determine if an auditory mimicry is involved here.

Black racers in the field seem to prefer to maintain their body temperature between 90° and 92° F.

### OVERWINTERING

As the weather turns colder, racers migrate, usually up forested slopes, to reach communal and historic den sites. Racers often linger for several weeks around the openings to den sites in the fall. They are believed to shed their skins prior to disappearing into the dens, but this does not always happen. Typically, racers overwinter near other species of snake, including copperheads, western and timber rattlesnakes, and striped whipsnakes.

There is little information available on how they are able to orient and navigate back to the dens each year, but some individuals use the same site each fall and winter. Several field studies indicate that a large proportion of a winter den population returns to the same den in the fall.

Racers have been found overwintering alone or in small groups, sometimes adjacent to large denning areas. Body temperatures taken of overwintering racers inside den sites indicate that they maintain a slightly higher temperature than the surrounding air. All snakes are able to move about underground during the winter; this may allow them some measure of safety from shifts in rocks, attacks by mammalian predators, or temperature changes that might occur.

At some den sites, populations of black racers have increased dramatically, often at the same time that other species decrease. One explanation might be that reduced competition for food and other resources allows the racers to increase their populations. It is unclear what causes the other species to decline, but it is not likely to be due directly to the behavior or activities of racers.

## Quick Reference Chart

**Length of Breeding Season:** From April to June
**Eggs Deposited:** Up to 25 eggs deposited in June or July
**Eggs Hatch:** Incubation about 2 months; hatching normally in August and September
**Age and Size at Sexual Maturity:** 2 years at the earliest, 3 more common; about 2 feet in length
**Lifespan of Adults:** Estimated up to 15 years

*Adult northern copperhead basking in spring*

# NORTHERN COPPERHEAD /
*Agkistrodon contortrix*

EVERY SPRING I take a short drive to a lovely mountain—a hill, really, by geologic standards—to look for the first copperheads of the year as they emerge from five months spent dormant beneath the basalt rock outcrops. They have been underground since last October, when their bodies, draped about the autumn leaves, provided an indescribable mix of color and texture. In the first warm days of late April, when last year's leaves are bleached to a pale brown and tan, it always impresses me how well the snake's body still matches its rocky forest habitat.

When a copperhead comes into view—perhaps just the sunlit edge of a coil pressing out from a rock crevice in the late afternoon, or a light yellow-pink snout and chin at the entrance of a den— the feeling is one of awe. This is a magnificent animal who is somehow surviving, though suburbia and second homes are constantly growing up on the periphery of its territory.

The copperhead is almost unknown. It is the nearby rattle-snakes that usually get the attention. This may be partly the reason why copperheads have held on so well; few people know they're around. On warm, sunny April afternoons, I love to sit near the snakes, watch some of the hawks return from Central America, and enjoy the woodland wildflowers that grow nearby. It is a rare but welcome event when I can recognize an individual from the previous year and know that at least this one made it through another winter.

## How to Recognize Northern Copperheads

### ADULTS

These snakes are called copperheads because they have a solid, unmarked, coppery-colored head. They have reddish brown, coppery bodies with darker reddish brown saddles along their back. Relatively thick-bodied, copperheads have keeled scales that give them a rough-looking texture.

As a member of the pit-viper family, copperheads have a temperature-sensitive pit organ on each side of the head, located between the eye and nostril.

There are several snakes in North America that look superficially like copperheads. Each lacks one or more of the following characteristics, however, all of which the copperhead possesses: a pit between the eye and the nostril, red or pink tongue, noticeable ridges on each scale, and a single row of scales beneath the tail. Copperheads can grow to be just over four feet in length, though most snakes in natural situations rarely reach three feet.

Copperheads are members of the pit-viper family, Viperidae, all of whom have curved, hollow fangs that can be rotated and venom glands that supply a potent toxin. Copperheads are closely related to, and in the same genus as, the water moccasin (*Agkistrodon piscivorous*).

### DISTINGUISHING THE SEXES

As is typical of most snakes, males have longer tails than females. Females grow to greater total lengths, however, reaching just over four feet at the maximum, while males rarely reach that length.

### YOUNG COPPERHEADS

A range of two to ten snakelings, seven to ten inches long, are born alive, but within a transparent membrane, to an adult female. They work their way out of the membrane in just a few minutes. Newborns and juveniles tend to be grayer in color than adults, and they also have a remarkable sulphur yellow–tipped tail. This coloration fades as they get older and is gone by their third or fourth year.

## How to Find Northern Copperheads

**Habitat:** Terrestrial to semiaquatic; rocky, forested hillsides, various wetlands
**Months of Activity:** Year-round (South); April to October (North)

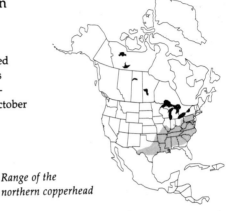

*Range of the northern copperhead*

Obviously, since these are poisonous snakes, all precautions and care should be taken around individuals and in areas that they inhabit. Most experienced field observers who watch venomous snakes have grown to understand that there is no need to push your luck or take chances. Most bites from venomous snakes occur when people become complacent about the potential danger and feel some dubious need to handle the snake. This is rarely done by professionals, despite what the media tends to highlight, and there is little reason for any of us to do so.

The easiest place to observe copperheads is definitely at or near their den sites in spring and autumn, when they are active in the daytime (in the heat of summer they become essentially nocturnal). These are usually rocky, wooded hillsides on the southern end of hills and mountains. Den sites are used for many years, perhaps indefinitely, so when you find a location you can expect to find the snakes, at least during two seasons, year after year. Usually some part of the population remains near the dens throughout the summer. It is always worth checking, no matter what month of the year you get out to look.

Each year, however, most copperheads migrate some distance, probably one or two miles, away from the den site. The best area to search for copperheads at the height of summer is near wetlands —wooded swamps and marshes—or lakes and reservoirs. Copperheads, though not as aquatic as their close relative the water moccasin, do show a slight preference toward wetlands, especially in the warmer parts of the year.

Other places that copperheads inhabit in the summertime are fields and meadows, wet woodlands, and quarries. In many parts of their range copperheads are active in the summer mainly at night, but in northern areas they usually can be observed during daylight hours, especially in the morning or late afternoon.

## What You Can Observe

### SPRING ACTIVITY

Copperheads begin to emerge from their den sites about the time that many birds of prey begin to return. In the northern edge of their range, this is about the middle of April; in southern and western areas, it may be as early as February or March. In the most southerly areas, copperheads may remain active every month of the year.

Sunning seems to be especially important in the spring and fall, and you can expect copperheads to be visible from late in the morning into the afternoon. Their body postures may have an effect on the heating and cooling of the snake's body and indicate delicate behavioral adjustments designed to keep the individual within a particular comfort range. Snakes in tight coils, for example, may heat up more quickly and to higher temperatures than snakes in loose coils, while snakes more or less stretched out may lose excess heat rapidly. Though the snakes may not be moving much, if at all, the slightly varied positions in which they put themselves indicate that they are finely tuned to their immediate environs.

Male copperheads have been observed in aggressive encounters during the spring and autumn mating seasons. Snakes will try to overpower each other, and one may even pin the other's body to the ground with coils or bends in its body. This behavior is known to occur in the presence of a female, but this is not always the case. Encounters between males may last for brief moments or longer than two hours.

These interactions often begin with two males' approaching each other and elevating the forward part of their body off the ground, as each begins swaying side to side. The object seems to be to attempt to get higher than the rival. One or the other will hook its neck and body partially around the raised body of the other, and this may cause one or both to drop to the ground. The snakes may continue to raise their bodies and sway until they completely entwine for almost their entire length. They may release and intertwine several times before one or the other leaves, almost always followed by the other. The snake that leaves first generally shows no further interest in the other.

Often, you will find several copperheads close to one another. Certainly this is true near the den sites, where the local population must share relatively few locations for sunning, courting, mating, eating, drinking, and avoiding predators, at least for a short period of time in the spring and fall. They can be found basking adjacent to and even touching timber rattlesnakes, milksnakes, black ratsnakes, and black racers, among others.

Copperheads are believed to migrate late in the spring to reach summer feeding territories, where they remain until reversing the migration early in the autumn. Recent field studies on other denning and migrating snakes indicate that those snakes that do leave the dens in the spring make a continuous and roughly circular migration away from and then back to the dens.

## COURTSHIP AND MATING

Most reports of copperhead mating behavior are made in the spring shortly after the snakes emerge from their winter dens.

However, there are ample reports of autumn courtship and mating as well, again near the den sites.

Several researchers have determined that males locate sexually active females by sensing with their tongues pheromones wafted through the air (tongue-flicking is a good indication of an alert and active copperhead). When a male senses a female he will approach her and begin moving his head or rubbing his chin on the ground. If the female moves away, the male will follow and attempt to move alongside and place his head on some part of her body. The female responds with a series of tail movements: slow back-and-forth waving; rapid back-and-forth whipping; or extremely rapid tail vibration.

A male will continue to rub his chin on the back and head of the female as he moves to align his body next to hers. This courtship may continue for an hour or more if the female does not respond. There is speculation that this may be one point at which females are making a choice as to a potential mate and that male courting behavior becomes an important process in sexual selection.

Once sufficiently stimulated, the female may lift and arch her tail and lower the scale that covers her cloaca. The male then arches his body and tail and everts one of his two sex organs and mates with the female. The two will remain together for varying lengths of time, though the range can be as much as three and a half to eight and a half hours.

This relatively long time when the two snakes are physically joined may serve several important functions. Since females mate with only one male at a time, a long mating lessens the number of other males that could possibly mate with her. During this period males may be producing a pheromone that makes females unattractive to other males. In fact, unmated males seem to pay little attention to females that are in the process of mating or have just mated.

Also, the female's interest in mating may be reduced after prolonged mating. In any case, females, following a successful mating, will show little interest or response to other males trying to initiate courtship behaviors. It is believed they will not mate with another male that year. Males begin searching for new females within twenty-four hours, though it is unknown what the percentage of multiple matings is in free-ranging populations.

BREEDING

A number of pregnant females who will be giving birth late in the summer or early in autumn do not leave the den areas in the spring. Females who will be giving birth late in the season tend to gather together in areas called *birthing rookeries,* which may be at their winter dens or sometimes up to a mile away. Lingering at or near the den, to which the newborn young must return shortly after birth, eliminates the need for a long and presumably dangerous migration for the newborn that would arise if she had migrated some distance away.

Female copperheads give birth in August or September. These births may be the result of a mating that occurred the previous spring or fall; storage and viability of sperm in the female's reproductive tract has been established. The few observations of birth in wild, free-ranging copperheads indicate that birth occurs during daylight hours. During this time the female remains relatively motionless, lifting her tail slightly when she is ready to give birth to the next snakeling. All the young are born within an hour or so, after which the female offers no direct care.

LIFE OF YOUNG COPPERHEADS

At birth the newborn copperhead takes nourishment from egg yolk inside its body, but although it grows in size, it tends to lose weight. Some biologists believe that this makes it imperative for the young snake to find and capture some food before it overwinters, to ensure that it has enough energy reserves to last until spring.

Rarely recorded in nature, tail-luring is one of the most interesting behaviors that you may hope to observe in copperheads. It is confined to young animals, usually less than three years old, who are born with and retain a yellow tail tip. In some newborn snakes the color can be quite vivid, while in others and in older snakes it

*Newborn copperhead with yellow-tipped tail approaching a wood frog*

can become relatively obscure. The belief is that the snake wiggles its tail as a sort of lure to frogs or insects that might be looking for small, caterpillarlike prey. When the animal gets close enough, the copperhead can strike out and thus acquire its meal. Young copperheads are known to eat a variety of insect and vertebrate prey, but the role of the tail tip in procuring this food is still largely a matter of speculation.

FOOD AND FEEDING

Young copperheads eat much different foods than adults do, probably helping to reduce competition between them. Juveniles rely heavily on a large supply of insects, particularly caterpillars, for survival, while adults feed mostly on amphibians and mammals.

One researcher has found that a copperhead eats only about eight meals in a single growing season (totaling no more than 200 percent of the snake's body weight). This may be due to a combination of a slow metabolism (with the snake thereby requiring only a small amount of food) and the difficulty of finding prey. Females who are carrying young may not eat at all during the summer due to the growing embryos that take up a large volume of her body cavity.

OVERWINTERING

During September and October copperheads congregate, sometimes in large numbers, at winter den sites that are used annually. Individual snakes seem to return to the same den area for years. The den sites are normally situated on rocky hillsides and have a southerly exposure, insuring the maximum amount of sunlight in the spring and fall.

Copperheads linger at the entrance to the den for three weeks or more. They sun themselves from midmorning to late afternoon on bright days. When it is overcast or cool, they remain just inside their den entrances or tuck themselves into the leaf litter. Eventually, in response to continued declining temperatures, all copperheads work their way underground. How deep they go and what their activity is during the winter remains undocumented.

---

## Quick Reference Chart

**Length of Breeding Season:** April to May or August to
   September, or both
**Young Born:** 2–10 young born in August or September
**Gestation Period:** 3–9 months
**Age and Size at Sexual Maturity:** 4 years for both sexes;
   about 2 feet in length
**Lifespan of Adults:** At least 18 years

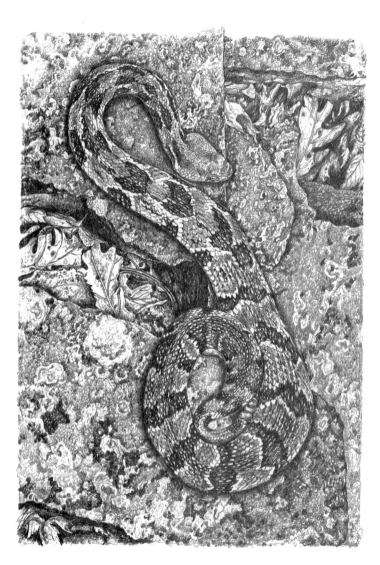

*Young timber rattlesnake basking*

# TIMBER RATTLESNAKE / *Crotalus horridus*

WHERE I GREW up stories of encounters with rattlesnakes were told often. There had always been some sort of population of timber rattlesnakes in the hills and mountains surrounding the broad river valley where I lived, and reports of their numbers ranged from thousands to millions. I figured it wouldn't be long before I got my chance at finding one. It wasn't until my first year of college, however, that I finally did.

A friend and I hiked up and around a hilltop where we had been many times before. It was early September, the day was sunny and warm, and many hawks were drifting by. We had been bush-whacking through the oak and hickory forest for hours. Near the uppermost ridge we came upon a service road that had originally been built in the late nineteenth century to haul tourists by a gravity-fed cable car to an opulent summit house. We followed it up as it cut through the basalt that forms the uppermost capping of many of the local hills.

It was in a jumbled pile of basalt rock that we saw our first rattlesnake. I had to stare for several seconds to make sure that it was in fact a snake that I was seeing. Its head and neck were exposed, while its body remained in the shadows beneath an overhanging rock. What impressed us most of all was its sheer bulk, especially compared to many of the common species that we were used to seeing. (In many parts of its range, the timber rattle-snake is the largest snake in the region.) As we approached the snake to take a photograph, it simply withdrew back into the crevice and disappeared completely from view. This was a week-end afternoon, and we both had to wait another week to get back there. When we did I learned a bit more about the autumn activi-ties of this species. With all the stealth and cunning we could muster, we inched over the fallen logs and briers at the edge of the road. The plan was to spot the rattlesnake before it spotted us. After several hours of climbing we were in place to view the exact location where the snake had been sitting a week earlier. No mat-ter how much we searched with binoculars, the rattlesnake was nowhere to be seen. We stood, examined every rock and crevice, and still came up empty. We walked up and down the road and into the woodland on either side. Suddenly, I looked down at my feet and there it was, coiled at the base of a small oak, within a yard of where it had been the week before. The rattlesnake, to its credit, was much calmer about the encounter than I—it never moved, never rattled, didn't even flick out its tongue.

Though I never did see that snake again, I have become quite familiar with many of the members of a dwindling population near my home. Local legends will have to be adjusted; there are less than a few dozen rattlesnakes left in these hills.

## How to Recognize Timber Rattlesnakes

### ADULTS

Timber rattlesnakes are very robust animals that can grow to a length of five feet or more, though the most commonly seen indi-viduals are usually much shorter. The distinctive rattle at the end of the tail is enough to distinguish this animal as a rattlesnake. Timber rattlesnakes, like other members of its family, Viperidae, have a temperature-sensitive opening, or pit, on each side of the face, between the eye and nostril. Their scales have obvious ridges running down their centers, giving the snake a relatively rough-skinned appearance.

Color patterns in the timber rattlesnake are extremely variable; some individuals are almost jet black, while others are a beautiful sulphur yellow with black, brown, or rust-colored blotches on the back and sides. Southern populations of timber rattlesnakes have a lovely chestnut stripe down the back.

The timber rattlesnake is distinguished from a dozen or so other North American species of rattlesnake by its range in the eastern two-thirds of the country, a lack of stripes or bands on its head and face, and a solid black tail. This is a medium-sized rattlesnake, the largest recorded being just over six feet in total length.

Rattlesnakes, with their specialized tail appendages, are found only in the New World.

## DISTINGUISHING THE SEXES

It is difficult to tell male and female timber rattlesnakes apart in the field from a safe distance. As with most snakes, males have longer tails than females. Late in summer, when they are filled with developing embryos, females can look especially massive and their short tail seemingly more so.

## YOUNG AT BIRTH

At birth timber rattlesnakes are nearly a foot in length. They emerge singly from the female, each encased in a transparent membrane. Within a few minutes the young force their way out of the membrane.

There is some variation in size at birth, including a small but significant difference between males and females. In general, males average just over a foot in length while females measure just under. Newborn rattlesnakes have a velvety texture, though their pattern is essentially the same as that of the adult.

## SHED SKIN

You may often be able to find the shed skins of timber rattlesnakes in and around the den site and also in the forestland surrounding it. The skins are frequently found at favorite sunning sites as well. They can be identified as rattlesnake skins because the tail does not come to a point as in all other snakes, but rather has a blunted and opened end.

The heavily keeled scales will be very obvious. The pattern that is left behind will also give you a good clue to the species and help to identify individual snakes that have any unusual patterns or injured scales. Be very sure the snake who just shed isn't still sitting there when you reach down to retrieve the skin.

### THE RATTLE

All rattlesnakes are so named because of the unique structure at the tip of their tail that, when vibrated, makes an extraordinary sound. Though the number of rattles, especially in free-ranging snakes, is variable, there are usually at least one or two there, making their tails different from the pointed tips of all other snakes in the country.

A rattlesnake adds a new rattle segment each time it sheds its skin. In natural situations, this occurs only once a year or twice in every three years on the average. Many-segmented rattles are rarely seen on wild snakes since they break off regularly.

## How to Find Timber Rattlesnakes

**Habitat:** Deciduous forests in rugged terrain; also, pine barrens and wetlands near mountains; occasionally fields and pastures
**Months of Activity:** From early April to November (South); from mid-May to mid-October (North)

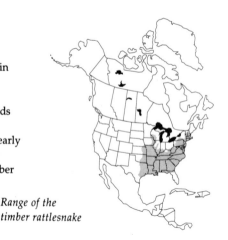

*Range of the
timber rattlesnake*

Most people interested in timber rattlesnakes concentrate their observations during the spring and fall when the snakes congregate at their dens. Here, one can observe a relatively high percentage of the population and watch any interactions and behaviors that occur. A word of caution, however, is in order. You may have to spend many hours observing timber rattlesnakes before you actually see any movement or action. At the dens they tend to spend much of their time sunning and resting. Still, you should be ready for anything to happen.

## What You Can Observe

### SPRING ACTIVITY

Timber rattlesnakes emerge from their winter den sites in April and May and linger in the area for several weeks. They can be found sunning themselves regularly (usually in the same spot), often with other rattlesnakes or other species nearby.

There is relatively little movement or feeding early in the spring, and the snakes may appear lethargic. They can be approached too closely, however, and will either rattle a warning or immediately retreat into the nearest crevice.

Timber rattlesnakes are active by day in the spring and autumn but may become nocturnal in the heat of midsummer, especially in southern and western populations.

### TERRITORIAL BEHAVIOR

After mating, most of the males and at least some of the females begin to migrate up to two or three miles from the den site (the home ranges of individuals can vary substantially).

There is some question as to whether the snakes actually set up summer feeding territories and remain within them for most of the summer, or if they continually move in a large, oval route that brings them eventually back to the den site early in the fall. There is little evidence to suggest that rattlesnakes defend summer feeding or resting sites from other rattlesnakes.

In the summer female timber rattlesnakes appear to prefer open forests or edges of fields where temperatures are higher than in surrounding locations. Males, on the other hand, seem to linger in thicker woods where the forest canopy is more completely covered.

### COURTSHIP AND MATING

Timber rattlesnakes are known to mate both in the spring and autumn. Males seem to be particularly active during courtship and are able to track females by a pheromone they leave behind.

*Yellow and black color forms of timber rattlesnake*

Courting males attempt to crawl along the length of the female and may engage in some chin rubbing. The pair may crawl over each other's bodies several times. If the female is ready to mate, she will lift the rear part of her body and tail off the ground slightly as the male maneuvers his tail around and under hers. Duration of actual mating is unknown.

### BREEDING

In the summer there may be a few lingering timber rattlesnakes at the dens. Most likely these are females who will be giving birth later in the year. On subsequent visits you might try to ascertain what particular sites an individual snake prefers or if there is a concentration of individuals in a certain area.

Some field researchers have found concentrations of gravid females in birthing rookeries some distance away from the winter den sites. It may be that these locations provide some important resource, such as a greater amount of heat or ample water.

At the highest estimates, just over half of all the females in a given population have young in any one year. In most locations, the proportion is probably lower than that. Certainly in northern latitudes and at the higher elevations where timber rattlesnakes are found, females give birth only every second or third year. Because gravid females generally fast for the summer and have little opportunity to eat in the autumn after giving birth, they may be under physical stress for some time and must use the next active season to restore their bodies.

If you follow enough of these females throughout the summer, or certainly year after year, you will eventually be rewarded with a view of the newborn young. The birth process is similar to that described for other live-bearing species of snakes. A female lifts her tail and the young are extruded, usually one at a time, within a minute or two of each other.

### LIFE OF YOUNG RATTLESNAKES

Five to nine young are born alive sometime between late August and mid-September. Each is equipped with venom, fangs, and a single, tiny rattle segment called a *button*. They remain near each other for a week or two and then shed their skins. Following this, the young have a tendency to move away from where they were born.

Because they are born in late summer, the young snakes must find suitable overwintering sites relatively quickly. Several interesting laboratory studies have shown that newborn timber rattlesnakes are able to detect the odors left by their mother or siblings, suggesting that newborn snakes, with no immediate knowledge of the distance or direction of a wintering den site, may actually follow a trail left by their mother.

## FOOD AND FEEDING

Field researchers have identified at least one method of hunting. The snake sits quietly for some time and then ambushes its prey when it moves within striking distance. Timber rattlesnakes attempting to feed this way coil their bodies next to a fallen log and rest their head or chin on the edge. They may actually be able to feel the vibration caused by a chipmunk or other small mammal that runs along the top, or they may sense the prey with their temperature-sensitive pit organs, or they may simply see something moving.

## OTHER FACTS ABOUT TIMBER RATTLESNAKES

Local legends continue to insist that there are millions of rattlesnakes in the hills. Unfortunately that isn't true today, if it ever was. Conservation groups around the country are beginning to focus their attentions on the plight of less glamorous threatened and declining populations of species. Several states have listed the timber rattlesnake and other snakes as endangered or threatened and display some interest in conserving them. Let's hope they are successful before the timber rattlesnake and others become nothing more than stories of long ago.

## OVERWINTERING

Concentrations of timber rattlesnakes occur in September and October around historic den sites. These dens usually are south-facing, rocky hillsides that provide late fall and early spring sunning locations and access to underground winter retreats. Historically, at least in some places, hundreds of timber rattlesnakes would gather and bask in the autumn sunlight. Today there are not very many locations that still claim such immense numbers since many colonies have been dramatically reduced or even eliminated.

Because of the difficulty in tracking them, very little is known about the characteristics of these underground refuges or the behavior of the snakes while they are there. However, at least one researcher, using radio telemetry, discovered that overwintering timber rattlesnakes initially showed a slowly declining body temperature in the autumn, reaching a low of about 40° F during most of the winter. In April their body temperature slowly increased to about 46° F and by mid-May was near 50° F. Snakes began moving about in their dens at this time and emerged for the first time shortly afterward.

## Quick Reference Chart

**Length of Breeding Season:** Typically May and June; sometimes in September or October
**Young Born:** Up to 14 young born alive in September
**Gestation Period:** 4–5 months
**Age and Size at Sexual Maturity:** About 5 months in males, 6–7 in females; about 2 feet in length
**Lifespan of Adults:** Estimated to be at least 10–15 years

# Appendix

## Amphibian and Reptile Watching—Special Sites and Resources

In North America, Georgia's *Okefenokee Swamp* has one of the highest concentrations of both amphibians and reptiles. The vast majority of the 400,000-acre area is protected as the Okefenokee National Wildlife Refuge, administered by the U.S. Fish and Wildlife Service. Sixty species of reptiles and thirty-seven different amphibians inhabit the pine and oak woods, cypress swamps, and floating prairies that make up much of Okefenokee. For a checklist of the amphibians and reptiles of the swamp and other natural history information, contact the Refuge Manager, Okefenokee National Wildlife Refuge, Route 2, Box 338, Folkston, Georgia 31537.

*Everglades National Park,* at the very southern tip of Florida, is a haven for many species of amphibians and reptiles. At least seventeen species of amphibian and forty-nine different reptiles live within its almost one and a half million acres. Species are found in the sawgrass prairies, tropical hardwood hummocks, freshwater sloughs, and mangrove swamps of the park. For details on the park and a checklist of species, write to the Park Superintendent, Everglades National Park, Box 279, Homestead, Florida 33030.

*Great Smoky Mountains National Park* in Tennessee and North Carolina has more species of salamanders than anyplace else. In total, there are thirty-seven different amphibian species and thirty-five species of reptiles within the half million acres of mountain forestland and streams. For general information write the Park Superintendent, Great Smoky Mountains National Park, Gatlinburg, Tennessee 37738.

The Sonoran desert, extending from southeastern California and southern Arizona into Mexico has a rich herpetofauna. Numerous federal, state, and city-owned parks provide visitors with ample opportunities to see many unique amphibians and reptiles, including nearly thirty species of snake alone. *Saguaro National Monument*, both east and west of Tucson, is one such park. Write to the Superintendent, Route 8, Box 695, Tucson, Arizona 85730, for maps, checklists, and other information.

The *Nature Conservancy* manages and protects many ecologically significant preserves throughout the country. Many of these are home to unique amphibians and reptiles, in addition to a generally rich complex of species that are indigenous to a particular locale. You can write to the staff for information on all their properties and access to them at their main office, Suite 800, 1800 North Kent Street, Arlington, Virginia 22209.

The *National Audubon Society* maintains wildlife sanctuaries in many states. Regional offices can give detailed information and lists of species found in particular spots. Write to their national office at 950 Third Avenue, New York, New York 10022, for complete details on the locations of their properties.

Many states have their own, independent Audubon Societies, and the natural-history staff of these nonprofit organizations can direct you within local areas. The *Massachusetts Audubon Society*, the first such group ever formed, has eighteen separate staffed nature centers and sanctuaries across the state. In addition, the society leads natural history tours throughout the world, some of them concentrating on herpetology. Their main office is at South Great Road, Lincoln, Massachusetts 01773.

Many states have their own statewide or regional herpetological societies where people with varying interests in amphibians and reptiles meet, often on a regular basis, to discuss particular subjects. News about most of them are included in the several publications of the *Society for the Study of Amphibians and Reptiles.* For information write to the current Regional Societies Editor, Stephen Hammack, Reptile Department, Dallas Zoo, 621 East Clarendon Drive, Dallas, Texas 75203. For general information about membership in the society, write to: Henri Seibert, Department of Zoological and Biomedical Sciences, Ohio University, Athens, Ohio 45701.

*In Search of Amphibians and Reptiles,* a recent book by Richard D. Bartlett (E.J. Brill 1988), is an exciting account of traveling to find common and rare species throughout North and South America. The book can direct you to more of the most herpetologically interesting places in this hemisphere.

Each state also has a department of fisheries and wildlife, conservation, or environmental protection. Get the address from your local library and write to ask for information about amphibians and reptiles and about the land the department manages. Check also with a local university, museum, or zoo for activities concerning amphibians and reptiles.

# Selected References

The following list of references includes only some of the more than 500 important or recent papers used during the preparation of this book. Numerous other papers were consulted but could not be listed here because of space limitations. Reading the "literature cited" sections of those that are included, however, will lead you to many of the earlier papers on any particular species.

## Amphibians and Reptiles

Behler, J. L., and F. W. King. 1979. *The Audubon Society field guide to North American amphibians and reptiles.* New York: Alfred A. Knopf.

Conant, R. 1975. *A field guide to reptiles and amphibians.* Boston: Houghton Mifflin.

Gibbons, W. 1983. *Their blood runs cold.* University, Ala.: University of Alabama Press.

Goin, C. J., and O. B. Goin. 1971. *Introduction to herpetology.* San Francisco: W. H. Freeman. 2nd ed.

Lazell, J. D., Jr. 1976. *This broken archipelago.* New York: Quadrangle.

Porter, K. R. 1972. *Herpetology.* Philadelphia: W. B. Saunders.

Rhodin, A. G. J., and K. Miyata, eds. 1983. *Advances in herpetology and evolutionary biology.* Cambridge, Mass.: Museum of Comparative Zoology.

Stebbins, R. C. 1966. *A field guide to western reptiles and amphibians.* Boston: Houghton Mifflin.

## Amphibians

Duellman, W. E., and L. Trueb. 1986. *Biology of amphibians.* New York: McGraw-Hill.

Goin, Coleman J., and Olive B. Goin. 1962. *Introduction to herpetology.* San Francisco: W. H. Freeman.

Hanken, J. 1989. Development and evolution in amphibians. *Am. Scientist* 77:336–43.

## Frogs

Altig, R. 1970. A key to the tadpoles of the continental United States and Canada. *Herpetologica* 26:180–207.

Crump, M. 1977. The many ways to beget a frog. *Natural History* 86:38–43.

Smith-Gill, S. J., and K. A. Berven. 1979. Predicting amphibian metamorphosis. *Am. Nat.* 113:563–85.

Taigen, E. L., and K. D. Wells. 1985. Energetics of vocalization by an anuran amphibian (*Hyla versicolor*). *J. Comp. Physiol.* B 155:163–70.

Wassersug, R. J. 1975. The adaptive significance of the tadpole stage with comments on the maintenance of complex life cycles in anurans. *Am. Zool.* 15:405–17.

———. 1984. Why tadpoles love fast food. *Natural History* 93:60–69.

Wells, K. D. 1986. The effect of social interactions on calling energetics in the gray treefrog (*Hyla versicolor*). *Behav. Ecol. and Sociobiol.* 19:9–18.

———. 1988. The effect of social interactions on anuran vocal behavior. In *The evolution of the amphibian auditory system.* New York: John Wiley & Sons.

## American Toad

Beiswenger, R. E. 1977. Diel patterns of aggregative behavior in tadpoles of *Bufo americanus,* in relation to light and temperature. *Ecology* 58:98–108.

Bider, J. R., and K. A. Morrison. 1981. Changes in toad (*Bufo americanus*) responses to abiotic factors at the northern limit of their distribution. *Am. Midland Nat.* 106:293–304.

Breeden, F., and C. H. Kelly. 1982. The effect of conspecific interactions on metamorphosis in *Bufo americanus. Ecol.* 63:1682–89.

Brockelman, W. Y. 1969. An analysis of density effects and predation in *Bufo americanus* tadpoles. *Ecol.* 50:632–44.

Brodie, E. D., Jr., and D. R. Formanowicz, Jr. 1983. Prey size preference of predators: Differential vulnerability of larval anurans. *Herpetologica* 39:67–75.

Fairchild, L. 1984. Male reproductive tactics in an explosive breeding toad population. *Am. Zool.* 24:407–18.

Fitzgerald, G. J., and J. R. Bider. 1974. Seasonal activity of the toad *Bufo americanus* in southern Quebec as revealed by a sand-transect technique. *Can. J. Zool.* 5:1–5.

Gatz, A. J., Jr. 1981. Non-random mating by size in American toads, *Bufo americanus*. *Animal Behavior* 29:1004–12.

Groves, J. D. 1980. Mass predation on a population of the American toad, *Bufo americanus*. *Am. Midland Nat.* 103:202–3.

Kruse, K. C. 1981. Mating success, fertilization potential, and male body size in the American toad (*Bufo americanus*). *Herpetologica* 37:228–33.

———. 1983. Optimal foraging by predaceous diving beetle larvae on toad tadpoles. *Oecologia* 58:383–88.

Licht, L. E. 1976. Sexual selection in toads. *Can. J. Zool.* 54:1277–84.

———. 1968. Unpalatability and toxicity of toad eggs. *Herpetologica* 24:93–98.

McNicholl, M. K. 1972. An observation of apparent death-feigning by a toad. *Blue Jay* 1972:54–55.

Oldham, R. S. 1966. Spring movements in the American toad, *Bufo americanus*. *Can. J. Zool.* 44:63–100.

Price, R. M., and E. R. Meyer. 1979. An amplexus call made by the male American toad, *Bufo americanus americanus*. *J. Herpetol.* 13:506–9.

Voris, H. K., and J. P. Bacon, Jr. 1966. Differential predation on tadpoles. *Copeia* 1966:594–98.

Waldman, B. 1985. Sibling recognition in toad tadpoles: Are kinship labels transferred among individuals? *Z. Tierpsychol.* 68:41–57.

Waldman, B., and K. Adler. 1979. Toad tadpoles associate preferentially with siblings. *Nature* 282:611–13.

Wilbur, H. M., D. I. Rubenstein, and L. Fairchild. 1978. Sexual selection in toads: The roles of female choice and male body size. *Evolution* 32:264–70.

Young, A. M. 1967. Predation in the larvae of *Dytiscus marginalis*. *Pan-Pacific Entomol.* 43:113–17.

*Eastern Spadefoot Toad*

Axtell, R. W. 1958 (1959). Female reaction to the male call in two anurans (Amphibia). *Southwestern Nat.* 3:70–76.

Ball, S. C. 1936. The distribution and behavior of the spadefoot toad in Connecticut. *Transac. Conn. Acad. Arts and Sciences* 32:351–79.

Bragg, A. 1965. *Gnomes of the night.* Philadelphia: Univ. Penn. Press.

Driver, E. C. 1936. Observations on *Scaphiopus holbrookii*. *Copeia* 1936:67–69.

Hampton, S. H., and E. P. Volpe. 1963. Development and interpopulation variability of the mouthparts of *Scaphiopus holbrooki*. *Am. Midland Nat.* 70:319–28.

Hansen, K. L. 1958. Breeding pattern of the eastern spadefoot toad. *Herpetologica* 14(2):57–67.

Moody, S. M. 1986. Geographic distribution, *Scaphiopus holbrooki*. *Herp. Rev.* 17(4):91.

Morin, P. J. 1985. Predation intensity, prey survival and injury frequency in an amphibian predator/prey interaction. *Copeia* 1985:638–44.

Neil, W. T. 1957. Notes on metamorphic and breeding aggregations of the eastern spadefoot, *Scaphiopus holbrooki*. *Herpetologica* 13:185–87.

Pague, C. A. 1983. Field notes. *Catesbeiana* 3:17.

Pearson, P. G. 1957. Further notes on population ecology of the spadefoot toad. *Ecol.* 38:580–86.

Prescott, R. 1978. Nature notes. *Cape Nat.* 7:35–37.

Richmond, N. D. 1947. Life history of *Scaphiopus h. holbrooki*. Part 1: Larval development and behavior. *Ecol.* 28:53–67.

Rothman, N., and R. Smith. 1960. Winter breeding records for *Scaphiopus h. holbrooki*. *Bull. Philadelphia Herp. Soc.* 8(4):10–11.

Semlitsch, R. D., and J. P. Caldwell. 1982. Effects of density on growth, metamorphosis, and survivorship in tadpoles of *Scaphiopus holbrooki*. *Ecol.* 63:905–11.

Stone, W. 1932. Terrestrial activity of spadefoot toads. *Copeia* 1932:35–36.

Wilbur, H. M., P. J. Morin, and R. N. Harris. 1983. Salamander predation and the structure of experimental communities: anuran responses. *Ecol.* 64:1423–29.

Woodward, B. D. 1983. Predator-prey interactions and breeding-pond use of temporary-pond species in a desert anuran community. *Ecol.* 64:1549–55.

## Spring Peeper

Brodie, E. D., Jr., and D. R. Formanowicz, Jr. 1983. Prey size preference on predators: Differential vulnerability of larval anurans. *Herpetologica* 39:67–74.

Crump, M. L. 1984. Intraclutch egg size variability in *Hyla crucifer*. *Copeia* 1984:302–8.

Fellers, G. M. 1979. Aggression, territoriality, and mating behavior in North American treefrogs. *Animal Behavior* 27:107–19.

Forester, D. C., and R. Czarnowsky. 1985. Sexual selection in the spring peeper, *Hyla crucifer*: Role of the advertisement call. *Behavior* 92: 113–28.

Forester, D. C., and D. V. Lykens. 1986. Significance of satellite males in a population of spring peepers. *Copeia* 1986:719–24.

Gatz, A. J., Jr. 1981. Size selective mating in *Hyla versicolor* and *Hyla crucifer*. *J. Herpetol.* 15:114–16.

Gosner, K. L., and D. A. Rossman. 1960. Eggs and larval development of the treefrogs, *Hyla crucifer* and *Hyla ocularis*. *Herpetologica* 16:225–32.

Kats, L. B., and R. G. Van Dragt. 1986. Background color–matching in the Spring peeper, *Hyla crucifer*. *Copeia* 1986:109–15.

Morin, P. J. 1986. Interactions between intraspecific competition and predation in an amphibian predator-prey system. *Ecol.* 67:713–20.

Oplinger, C. S. 1967. Food habits and feeding activity of recently transformed and adult *Hyla crucifer*. *Herpetologica* 23:209–17.

Pechmann, J. H., and R. D. Semlitsch. 1986. Diel activity patterns in the breeding migrations of winter-breeding anurans. *Can. J. Zool.* 64:1116–20.

Rosen, M., and R. E. Lemon. 1974. The vocal behavior of spring peepers, *Hyla crucifer*. *Copeia* 1974:940–50.

Storey, K. B., and J. M. Storey. 1987. Persistence of freeze tolerance in terrestrially hibernating frogs after spring emergence. *Copeia* 1987: 720–26.

### Gray Treefrog

Brodie, E. D., Jr., and D. R. Formanowicz, Jr. 1981. Palatability and antipredator behavior of the treefrog *Hyla versicolor* to the shrew *Blarina brevicauda*. *J. Herpetol.* 15:235–36.

Fellers, G. M. 1979. Mate selection in the gray treefrog, *Hyla versicolor*. *Copeia* 1979:286–90.

Gayou, D. C. 1984. Effects of temperature on the mating call of *Hyla versicolor*. *Copeia* 1984:733–38.

Green, D. M. 1981. Adhesion and the toe-pads of treefrogs. *Copeia* 1981:790–96.

Klump, G. B., and H. C. Gerhardt. 1987. Use of non-arbitrary acoustic criteria in mate choice by female gray tree frogs. *Nature* 326:286–88.

McComb, W. C., and R. E. Noble. 1981. Herpetofaunal use of natural tree cavities and nest boxes. *Wildl. Soc. Bull.* 9:261–67.

Morris, M. 1984. The mating behavior of the treefrog, *Hyla versicolor*. *Proc. Indiana Acad. Science* 92:460.

Roble, S. M. 1979. Dispersal movements and plant associations of juvenile gray treefrogs, *Hyla versicolor*. *Transac. Kansas Acad. of Science* 82:235–45.

Storey, K. B., and J. M. Storey. 1987. Persistence of freeze tolerance in terrestrially hibernating frogs after spring emergence. *Copeia* 1987:720–26.

Wells, K. D., and T. L. Taigen. 1986. The effect of social interactions on calling energetics in the gray treefrog (*Hyla versicolor*). *Behav. Ecol. and Sociobiol.* 19:9–18.

## Green Frog

Adler, K. 1980. Individuality in the use of orientation cues by green frogs. *Animal Behavior* 28:413–25.

Breven, K. A., D. E. Gill, and S. J. Smith-Gill. 1979. Countergradient selection in the green frog, *Rana clamitans. Evolution* 33:609–23.

Brode, W. E. 1959. Territoriality in *Rana clamitans. Herpetologica* 15:140.

Etges, W. J. 1987. Call site choice in male anurans. *Copeia* 1987:910–23.

Formanowicz, D. R., Jr. 1986. Anuran tadpole/aquatic insect predator-prey interactions: tadpole size and predator capture success. *Herpetologica* 42:367–373.

Gascon, C., and J. R. Bider. 1984. The effect of pH on bullfrog, *Rana catesbeiana,* and green frog, *Rana clamitans melanota,* tadpoles. *Can. Field Nat.* 99:259–61.

Jenssen, T. A. 1967. Food habits of the green frog, *Rana clamitans,* before and during metamorphosis. *Copeia* 1967:214–18.

———. 1968. Some morphological and behavioral characteristics of an intergrade population of the green frog, *Rana clamitans,* in southern Illinois. *Ill. Acad. Science* 61:252–59.

Jenssen, T. A., and W. B. Preston. 1968. Behavioral responses of the male green frog, *Rana clamitans,* to its recorded call. *Herpetologica* 24:181–82.

Martoff, B. S. 1953. Territoriality in the green frog, *Rana clamitans. Ecol.* 34:165–74.

———. 1953. Home range and movements of the green frog, *Rana clamitans. Ecol.* 34:529–43.

Oldham, R. S. 1967. Orienting mechanisms of the green frog, *Rana clamitans. Ecol.* 48:477–90.

Ramer, J. D., T. A. Henssen, and C. J. Hurst. 1983. Size-related variation in the advertisement call of *Rana clamitans* and its effect on conspecific males. *Copeia* 1983:141–55.

Richmond, N. D. 1964. The green frog developing in one season. *Herpetologica* 20:132.

Schroeder, E. E. 1968. Aggressive behavior in *Rana clamitans. J. Herpetol.* 1:95–96.

Stewart, M. M. 1983. *Rana clamitans.* Catalog of American Amphibians and Reptiles 337.1–4. Albany, N.Y.: State Univ. of New York.

Stewart, M. M., and P. Sandison. 1972. Comparative food habits of sympatric mink frogs, bullfrogs, and green frogs. *J. Herpetol.* 6:241–44.

Wells, K. D. 1976. Multiple egg clutches in the green frog (*Rana clamitans*). *Herpetologica* 32:85–87.

———. 1977. Territoriality and male mating success in the green frog (*Rana clamitans*). *Ecol.* 58:750–62.

———. 1978. Territoriality in the green frog (*Rana clamitans*): Vocalizations and agonistic behavior. *Animal Behavior* 26:1051–63.

## Bullfrog

Aronson, L. R. 1943. The sexual behavior of anura. Oviposition in the green frog, *Rana clamitans*, and the bullfrog, *Rana catesbeiana*. *Am. Mus. Novitates* 1224:1–6.

Clarkson, R. W., and J. C. deVos, Jr. 1986. The bullfrog, *Rana catesbeiana* Shaw, in the lower Colorado river, Arizona-California. *J. Herpetol.* 20:42–49.

Currie, W., and E. D. Bellis. 1969. Home range and movements of the bullfrog, *Rana catesbeiana* Shaw, in an Ontario pond. *Copeia* 1969:688–92.

Emlen, S. T. 1968. Territoriality in the bullfrog, *Rana catesbeiana*. *Copeia* 1968:240–43.

———. 1976. Lek organization and mating strategies in the bullfrog. *Behav. and Ecol. Sociobiol.* 9:283–313.

Howard, R. D. 1978. The evolution of mating strategies in bullfrogs, *Rana catesbeiana*. *Evolution* 32:850–71.

———. 1978. The influence of male-defended ovipoition sites on early embryo mortality in bullfrogs. *Ecol.* 59:789–98.

———. 1981. Sexual dimorphism in bullfrogs. *Ecol.* 62:303–10.

Lilywhite, H. B. 1970. Behavioral temperature regulation in the bullfrog, *Rana catesbeiana*. *Copeia* 1970:158–68.

Ryan, M. J. 1980. The reproductive behavior of the bullfrog (*Rana catesbeiana*). *Copeia* 1980:108–14.

Steinwascher, K. 1978. The effect of coprophagy on the growth of *Rana catesbeiana* tadpoles. *Copeia* 1978:130–34.

Wiewandt, T. A. 1969. Vocalization, aggressive behavior, and territoriality in the bullfrog, *Rana catesbeiana*. *Copeia* 1969:276–85.

Willis, Y. L., D. L. Moyle, and T. S. Baskett. 1956. Emergence, breeding, hibernation, movements and transformation of the bullfrog, *Rana catesbeiana*, in Missouri. *Copeia* 1956:30–41.

## Northern Leopard Frog

Brown, L. E., and J. R. Brown. 1972. Call types of the *Rana pipiens* complex in Illinois. *Science* 176:928–29.

Cochran, P. A. 1986. The herpetofauna of the Weaver Dunes, Wabasha County, Minnesota. *Prairie Nat.* 18:143–50.

Collins, J. P. 1979. Overwintering tadpoles and breeding season variation in the *Rana pipiens* complex. *Southwestern Nat.* 24:371–96.

Cunjak, R. A. 1986. Winter habitat of northern leopard frogs, *Rana pipiens,* in a southern Ontario stream. *Can. J. Zool.* 64:255–57.

Dole, J. W. 1965. Summer movements of adult leopard frogs, *Rana pipiens,* in Northern Michigan. *Ecol.* 46:236–54.

Emery, A. R., A. H. Berst, and K. Kodaira. 1972. Under-ice observations of wintering sites of leopard frogs. *Copeia* 1972:123–26.

Noble, G. K., and L. R. Aronson. 1942. The sexual behavior of anura. The normal mating pattern in *Rana pipiens. Bull. Am. Mus. Nat. Hist.* 80:127–42.

Schmid, W. D. 1982. Survival of frogs in low temperature. *Science* 215:697–98.

Shinn, E. A., and J. W. Dole. 1978. Evidence for a role for olfactory cues in the feeding response of leopard frogs, *Rana pipiens. Herpetologica* 34:167–72.

## Wood Frog

Berven, K. A. 1981. Mate choice in the wood frog, *Rana sylvatica. Evolution* 35:707–22.

Hassinger, D. D. 1970. Notes on the thermal properties of frog eggs. *Herpetologica* 26:49–51.

Haynes, C. M., and S. D. Aird. 1981. The distribution and habitat requirements of the wood frog in Colorado. Special Report No. 50. Ft. Collins, Colo.: Colorado Div. Wildl.

Howard, R. D. 1980. Mating behavior and mating success in woodfrogs, *Rana sylvatica. Animal Behavior* 28:705–16.

Ling, R. W., J. P. VanAmberg, and J. K. Werner. 1986. Pond acidity and its relationship to larval development of *Ambystoma maculatum* and *Rana sylvatica* in Upper Michigan. *J. Herpetol.* 20:230–36.

Nyman, S. 1986. Mass mortality in larval *Rana sylvatica* attributable to the bacterium, *Aeromonas hydrophila. J. Herpetol.* 20:196–201.

Pierce, B. A., J. B. Hoskins, and E. Epstein. 1984. Acid tolerance in Connecticut wood frogs (*Rana sylvatica*). *J. Herpetol.* 18:159–67.

Seale, D. B. 1982. Physical factors influencing oviposition by the woodfrog, *Rana sylvatica,* in Pennsylvania. *Copeia* 1982:627–35.

Waldman, B. and M. J. Ryan. 1983. Thermal advantages of communal egg mass deposition in wood frogs (*Rana sylvatica*). *J. Herpetol.* 17:70–72.

Werner, J. K., and M. B. McCune. 1979. Seasonal changes in anuran populations in a northern Michigan pond. *J. Herpetol.* 13:101–4.

Wilbur, H. M. 1972. Competition, predation, and the structure of the *Ambystoma–Rana sylvatica* community. *Ecol.* 53:3–21.

Zweifel, R. G. 1989. Calling by the frog, *Rana sylvatica*, outside the breeding season. *J. Herpetol.* 23:185–86.

## Salamanders

Dunn, E. R. 1926. The salamanders of the family Plethodontidae. Northampton, Mass.: Smith Coll. 50th Ann.

Hairston, N. G., Sr. 1987. *Community ecology and salamander guilds.* Cambridge: Cambridge University Press.

Nunes, V. d. S., and R. G. Jaeger. 1989. Salamander aggressiveness increases with length of territorial ownership. *Copeia* 1989:712–18.

## Mudpuppy

Anderson, K. A., and T. L. Beitinger. 1979. Body heating and cooling in the mudpuppy, *Necturus maculosus. Herpetologica* 35:234–39.

Harris, J. P., Jr. 1959. The natural history of *Necturus:* I. Habitats and habits. II. Respiration. III. Food and feeding. *Field and Lab.* 27:11–20, 71–77, 105–111.

———. 1960. The natural history of *Necturus:* IV. Reproduction. *J. Graduate Research Center:* 69–81.

Hutchinson, V. H., and L. G. Hill. 1976. Thermal selection in the hellbender, *Cryptobranchus allenganiensis,* and the mudpuppy, *Necturus maculosus. Herpetologica* 32:327–31.

Hutchinson, V. H., and K. K. Spriestersbach. 1986. Diel and seasonal cycles of activity and behavioral thermoregulation in the salamander *Necturus maculosus. Copeia* 1986:612–18.

Hutchinson, V. H., and J. P. Ritchart. 1989. Annual cycle of thermal tolerance in the salamander, *Necturus maculosus. J. Herpetol.* 23:73–76.

## Red-Spotted Newt

Brodie, E. D., Jr. 1968. Investigations on the skin toxin of the red-spotted newt, *Notophthalmus viridescens. Am. Midland Nat.* 80:276–80.

Burton, T. M. 1977. Population estimates, feeding habits and nutrient and energy relationships of *Notophthalmus v. viridescens,* in Mirror Lake, New Hampshire. *Copeia* 1977:139–43.

Gill, D. E. 1978. The metapopulation ecology of the red-spotted newt, *Notophthalmus viridescens*. *Ecolog. Monog.* 48:145–66.

———. 1979. Density dependence and homing behavior in adult red-spotted newts, *Notophthalmus viridescens*. *Ecol.* 60:800–813.

Harris, R. N. 1989. Ontogenetic changes in size and shape of the facultatively paedomorphic salamander, *Notophthalmus viridescens dorsalis*. *Copeia* 1989:35–42.

Healy, W. R. 1974. Population consequences of alternative life histories in *Notophthalmus v. viridescens*. *Copeia* 1974:221–29.

Hurlbert, S. H. 1969. The breeding migrations and interhabitat wandering of the vermilion-spotted newt, *Notophthalmus viridescens*. *Ecol. Monographs* 39:465–88.

———. 1970. The post-larval migration of the red-spotted newt, *Notophthalmus viridescens*. *Copeia* 1970:515–28.

Morin, P. J., H. M. Wilbur, and R. N. Harris. 1983. Salamander predation and the structure of experimental communities: responses of *Notophthalmus* and microcrustacea. *Ecol.* 64:1430–36.

Verrell, P. A. 1985. Female availability and multiple courtship in male red-spotted newts: Decisions that maximize male mating success. *Behavior* 94:244–53.

## Spotted Salamander

Cook, R. P. 1983. Effects of acid precipitation on embryonic mortality of *Ambystoma* salamanders in the Connecticut Valley of Massachusetts. *Biol. Conservation* 27:77–88.

Ducey, P. K., and P. Ritsema. 1988. Intraspecific aggression and responses to marked substrates in *Ambystoma maculatum*. *Copeia* 1988:1008–13.

McGregor, J. H., and W. R. Teska. 1989. Olfaction as an orientation mechanism in migrating *Ambystoma maculatum*. *Copeia* 1989:779–81.

O'Donnell, D. J. 1935. Natural history of the Ambystomid salamanders of Illinois. *Am. Midland Nat.* 47:1063–71.

Phillips, C. A., and O. J. Sexton. 1989. Orientation and sexual differences during breeding migrations of the spotted salamander, *Ambystoma maculatum*. *Copeia* 1989:17–22.

Pough, F. H. 1976. Acid precipitation and embryonic mortality of spotted salamanders, *Ambystoma maculatum*. *Science* 192:68–70.

Shoop, C. R. 1968. Migratory orientation of *Ambystoma maculatum*: movements near breeding ponds and displacements of migrating individuals. *Biol. Bull.* 135:230–38.

———. 1974. Yearly variation in larval survival of *Ambystoma maculatum*. *Ecol.* 55:440–44.

Stenhouse, S. L. 1987. Embryo mortality and recruitment of juveniles of *Ambystoma maculatum* and *Ambystoma opacum* in North Carolina. *Herpetologica* 43:496–501.

Whitford, W. G., and A. Vinegar. 1966. Homing, survivorship, and overwintering of larvae in spotted salamanders, *Ambystoma maculatum*. *Copeia* 1966:515–19.

## Tiger Salamander

Brandon, R. A. 1967. Overwintering of larval tiger salamanders in southern Illinois. *Herpetologica* 23:67–68.

Fernandez, P. J., Jr., and J. P. Collins. 1988. Effect of environment and ontogeny on color pattern variation in Arizona tiger salamanders (*Ambystoma tigrinum nebulosum* Hallowell). *Copeia* 1988:928–38.

Holomuzki, J. R. 1986. Effect of microhabitat on fitness components of larval tiger salamanders. *Ambystoma tigrinum nebulosum*. *Oecologia* 71:142–48.

Holomuzki, J. R., and J. P. Collins. 1987. Trophic dynamics of a top predator, *Ambystoma tigrinum nebulosum* (Caudata: Ambystomatidae), in a lentic community. *Copeia* 1987:949–57.

Leff, L. G., and M. D. Bachmann. 1986. Ontogenetic changes in predatory behavior of larval tiger salamanders (*Ambystoma tigrinum*). *Can. J. Zool.* 64:1337–44.

Lindquist, S. B., and M. D. Bachmann. 1980. Feeding behavior of the tiger salamander, *Ambystoma tigrinum*. *Herpetologica* 36:144–58.

Miller, B. T., and J. H. Larsen, Jr. 1986. Feeding habits of metamorphosed *Ambystoma tigrinum melanostictum* in ponds of high pH (>9). *Great Basin Nat.* 46:299–301.

Norris, D. O. 1989. Seasonal changes in diet of paedogenetic tiger salamanders (*Ambystoma tigrinum mavortium*). *J. Herpetol.* 23:87–89.

Rogers, K. L. 1985. Facultative metamorphosis in a series of high altitude fossil populations of *Ambystoma tigrinum*. *Copeia* 1985:926–32.

Semlitsch, R. D., and J. H. K. Pechmann. 1985. Diel pattern of migratory activity for several species of pond-breeding salamanders. *Copeia* 1985:86–91.

Sexton, O. J., and J. R. Bizer. 1978. Life history patterns of *Ambystoma tigrinum* in Montane Colorado. *Am. Midland Nat.* 99:101–18.

Stine, C. J., Jr., J. A. Fowler, and R. S. Simmons. 1954. Occurrence of the eastern tiger salamander, *Ambystoma tigrinum tigrinum*, in Maryland, with notes on its life history. *Ann. Carnegie Mus.* 33:145–48.

Woodward, B., and P. Johnson. 1985. *Ambystoma tigrinum* predation on *Scaphiopus couchi* tadpoles of different sizes. *Southwestern Nat.* 30:460–61.

## Marbled Salamander

Anderson, J. D., and R. E. Graham. 1967. Vertical migration and stratification of larval *Ambystoma*. *Copeia* 1967:371–74.

Dunn, E. R. 1917. The breeding habits of *Ambystoma opacum*. *Copeia* 1917:40–43.

Graham, R. E. 1971. Environmental effects on deme structure, dynamics and breeding strategy of *Ambystoma opacum*. Ph.D. diss. Rutgers Univ.

Hassinger, D. D., J. D. Anderson, and G. H. Dalrymple. 1970. The early life history and ecology of *Ambystoma tigrinum* and *Ambystoma opacum* in New Jersey. *Am. Midland Nat.* 84:474–95.

Lazell, J. D., Jr. 1979. Teetering toward oblivion. *Mass. Wildl.* 30:15–18.

Nobel, G. K., and M. K. Brady. 1933. Observations on the life history of the Marbled salamander, *Ambystoma opacum*. *Zoologica* 11:89–132.

Petranka, J. W., and J. G. Petranka. 1981. On the evolution of nest site selection in the marbled salamander, *Ambystoma opacum*. *Copeia* 1981:387–91.

Shoop, R. C., and T. L. Doty. 1972. Migratory orientation by marbled salamanders (*Ambystoma opacum*) near a breeding area. *Behav. Biol.* 7:131–36.

## Redback Salamander

Bachmann, M. D. 1984. Defensive behavior of brooding female red-backed salamanders (*Plethodon cinereus*). *Herpetologica* 40:436–43.

Brodie, E. D., Jr., and E. D. Brodie, III. 1980. Differential avoidance of mimetic salamanders by free-ranging birds. *Science* 208:181–82.

Caldwell, R. S. 1975. Observations on the winter activity of the red-backed salamander, *Plethodon cinereus*, in Indiana. *Herpetologica* 31:21–22.

Caldwell, R. S., and G. S. Jones. 1973. Winter congregations of *Plethodon cinereus* in ant mounds, with notes on their food habits. *Am. Midland Nat.* 90:482–85.

David, R. S., and R. G. Jaeger. 1981. Prey location through chemical cues by a terrestrial salamander. *Copeia* 1981:435–40.

Dawley, E. M. 1987. Species discrimination between hybridizing and non-hybridizing terrestrial salamanders. *Copeia* 1987:924–31.

Ducey, P. K., and E. D. Brodie, Jr. 1983. Salamanders respond selectively to contacts with snakes: Survival advantage of alternative antipredator strategies. *Copeia* 1983:1036–41.

Greer, A. E., Jr. 1973. The color phases of the red-backed salamander in New England. *Man and nature* (Massachusetts Audubon Society), March, 27–32.

Heatwole, H. 1962. Environmental factors influencing local distribution and activity of the salamander, *Plethodon cinereus*. *Ecology* 43:460–72.

Highton, R., and T. Savage. 1961. Functions of the brooding behavior in the female red-backed salamander, *Plethodon cinereus*. *Copeia* 1961:95–98.

Horne, E. A. 1988. Aggressive behavior of female red-backed salamanders. *Herpetologica* 44:203–9.

Jaeger, R. G. 1981. Dear enemy recognition and the costs of aggression between salamanders. *Am. Nat.* 117:962–74.

———. 1984. Agonistic behavior of the red-backed salamander. *Copeia* 1984:309–14.

Jaeger, R. G., J. M. Goy, M. Tarver, and C. E. Marquez. 1986. Salamander territoriality: Pheromonal markers as advertisement by males. *Animal Behavior* 34:860–64.

Kleeberger, S. R., and J. K. Werner. 1982. Home range and homing behavior of *Plethodon cinereus* in Northern Michigan. *Copeia* 1982:409–15.

Nunes, V. d. S., and R. G. Jaeger. 1989. Salamander aggressiveness increases with length of territorial ownership. *Copeia* 1989:712–18.

Sayler, A. 1966. The reproductive ecology of the red-backed salamander, *Plethodon cinereus*, in Maryland. *Copeia* 1966:183–93.

Taub, F. B. 1961. The distribution of the red-backed salamander, *Plethodon c. cinereus*, within the soil. *Ecology* 42:681–98.

Test, F. H., and H. Heatwole. 1962. Nesting sites of the red-backed salamander, *Plethodon cinereus*, in Michigan. *Copeia* 1962:206–7.

Thurow, G. R. 1961. A salamander color variant associated with glacial boundaries. *Evolution* 15:281–87.

Tilley, S. G., B. L. Lundrigan, and L. P. Brower. 1982. Erythrism and mimicry in the salamander *Plethodon cinereus*. *Herpetologica* 38:409–17.

Vania da Silva, N. 1988. Feeding assymmetry affects territorial disputes between males of *Plethodon cinereus*. *Herpetologica* 44:386–91.

## Reptiles

Ashton, R. E, Jr., and P. S. Ashton. 1985. *Handbook of reptiles and amphibians of Florida*. Miami: Windward Publications.

Bakker, R. T. 1986. *The dinosaur heresies*. New York: William Morrow.

Behler, J. L., and F. W. King. 1979. *The Audubon Society field guide to North American reptiles and amphibians*. New York: Alfred A. Knopf.

Dodd, C. K., Jr., K. M. Enge, and J. N. Stuart. 1989. Reptiles on highways in north-central Alabama, USA. *J. Herpetol.* 23:197–200.

Pough, F. H. 1981. Herpetology laboratory manual. Cornell Univ. Photocopy.

Smith, H. M., and E. D. Brodie, Jr. 1982. *A guide to field identification of reptiles of North America.* New York: Golden Press.

Stebbins, R. C. 1966. *A field guide to western reptiles and amphibians.* Boston: Houghton Mifflin Co.


## Turtles

Boyer, D. R. 1965. Ecology of the basking habit in turtles. *Ecology* 46:99–118.

Bull, J. J., and R. C. Vogt. 1979. Temperature-dependent sex determination in turtles. *Science* 206:1186–88.

Bull. J. J., R. C. Vogt, and C. J. McCoy. 1982. Sex determining temperatures in turtles: A geographic comparison. *Evolution* 36:326–32.

Carr, A. 1952. *Handbook of turtles.* Ithaca, N.Y.: Cornell Univ. Press.

Ernst, C. H., and R. W. Barbour. 1972. *Turtles of the United States.* Lexington, Ky.: Univ. of Kentucky Press.

———. 1989. *Turtles of the world.* Washington, D.C., and London: Smithsonian Institution Press.

Gibbons, J. W., and D. H. Nelson. 1978. The evolutionary significance of delayed emergence from the nest by hatchling turtles. *Evolution* 32:297–303.

Harless, M., and H. Morlock, eds. 1979. *Turtles: Perspectives and research.* New York: John Wiley & Sons.

Pritchard, P. H. 1979. *Encyclopedia of turtles.* Neptune, N.J.: TFH Publications.

Smith, H. M., and E. D. Brodie, Jr. 1982. *A guide to field identification: Reptiles of North America.* New York: Golden Press.


## Painted Turtle

Belusz, L. C., and R. J. Reed. 1969. Some epizoophytes on six turtle species collected in Massachusetts and Michigan. *Am. Midland Nat.* 81:598–601.

Congdon, J. D., and R. E. Gatten, Jr. 1989. Movements and energetics of nesting *Chrysemys picta. Herpetologica* 45:94–100.

Ernst, C. H. 1971. Population dynamics and activity cycles of *Chrysemys picta* in southeastern Pennsylvania. *J. Herpetol.* 5:151–60.

———. 1972. Temperature-activity relationship in the painted turtle, *Chrysemys picta. Copeia* 1972:217–22.

Gaten, R. E., Jr. 1981. Anaerobic metabolism in freely diving painted turtles. *J. Exper. Zool.* 216:377–85.

Gutzke, W. H. N., and G. C. Packard. 1985. Hatching success in relation to egg size in painted turtles. *Can. J. Zool.* 63:67–70.

Gutzke, W. H. N., G. C. Packard, M. J. Packard, and T. J. Boardman. 1987. Influence of the hydric and thermal environments on eggs and hatchlings of painted turtles (*Chrysemys picta*). *Herpetologica* 43:393 – 404.

Gutzke, W. H. N., and G. L. Paukstis. 1984. A low threshold temperature for sexual differentiation in the painted turtle, *Chrysemys picta. Copeia* 1984:546 – 47.

Lovich, J. 1988. Aggressive basking behavior in eastern painted turtles. *Herpetologica* 44:197 – 202.

Waters, J. H. 1969. Additional observations of southeastern Massachusetts insular and mainland populations of painted turtles. *Copeia* 1969: 179 – 82.

Woolverton, E. 1963. Winter survival of hatchling painted turtles in northern Minnesota. *Copeia* 1963:569 – 70.

## Snapping Turtle

Christiansen, J. L., and R. R. Burken. 1979. Growth and maturity of the snapping turtle (*Chelydra serpentina*) in Iowa. *Herpetologica* 35:261 – 66.

Congdon, J. D., G. L. Breitenbach, R. C. van Loben Sels, and D. W. Tinkle. 1987. Reproduction and nesting ecology of snapping turtles (*Chelydra serpentina*) in southeastern Michigan. *Herpetologica* 43:39 – 54.

Hammer, D. A. 1969. Parameters of a marsh snapping turtle population in Lacreek Refuge, South Dakota. *J. Wildl. Manage.* 33:995 – 1005.

Obbard, M. E., and R. J. Brooks. 1979. Factors affecting basking in a northern population of the common snapping turtle, *Chelydra serpentina. Can. J. Zool.* 57:435 – 40.

——. 1981. A radio-telemetry mark and recapture study of activity in the common snapping turtle, *Chelydra serpentina. Copeia* 1981:630 – 37.

Robinson, C., and J. R. Bider. 1988. Nesting synchrony—a strategy to decrease predation of snapping turtle (*Chelydra serpentina*) nests. *J. Herpetol.* 22:470 – 73.

Vogt, R. C., and J. J. Bull. 1982. Temperature controlled sex-determination in turtles: Ecological and behavioral aspects. *Herpetologica* 38:156 – 64.

White, J. B., and G. G. Murphy. 1973. The reproductive cycle and sexual dimorphism of the common snapping turtle, *Chelydra serpentina serpentina. Herpetologica* 29:240 – 46.

Wilhoft, D. C., and E. Houghtaling. 1984. Temperature-dependent sex determination in the snapping turtle, *Chelydra serpentina. ASRA Journal* 2:34 – 46.

Wilhoft, D. C., M. G. Del Baglivo, and M. D. Del Baglivo. 1979. Observations on mammalian predation of snapping turtle nests. *J. Herpetol.* 13:435–38.

Yntema, C. L. 1979. Temperature levels and periods of sex determination during incubation of eggs of *Chelydra serpentina. J. Morphol.*159:17–28.

## Stinkpot

Berry, J. F. 1975. The population effects of ecological sympatry on musk turtles in northern Florida. *Copeia* 1975:692–701.

Ernst, C. H. 1986. Ecology of the turtle, *Sternotherus odoratus,* in southeastern Pennsylvania. *J. Herpetol.* 20:341–52.

Graham, T. E., and J. E. Forsberg. 1986. Clutch size in some Maine turtles. *Bull. Maryland Herp. Soc.* 22:146–48.

Graham, T. E., and V. H. Hutchinson. 1979. Effect of temperature and photoperiod acclimatization on thermal preferences of selected freshwater turtles. *Copeia* 1979:165–69.

Mahmoud, I. Y. 1968. Feeding behavior in Kinosternid turtles. *Herpetologica* 24:300–305.

McPherson, R. J., and K. R. Marion. 1981. The reproductive biology of female *Sternotherus odoratus* in an Alabama population. *J. Herpetol.* 15:389–96.

Mitchell, J. C. 1985. Variation in the male reproductive cycle in a population of stinkpot turtles, *Sternotherus odoratus,* from Virginia. *Copeia* 1985:941–49.

Reynolds, S. L., and M. E. Seide. 1983. Morphological homogeneity in the turtle *Sternotherus odoratus* (Kinosternidae) throughout its range. *J. Herpetol.* 17:113–120.

Vogt, R. C. 1982. Incubation temperature influences sex determination in Kinosternid turtles. *Copeia* 1982:480–82.

## Spotted Turtle

Cook, F. R., J. D. Lafontaine, S. Black, L. Luckuk, and R. V. Lindsay. 1980. Spotted turtles (*Clemmys guttata*) in eastern Ontario and adjacent Quebec. *Can. Field Nat.* 94:411–15.

Ernst, C. H. 1970. Reproduction in *Clemmys guttata. Herpetologica* 26:228–32.

——— . 1970. Home range of the spotted turtle, *Clemmys guttata. Copeia* 1970:391–93.

——— . 1982. Environmental temperatures and activities in wild spotted turtles, *Clemmys guttata. J. Herpetol.* 16:112–20.

Graham, T. E. 1970. Growth rate of the spotted turtle, *Clemmys guttata,* in southern Rhode Island. *J. Herpetol.* 4:87–88.

Lovich, J. E. 1988. Geographic variation in the seasonal activity cycle of spotted turtles, *Clemmys guttata. J. Herpetol.* 22:482–85.


## Wood Turtle

Barzilay, S. 1980. Aggressive behavior in the wood turtle, *Clemmys insculpta. J. Herpetol.* 14:89–91.

Brewster, C. M. 1985. Wood turtle, *Clemmys insculpta,* research in northern Wisconsin. *Bull. Chicago Herp. Soc.* 20:13–20.

Bull, J. J. 1985. Non-temperature dependant sex determination in two suborders of turtles. *Copeia* 1985:784–86.

Graham, T. E., and J. E. Forsberg. 1986. Clutch size in some Maine turtles. *Bull. Maryland Herp. Soc.* 22:146–48.

Kaufmann, J. H. 1986. Stomping for earthworms by wood turtles, *Clemmys insculpta:* A newly discovered foraging technique. *Copeia* 1986:1001–4.

Meritt, D. A., Jr. 1980. The wood turtle, *Clemmys insculpta:* Natural history, behavior, and food habits. *Bull. Chicago Herp. Soc.* 15:6–9.

Strang, C. A. 1983. Spatial and temporal activity patterns in two terrestrial turtles. *J. Herpetol.* 17:43–47.


## Eastern Box Turtle

Babcock, H. L. 1928. The long life of turtles. *Bull. Boston Mus. Nat. Hist.* 46:9–10.

Cahn, A. R., and E. Conder. 1932. Mating of the box turtles. *Copeia* 1932:86–88.

Carr, J. L., and T. W. Houseal. 1981. Post-hibernation behavior in *Terrapene carolina triunguis. Southwest Nat.* 26:199–200.

Congdon, J. D., R. E. Gatten, Jr., and S. J. Morreale. 1989. Overwintering activity of box turtles (*Terrapene carolina*) in South Carolina. *J. Herpetol.* 23:179–81.

Ernst, C. H. 1981. Courtship behavior of male *Terrapene carolina major. Herp. Rev.* 12:7–8.

Kiester, A. R., C. W. Schwartz, and E. R. Schwartz. 1982. Promotion of gene flow by transient individuals in an otherwise sedentary population of box turtles (*Terrapene carolina triunguis*). *Evolution* 36:617–19.

Reagan, D. P. 1974. Habitat selection in the three-toed box turtle, *Terrapene carolina triunguis. Copeia* 1974:512–27.

Riemer, D. N. 1981. Multiple nesting by a female box turtle, *Terrapene carolina carolina. Chelonologica* 2:53–55.

Rust, R. W., and R. R. Roth. 1981. Seed production and seedling establishment in the may apple, *Podophyllum peltatum*. *Am. Midland Nat.* 105:51–60.

Stickel, L. F. 1989. Home range behavior among box turtles (*Terrapene c. carolina*) of a bottomland forest in Maryland. *J. Herpetol.* 32:40–44.

## Lizards

Huey, R. B., E. R. Pianka, and T. W. Schoener, eds. 1983. *Lizard ecology, studies of a model organism.* Cambridge: Harvard University Press.

Smith, H. M. 1946 (1971). *Handbook of lizards.* Ithaca, N.Y.: Cornell Univ. Press.

Smith, H. M., and E. D. Brodie, Jr. 1982. *A guide to field identification: Reptiles of North America.* New York: Golden Press.

## Green Anole

Andrews, R. M. 1985. Oviposition frequency of *Anolis carolinensis. Copeia* 1985:259–262.

Cooper, W. E., Jr. 1979. Variability and predictability of courtship in *Anolis carolinensis. J. Herpetol.* 13:233–43.

Fitch, H. S., and D. M. Hillis. 1984. The *Anolis* dewlap: Interspecific variability and morphological associations with habitat. *Copeia* 1984:315–23.

McLain, D. K. 1983. Coevolution: mulerian mimicry between a plant bug and a seed bug and the relationship between host plant choice and unpalatability. *Oikos* 43:143–48.

Tokarz, R. R., and R. E. Jones. 1979. A study of egg-related maternal behavior in *Anolis carolinensis. J. Herpetol.* 13:283–88.

## Five-Lined Skink

Cooper, W. E., Jr., and L. J. Vitt. 1987. Intraspecific and interspecific aggression in lizards of the scincid genus *Eumeces:* Chemical detection of conspecific sexual competitors. *Herpetologica* 43:7–14.

Cooper, W. E., Jr., L. J. Vitt, L. D. Vangilder, and J. W. Gibbons. 1983. Natural nest sites and brooding behavior of *Eumeces fasciatus. Herp. Rev.* 14:65–66.

Duvall, D., R. Herskowitz, and J. Trupiano-Duvall. 1980. Responses of five-lined skinks (*Eumeces fasciatus*) and ground skinks (*Scincella lateralis*) to conspecific and interspecific chemical cues. *J. Herpetol.* 14:121–27.

Fitch, H. S. 1954. Life history and ecology of the five-lined skink, *Eumeces fasciatus. Pub. Mus. Nat. Hist.* (Univ. of Kansas) 8:1–156.

Groves, J. D. 1981. Egg-eating behavior of brooding five-lined skinks, *Eumeces fasciatus. Copeia* 1982:969–71.

## Gila Monster

Jones, K. B. 1983. Movement patterns and foraging ecology of Gila monsters (*Heloderma suspectum*) in northwestern Arizona. *Herpetologica* 39:247–53.

Lowe, C. H., C. R. Schwalbe, and T. B. Johnson. 1986. *The venomous reptiles of Arizona.* Phoenix: Arizona Game and Fish Dept.

Miller, D. M., R. A. Young, T. W. Gatlin, and J. A. Richardson. 1982. *Amphibians and reptiles of the Grand Canyon.* Grand Canyon Nat. Hist. Assoc. Monog. no. 4.

Stebbins, R. C. 1972. *California amphibians and reptiles.* Berkeley and Los Angeles: Univ. of California Press.

## Regal Horned Lizard

Baharav, D. 1975. Movement of the horned lizard, *Phrynosoma solare. Copeia* 1975:649–57.

Baur, B. E. 1986. Longevity of horned lizards of the genus *Phrynosoma. Bull. Maryland Herp. Soc.* 22:149–51.

Sherbrooke, W. C. 1981. *Horned lizards.* Series No. 31. Globe, Ariz.: Southwest Parks and Monuments Assoc.

Van Devender, T. R., and C. W. Howard. 1973. Notes on natural nests and hatching success in the regal horned lizard (*Phrynosoma solare*) in southern Arizona. *Herpetologica* 29:238–39.

Vitt, L. J. 1977. Observations on clutch and egg size and evidence for multiple clutches in some lizards of southwestern United States. *Herpetologica* 33:333–38.

## American Alligator

Ashton, R. E., Jr., and P. S. Ashton. 1985. *Handbook of reptiles and amphibians of Florida.* Part Two. Lizards, turtles, and crocodilians. Miami: Windward Publications.

Brisbin, I. L., Jr., E. A. Standora, and M. J. Vargo. 1982. Body temperatures and behavior of American alligators during cold winter weather. *Am. Midland Nat.* 107:209–18.

Chabreck, R. H., and T. Joanen. 1979. Growth rates of American alligators in Louisiana. *Herpetologica* 35:51–57.

Deitz, D. C., and T. C. Hines. 1980. Alligator nesting in north-central Florida. *Copeia* 1980:249–58.

Deitz, D. C., and D. R. Jackson. 1979. Use of American alligator nests by nesting turtles. *J. Herpetol.* 13:510–12.

Ferguson, M. W. J. 1982. Temperature of egg incubation determines sex in *Alligator mississippiensis*. *Nature* 296:850–52.

Goodwin, T. M., and W. R. Marion. 1979. Seasonal activity ranges and habitat preferences of adult alligators in a north-central Florida lake. *J. Herpetol.* 13:157–63.

Kushlan, J. A. 1973. Observations on maternal behavior in the American alligator, *Alligator mississippiensis*. *Herpetologica* 29:256–57.

———. 1974. Observations on the role of the American alligator (*Alligator mississippiensis*) in the southern Florida wetlands. *Copeia* 1974: 993–96.

Kushlan, J. A., and M. S. Kushlan. 1980. Function of nest attendance in the American alligator. *Herpetologica* 36:27–32.

Murphy, P. A. 1981. Celestial compass orientation in juvenile American alligators (*Alligator mississippiensis*). *Copeia* 1981:638–45.

Nichols, J. D., and R. H. Chabreck. 1980. On the variability of alligator sex ratios. *Am. Nat.* 116:125–37.

Toops, C. 1988. *The alligator, monarch of the marsh.* Homstead, Fla.; Florida National Parks and Monuments Assoc., Inc.

*Snakes*

Engelmann, W., and F. J. Obst. 1981. *Snakes.* New York: Simon and Schuster.

Ernst, C. H., and R. W. Barbour. 1989. *Snakes of eastern North America.* Fairfax, Va.: George Mason University Press.

Parker, H. W., and A. G. G. Grandison. 1977. *Snakes: A natural history.* London: British Mus. Nat. Hist.

Seigel, R. A., J. T. Collins, and S. S. Novak, eds. 1987. *Snakes: Ecology and evolutionary biology.* New York: Macmillan.

*Common Garter Snake*

Arnold, S. J. 1978. Differential predation on metamorphic anurans by garter snakes (*Thamnophis*): Social behavior as a possible defense. *Ecology* 59:1014–22.

Blaesing, M. E. 1979. Some aspects of the ecology of the eastern garter snake (*Thamnophis sirtalis sirtalis*) in a a semi-disturbed habitat in west-central Illinois. *J. Herpetol.* 13:177–81.

Catling, P. M., and B. Freedman. 1980. Food and feeding behavior of sympatric snakes at Amherstburg, Ontario. *Can. Field Nat.* 94:28–33.

Crews, D. 1977. Copulatory plugs, restricted mating opportunities and reproductive competition among male garter snakes. *Nature* 267: 345–46.

Ford, N. B. 1981. Seasonality of pheromone trailing behavior in two species of garter snake, *Thamnophis*. *Southwestern Nat.* 26:385–88.

Garstka, W. A., and D. Crews. 1981. Female sex pheromone in the skin and circulation of a garter snake. *Science* 214:681–83.

———. 1985. Mate preference in garter snakes. *Herpetologica* 41:9–19.

Gordon, D. M., and F. R. Cook. 1980. An aggregation of gravid snakes in the Quebec Laurentians. *Can. Field Nat.* 94:456–57.

Gregory, P. T. 1984. Correlations between body temperature and environmental factors and their variations with activity in garter snakes (*Thamnophis*). *Can. J. Zool.* 62:2244–49.

Jansen, D. W., and R. C. Foehring. 1983. The mechanism of venom secretion from Duvernoy's gland of the snake *Thamnophis sirtalis*. *J. Morphol.* 175:271–77.

Kephart, D. G. 1982. Microgeographic variation in the diets of garter snakes. *Oecologia* 52:287–91.

Kephart, D. G., and S. J. Arnold. 1982. Garter snake diets in a fluctuating environment: A seven-year study. *Ecology* 63:1232–36.

Mason, R. T., and D. Crews. 1985. Female mimicry in garter snakes. *Nature* 316:59–60.

Ross, P., Jr., and D. Crews. 1977. Influence of the seminal plug on mating behaviour in the garter snake. *Nature* 267:344–45.

Seigel, R. A., and H. S. Fitch. 1985. Annual variation in reproduction in snakes in a fluctuating environment. *J. Animal Ecol.* 54:497–505.

### Northern Water Snake

Bauman, M. A., and D. E. Metter. 1977. Reproductive cycle of the northern watersnake, *Natrix s. sipedon*. *J. Herpetol.* 11:51–59.

Beatso, R. R. 1976. Environmental and genetical correlates of disruptive coloration in the water snake, *Natrix s. sipedon*. *Evolution* 30:241–52.

Blaney, R. M., and P. K. Blaney. 1979. The *Nerodia sipedon* complex of water snakes in Mississippi and southeastern Louisiana. *Herpetologica* 35:350–59.

Conant, R., and J. D. Lazell. 1973. The Carolina salt marsh snake: A distinct form of *Natrix sipedon*. *Breviora* 400:1–13.

Fraker, M. A. 1970. Home range and homing in the watersnake, *Natrix sipedon sipedon*. *Copeia* 1970:665–73.

King, R. B. 1986. Population ecology of the Lake Erie water snake, *Nerodia sipedon insularum*. *Copeia* 1986:757–72.

Mushinsky, H. R. 1979. Mating behavior of the common water snake,

Nerodia sipedon sipedon, in eastern Pennsylvania. *J. Herpetol.* 13:127 – 29.

Shine, R. 1978. Sexual size dimorphism and male combat in snakes. *Oecologia* 33:269 – 77.

Tiebout, H. M., III, and J. R. Cary. 1987. Dynamic spatial ecology of the water snake, *Nerodia sipedon. Copeia* 1987:1 – 18.


## Milk Snake

Fitch, H. S., and R. R. Fleet. 1970. Natural history of the milk snake (*Lampropeltis triangulum*) in northeastern Kansas. *Herpetologica* 26:387 – 96.

Henderson, R. W., M. H. Binder, R. A. Sajdak, and J. A. Buday. 1980. Aggregating behavior and exploitation of subterranean habitat by gravid eastern milk snakes (*Lampropeltis t. triangulum*). *Milwaukee Publ. Mus. Contributions in Biol. and Geol.* 32:1 – 9.

Williams, K. L. 1978. Systematics and natural history of the American milk snake, *Lampropeltis triangulum. Milwaukee Pub. Mus. Contributions in Biol. and Geol.* 2:1 – 258.


## Eastern Hognose Snake

Clark, H. 1952. Note on the egg-laying habits of *Heterodon platyrhinos. Herpetologica* 8:28 – 29.

Edgren, R. A. 1955. The natural history of the hog-nosed snakes, genus *Heterodon:* A review. *Herpetologica* 11:105 – 17.

Grogran, W. L., Jr. 1974. Effects of accidental envenomation from the saliva of the eastern hognose snake, *Heterodon platyrhinos. Herpetologica* 30:248 – 49.

Kroll, J. C. 1976. Feeding adaptations of hognose snakes. *Southwestern Nat.* 20:537 – 57.

Michener, M. C., and J. D. Lazell, Jr. 1989. Distribution and relative abundance of the hognose snake, *Heterodon platyrhinos,* in eastern New England. *J. Herpetol.* 23:35 – 40.

Munyer, E. A. 1967. Behavior of an eastern hognose snake, *Heterodon platyrhinos,* in water. *Copeia* 1967:668 – 70.

Platt, D. R. 1969. Natural history of the hognose snakes, *Heterodon platyrhinos* and *Heterodon nascius. Publ. Mus. Nat. Hist.* (Univ. of Kansas) 18:253 – 420.

Rodgers, R. B. 1985. Life history notes. Serpentes. *Heterodon platyrhinos. Herp. Rev.* 16:111.

Scott, D. 1986. Notes on the eastern hognose snake *Heterodon platyrhinos,* on a Virginia barrier beach island. *Brimleyana* 12:51 – 55.

## Black Racer

Brown, W. S., and W. S. Parker. 1984. Growth, reproduction, and demography of the racer, *Coluber constrictor mormon,* in northern Utah. In *Vertebrate ecology and systematics: A tribute to Henry S. Fitch,* 13–40. University of Kansas Museum of Natural History Special Publication no. 10. Lawrence.

Herzog, H. A., and G. M. Burghardt. 1974. Prey movement and predatory behavior of juvenile western yellow-bellied racers. *Herpetologica* 30:285–89.

Parker, W. S., and W. S. Brown. 1973. Species composition and population changes in two complexes of snake hibernacula in northern Utah. *Herpetologica* 29:319–26.

Sexton, O. J., and S. R. Hunt. 1980. Temperature relationships and movements of snakes (*Elaphe obsoleta, Coluber constrictor*) in a cave hibernaculum. *Herpetologica* 36:20–26.

## Copperhead

de Wit, C. A. 1982. Resistance of the prairie vole (*Microtis ochrogaster*) and the woodrat (*Neotoma floridana*), in Kansas, to the venom of the osage copperhead (*Agkistrodon contortrix phaeogaster*). *Toxicon* 20:709–14.

Fitch, H. S. 1960. Autecology of the copperhead, 85–288. University of Kansas Museum of Natural History Special Publication no. 13. Lawrence.

Reinert, H. K. 1984. Habitat variation within sympatric snake populations. *Ecology* 65:1673–82.

Sanders, J. S., and J. S. Jacob. 1981. Thermal ecology of the copperhead (*Agkistrodon contortrix*). *Herpetologica* 37:264–70.

Schuett, G. W. 1982. A copperhead (*Agkistrodon contortrix*) brood produced from autumn copulations. *Copeia* 1982:700–702.

Schuett, G. W., and J. C. Gillingham. 1986. Sperm storage and multiple paternity in the copperhead, *Agkistrodon contortrix. Copeia* 1986:807–11.

Stechert, R. 1980. Observations on northern snake dens. *Herp. Bull. N.Y. Herp. Soc.* 15:7–14.

## Timber Rattlesnake

Brown, C. W., and C. H. Ernst. 1986. A study of variation in eastern timber rattlesnakes, *Crotalus horridus. Brimleyana* 12:57–74.

Brown, W. S. 1982. Overwintering body temperatures of timber rattlesnakes (*Crotalus horridus*) in northeastern New York. *J. Herpetol.* 16:145–50.

Brown, W. S., and F. M. MacLean. 1983. Conspecific scent-trailing by newborn timber rattlesnakes, *Crotalus horridus. Herpetologica* 39:430–36.

Brown, W. S., D. W. Pyle, K. R. Greene, and J. B. Friedlaender. 1982. Movements and temperature relationships of timber rattlesnakes (*Crotalus horridus*) in northeastern New York. *J. Herpetol.* 16:151–61.

Galligan, J. H., and W. A. Dunson. 1979. Biology and status of timber rattlesnake (*Crotalus horridus*) populations in Pennsylvania. *Biolog. Conservation* 15:13–58.

Keenlyne, K. D. 1972. Sexual differences in the feeding habits of *Crotalus horridus horridus. J Herpetol.* 6:234–37.

Kimball, D., ed. 1978. The timber rattlesnake in New England: A symposium. Western Mass. Herpetological Society. Springfield Science Museum, Springfield, Mass.

Martin, W. H. 1982. The timber rattlesnake in the northeast: Its range, past and present. *Herp. Bull. N.Y. Herp. Soc.* 17:15–20.

Newman, E. A., and P. H. Harline. 1982. The infrared "vision" of snakes. *Scientific American* 246:116–27.

Odum, R. A. 1979. The distribution and status of the New Jersey timber rattlesnake including an analysis of Pine Barrens populations. *Herp. Bull. N.Y. Herp. Soc.* 15(1).

Reinert, H. K. 1984. Habitat variation within sympatric snake populations. *Ecology* 65:1673–82.

Reinert, H. K., D. Cundall, and L. M. Bushar. 1984. Foraging behavior of the timber rattlesnake, *Crotalus horridus. Copeia* 1984:976–81.

Reinert, H. K., and R. T. Zappalorti. 1988. Timber rattlesnakes (*Crotalus horridus*) of the pine barrens: Their movement patterns and habitat preference. *Copeia* 1988:964–78.

——. 1988. Field observations of the association of adult and neonatal timber rattlesnakes, *Crotalus horridus,* with possible evidence for conspecific trailing. *Copeia* 1988:1057–59.

Savage, T. 1967. The diet of rattlesnakes and copperheads in the Great Smoky Mountains National Park. *Copeia* 1967:226–27.

Schaefer, G. C. 1969. Sex independent ground color in the timber rattlesnake, *Crotalus horridus horridus. Herpetologica* 25:65–66.

Stechert, R. 1982. Historical depletion of timber rattlesnake colonies in New York State. *Herp. Bull. N.Y. Herp. Soc.* 17:23–24.

Stewart, M. M., G. E. Larson, and T. H. Matthews. 1960. Morphological variation in a litter of timber rattlesnakes. *Copeia* 1960:366–67.

JUN    7 1991